Work Smarts for Women

PATTI PANICCIA

WORK SMARTS FOR WOMEN

THE ESSENTIAL SEX DISCRIMINATION SURVIVAL GUIDE

BALLANTINE BOOKS • NEW YORK

A Ballantine Book
Published by The Ballantine Publishing Group

 Published in the United States by The Ballantine Publishing Group, a division of Random House, Inc., New York, and simultaneously in Canada by Random House of Canada Limited, Toronto.

www.randomhouse.com/BB/

Library of Congress Cataloging-in-Publication Data
Paniccia, Patti.
Work smarts for women: the essential sex discrimination survival guide / Patti Paniccia.
p.   cm.
Includes bibliographical references and index.
ISBN 0-345-42261-9 (pbk.: alk. paper)
1. Sex discrimination in employment—United States.
2. Sex discrimination against women—United States
3. Women—Employment—United States I. Title
HD6060.5.U5P36   2000
331.4'133'0973—dc21   99-41292
CIP

Text design by Ann Gold
Cover design by Cathy Colbert

Manufactured in the United States of America

First Edition: January 2000

10 9 8 7 6 5 4 3 2 1

Contents

Acknowledgments

The process of writing this book goes far beyond the day I first sat down to put words to paper. It originated the day I was fired from CNN and concludes only now as this book goes to press. Therefore, my acknowledgments include not only those people who helped me in the writing and research but also those who have been with me throughout my entire ordeal.

I found the process of writing a book to be all-consuming, if not devouring, of my time and thoughts. On one occasion, I inadvertently threw away an entire chapter, only to find myself curbside, digging through the trash. Nose-first inside a forty-gallon garbage barrel, I heard my phone ringing and rushed inside to answer. "I just thought you'd want to know," said the neighbor who was calling. "There's a homeless lady digging through your garbage." I'm sure there must be a happy medium between commitment to finishing a book and having a life. Unfortunately, I never found it.

Sincerest thanks . . .

To my former colleagues at CNN all around the globe who

came forward to testify or offered their support, especially to Lisa Briton, Greg Canes, Candy Crowley, Tena Ezzedine, Merrill Horowitz, John Gilmore, Julie Jorgensen, Bill Langley, Tom Larssen, Veronica McGregor, Ellie Miller, Lynda Arnel Nikula, Patricia Ochs, Jeff Ofgang, Cathryn Reardon, David Saeger, and Nina Zirato.

To my lawyers, John C. Taylor and Christine Spagnoli, for never once doubting my story, for believing it was the right thing to do, and for never making money an issue.

To the men who fired me and the attorneys who represented them—thank you. I've become a much stronger and better person than I ever imagined I could be.

To Lorraine Loder for her savvy legal advice when I needed it most (on the day I was fired).

To my pastor, John Day, for his kind counsel.

To my cousin Debra Cunningham for her friendship and support throughout, and also for reviewing parts of this manuscript as a wife, mother of two children, owner of a two-car garage, and professional outside the home.

To Ron Phillips, former dean at Pepperdine School of Law, for his mentorship and support. Also at Pepperdine to Dean Richard Lynn for his willingness and encouragement in allowing me to institute a Gender Law class, and to Dotty Aiken, Phil Bohl, Cynthia Greer, Ron Hall, Hazel Harrington, Cheryl MacDonald, Dan Martin, Chip Moore, Charles Nelson, John Peele, Shelly Saxer, and law librarian Mona Stahl for her assistance and familiar face over the years.

To my law students, who have demanded excellence and caused me to become truly an expert in this field, less they slice off my head with their "reasonable" line of questioning. Special thanks to my student intern, Julie McCormick.

To my law clerk, Carol Sovinski, for her professional abilities and swift, accurate research. Also to law clerk Julie Trotter for her last-minute cite checking.

To Christine Craft for sharing her experiences and offering her perspective and advice.

To Vivien Santana Hughes for her patience in editing my early attempts to switch from broadcast writing to print, for her critical reads of my first few chapters, and especially for her Miss Smarty-pants sense of humor.

To Alexandra Siegal for her encouragement to write this book, for her knowledgeable comments and feedback, and for graciously and eagerly sharing her knowledge of the publishing world.

To the many employment defense lawyers who shared their insight and expertise but who prefer not to be named as having shared legal strategies with the opposing side.

Also thanks to Jim Herman, Bonnie Nelson, Ken deRussy, Dinah Hoyland, Susan Hirasuna, Megan Klee, Matt Dettman, Lauren Diehl, Janis Moore, Sally Anderson, Susan Boyd, Deborah Kranze Feess, Jay Jovanov, Rose Nowak Smith, Anna Masters, Rebecca Westerfield, Ruth Handler, Jemela Macer, Elizabeth Orozco, Jack Popejoy, Ginny Waters, and countless others who offered feedback, advice, or assistance, or who have shared their stories.

It was at the suggestion of both my literary agent and my editor that I include my own story throughout this book. I realize that my own experiences add life and understanding to what might otherwise be complex and cloudy legal issues. For me, however, it meant taking a step backward in my life in order to relive the pain and humiliation I endured throughout my discrimination lawsuit. Nevertheless, it did produce a better book, and I thank them for suggesting it.

Most specifically, to my agent, Robin Rue, for her candid enthusiasm from the very beginning and for managing to keep it up throughout the entire process. I am grateful for her professional attitude, for being diligent about the smallest of details, for her firsthand understanding of "mommydom," and especially for wearing nylons to all the important meetings. Thanks to her assistant, Mark Chelius.

Also, sincere thanks to my editor, Shauna Summers, for choosing to undertake this book. In doing so, she not only gave it life but infused it with a straighter path and a more meaningful scope. I'm especially appreciative of her professional consistency and of her confidence in me throughout. Thanks also to Charlotte Herscher and to the many others at Ballantine who shared their talents and provided assistance in getting this book to print.

To my sister Laurie for her ever-patient listening skills and for all those early-morning phone conversations when I needed her most.

To my parents for teaching me the importance of having a cast-iron stomach in the face of adversity.

To my husband, Jeff, for his enduring love, friendship, and strength.

Finally, to my daughters, Alana and Malia, who on the momentous occasions of their births, brought about everlasting change in my life. I thank God.

AUTHOR'S NOTE

Some of the names of the women who have shared their stories with me have been changed at their request. Some of their job titles or occupations have also been changed. In some cases, I've merged several of their stories into one for the sake of clarity and brevity.

Work Smarts for Women

Introduction

"You're not fired. You're just being replaced." I sat stunned, unable to reply to my boss, the CNN Los Angeles bureau chief, Dave Farmer. "You've been one of my best and favorite employees, Patti, but as you are well aware, Jim's here now from the New York bureau." Just a few days earlier, Dave had told me that "Jim" had no children and was probably available to work any day, including holidays. I had wondered why Dave had even brought it up, considering that I had worked almost every weekend and holiday for the past four years.

Now I listened as he continued, "Ed and I thought you wouldn't mind, since you had the baby and all."

Wouldn't mind? If somebody else took my job? It was a job that had been the culmination of years of hard work and sacrifice. Again I was stunned, unable to even speak. Me, a CNN news correspondent who often spoke to half the planet, a lawyer trained to stand up and argue a case—unable to speak.

I mustered up all my resolve, my professionalism, my experience, my stamina . . . and then burst into tears.

Looking back, I know I should have seen the writing on the wall. Three years earlier, when I became pregnant with my first child, CNN had not taken kindly to the news. In fact, CNN Executive Vice President Ed Turner (no relation to Ted) had openly complained about my pregnancy. When I was five months pregnant, Atlanta-based Turner had seen one of my news stories and remarked, "Paniccia's looking fat these days." "She's not fat," someone had replied, "she's pregnant." Coworkers would later tell me that Turner had appeared visibly annoyed with the news and had remarked sourly, "Another good reporter down the drain."

I wrote him a letter, but decided not to tell him what I'd heard. I didn't want to antagonize the most important person in the network with respect to hiring and firing reporters, but at the same time I wanted to send a clear message that I wasn't going "down the drain."

When I had first met Ed, I'd told him I was willing to work a weekend-only job at CNN since there were no weekday shifts available at the Los Angeles bureau. I knew I was making less money than my full-time counterparts, but I figured I was paying dues, and I anticipated moving into a full-time weekday slot as soon as one opened up. Now I wrote to Ed suggesting that rather than wait for a Monday-through-Friday slot, why not sign me to a full-time contract for a Wednesday-through-Sunday shift? I realized the likelihood of that was slim, but at least my suggestion would communicate to him that I still intended to work full-time, despite whatever notions he might have that my pregnancy somehow indicated otherwise.

His reply arrived the same day my baby was born. "Dear Patti . . . Whatsamattah? You can't just have the baby during your lunch hour? Gone soft? We cannot add a [full-time] correspondent at the bureau until there is an opening but if/when that happens we would be happy to talk with you. Assuming you have not gone all goo-goo on us. Meantime, quit thinking CNN and start considering Mommydom; I'm sure you will come up with a good five part series on childbearing-while-editing-a-late-breaking story. Regards, Ed T."

I read the note over and over again, trying to decipher exactly what to make of it. Was it a joke? Perhaps if it had come from one of my newsroom colleagues, I might have taken it that way, but this was from someone I barely knew, someone in a position of authority whom I'd met briefly only twice before. Taken in conjunction with his remark about my "going down the drain," it was no joke. Maybe he'd felt duped that when we had last spoken about my future at CNN, I hadn't mentioned I was pregnant. It had been so early in my pregnancy that I didn't think it appropriate to bring it up. Imagine saying, "Oh, by the way, Ed, my period is two weeks late." On my doctor's advice, I did not officially notify my bureau chief until I was three months pregnant. Perhaps my bureau chief had never told Ed?

Throughout my maternity leave I wondered how to respond to the "mommydom memo." At one point, I took my newborn baby with me to a library and checked out every book I could find on women in the workplace. Another day, I went to a bookstore and bought every single book that looked remotely as if it had the answers to my dilemma. Each book gave different advice. "Immediately file a complaint with the EEOC!" urged one. "Complain to his superior," said another. "Laugh it off and respond in kind," urged yet another, adding, "then try to get transferred to another department with a more sympathetic supervisor." Not a bad idea, I thought. I applied for an opening as the West Coast correspondent for CNN Business News, a division *not* under Ed Turner. I would be working with Los Angeles–based David Saeger, a witty guy who had a secret life as a stand-up comedian. He was among the brightest producers I'd encountered at CNN, and according to David, I was on a shortlist of three to be hired, but then the Gulf War unexpectedly began heating up and plans for a West Coast business reporter were temporarily scrapped. I was left wondering what to do.

In the end, I chose to continue working as if nothing had happened. I shared the memo with only one other person at CNN, reporter Anne McDermott. Anne was a close friend and the only other woman news correspondent in the L.A. bureau. I swore her to secrecy, feeling ashamed and frightened that if others should learn of my fall from grace, they would treat me poorly. Assignment desk managers, responsible for divvying up news stories among the correspondents, would be fearful of assigning the best stories to a reporter who, for whatever reason, raised the ire of some exec or producer in Atlanta. Someone in Atlanta would holler, "Who the hell sent so-and-so to cover that?" Inevitably, the assignment editor would get blamed. For me, allowing my coworkers—even my own bureau chief—to know about the note would make me feel like the weakest member of the Donner party.

CNN neglected to inform me that the network had recently implemented a complaint procedure for sex-discrimination problems. As a result, I didn't know that I should have reported the matter to the human resources department at CNN Center in Atlanta. Even so, how comfortable can one feel lodging a complaint by telephone with a stranger two thousand miles away? The employee handbook I had received on my hire date stated only that I should talk to a department head or my immediate supervisor. My bureau chief? Surely the kiss of death.

So I continued to work, every weekend and every holiday, for another three years. Maybe if I do good work, I thought, they'll forget I'm a "mommy." Whenever I had confronted sexual bias in the past, I had used my wits and sense of humor to outsmart it. Why should this time be any different?

I worked with a Pollyanna-like enthusiasm that I'm sure made my fellow reporters want to gag. I thought I was succeeding.

But two and a half years later I became pregnant with my second child. Although the pregnancy was a difficult one, I was careful not to allow it to interfere with my story assignments. During the Los Angeles riots I hit the streets pregnant, with a microphone and a bulletproof vest. At times I worked twelve- to fourteen-hour days. Exhausted and sick to my stomach, I would come home and fall into bed, unable to move until the next day. I didn't want anyone saying, "Paniccia can't handle the job because she's pregnant." Once, I was assigned to cover a white supremacist rally in Simi Valley. Unexpectedly, crowds of African-Americans and Latinos showed up to confront the rallyers, and violence broke out. My photographer, Greg Canes, and I were caught between police and rioters. Greg continued to roll video and asked me to walk him backward out of the center of the small riot. It's a small courtesy reporters often do for photographers. The photographer continues to roll tape while a reporter holds the back of his belt. I would be Greg's eyes and slowly lead him backward, instructing him when to step up or down. Most important, I would watch his right side where the large camera mounted on his shoulder blinded him to flying debris, or even an angry punch.

Rocks and bottles flew. A reporter standing just inches from me fell to the ground, his head cut open and bloody. My baby was kicking. I calmly guided Greg to safety. Suddenly I felt an enormous pain as a rock bounced off my pregnant belly. I retreated to our news van and telephoned our bureau, asking that additional people be sent, along with the bureau's supply of goggles and bulletproof vests. I informed her about the rock and said I should probably see my doctor.

The Los Angeles-based assignment editor said she would check with Atlanta. Two minutes later, I had my answer. CNN Center had instructed her to ask if I could file the story even earlier—by 5:00 eastern. I stayed and worked, racing to meet the new deadline. Not only did I make it, I got the story on the air even sooner than they had requested.

I gave birth five months later. Preeclampsia, a dangerous maternal condition that had gripped my earlier pregnancy, returned—only worse this time. I received an emergency C-section and spent nearly a week in the hospital. Despite the fact that California law allows four months' maternity leave following cesareans, I chose to return after only three.

CNN, however, had something else in mind.

In February of 1993, I telephoned Dave Farmer, reminding him that I would be returning to work in March and asking which particular weekend I should start back. We initially agreed on the first weekend in March, but the next day he phoned back and told me that Ed Turner had asked him to give some work to Jim Hill, a correspondent from CNN's New York bureau who had just moved to Los Angeles. Dave asked whether I would mind if Jim worked my shift every other weekend. "Yes, I do mind," I said, but Dave insisted. "Just do this favor for me. For two months, alternate weekends with Jim and then you can have your job back." He implied that he would be in hot water with Ed if I refused. Against my better judgment, I agreed. After all, what choice did I have? If I insisted otherwise, my own bureau chief would hate my guts.

I was one of the few females my bureau chief tolerated, and I wanted to keep it that way. He had demoted or transferred most of the women who were directly underneath him, and brought in men to take their places. One man had no college degree; nor did he have any significant newswriting or reporting experience. In fact, his only management background had been a short stint as an underling on the assignment desk in the New York bureau. Dave eventually promoted him to second in command, responsible for reviewing every reporter script before it went on the air. Farmer's number three in command regularly sent one female employee home in tears, ridiculing her about her work and her long crinkly hair. He made comments about another woman's body, and even assigned an experienced newswoman to answer his phone.

At the end of two months, almost to the day, I told Dave I wanted my job back. "I'll check with Ed," he said. I wondered why he needed to check at all, but in just a few days I had my answer. Dave called me into his office to tell me I was being "replaced."

"Well, Patti, I was being polite when I *asked* whether Jim could work part of your shift. Actually, it was an audition, and Ed chose Jim."

An *audition* for my own job? I had been on air at CNN for four years; Jim for three out of New York. The "audition" excuse, like several other excuses CNN would eventually come up with, made no sense at all.

I thought back to a story my own mother had often told me. When she announced to her boss that she was two months pregnant, he immediately sent her home. "Of course you won't be wanting to work now that you are going to be a mother!" he had told her as he ushered her out the office door before she could say the word "income." My parents were poor. The sizable dent her job loss put in their budget made their lives difficult. Five years later, when she became pregnant again, she conveniently "forgot" to mention it to her new boss until she was six months along. Whenever I'd heard the story, I'd always thought how much things had changed since then.

Yet here I was, forty years old, crying in my boss's office as he told me I was being "replaced." I left the bureau head down, ashamed and embarrassed. Once at home, I sat on my couch and cried some more. My then three-year-old daughter, Alana, put her hand on my shoulder. "Mommy," she said, "I don't think it was very nice what CNN did to you. I think you should take some of their toys away." "Yes, Alana," I said. "It's called punitive damages." Then I picked up the phone.

Unfortunately, the first lawyer I chose was not the one for me. Although he has quite a reputation in discrimination cases, he seemed busy and distracted, and I ended up doing much of the work for him. He had me prepare two huge, tabbed binders full of facts and relevant items. Then he had me contact potential witnesses and prepare lengthy memos for his investigator, a woman who read my memos, telephoned each witness to verify what I had written, and rewrote almost word for word what I had given her. He also sent me alone to the EEOC, without advising me how to word my complaint. As I was to learn more than a year later, every word I stated—and the manner in which I stated it—would prove critical in my case. During the four months I spent with him, he returned only one of my phone calls, and took $3,000 from me for expenses. Eventually, I wrote him an angry letter instructing him either to return my call or refrain from working on my case, but he never called. It was my darkest hour.

Unable to sleep much at night, I had spent my days since being fired in a continual state of exhaustion. I was absentminded and distracted. Once, while driving, I inadvertently turned left in front of oncoming traffic. Had the other driver not been quick to react, I probably would have been killed. I developed constant headaches, which my doctor attributed to stress, and for which he prescribed drugs. I spent six weeks on Xanax, during which time my life seemed a blur. At one point I was scheduled to speak at a seminar by the California Judges' Association. I showed up an hour late, exhausted and hungry, yet unable to hold down any food. To this day, I remember nothing about the afternoon other than shaking hand after hand of both judges and journalists, nodding and smiling.

Finally, almost seven months after I'd been fired, I telephoned an acquaintance at one of the largest law firms in the country, which represents many high-profile employers against discrimination claims. "Which lawyer's name do you see on a complaint," I asked her, "that makes your side want to die?" She thought about it for a moment and then replied, "There was one lawyer who brought our firm to its knees."

That was John C. Taylor. I scheduled an appointment with him for January 17, 1994. It was a tumultuous beginning. At 4:32 that morning, the Northridge earthquake started with a jolt, purred into a gentle rumble, and then ended with what seemed like an eternity of violent shaking. Between my home in the Los Angeles foothills and John's Santa Monica office lay burning buildings, exploding gas lines, and shattered freeways. I didn't even try to make the appointment. My husband, a television news photographer for a local station, began working long days to cover the earthquake, gauged 6.7 on the Richter scale. I stayed home, huddled with the kids, and realized it was the first major news story in more than a decade that I wasn't covering.

Two weeks later, I signed John as my lawyer. He asked me to meet Christine Spagnoli, an associate in his office whom he wanted on the case with him. I liked her the moment I met her, and I later learned that when I had first faxed a letter to John outlining my case and asking him to represent me, he had asked Christine for her opinion. "You *have* to call her, John. You *have* to represent her," she had emphatically declared.

Over time, I would learn how they worked together. John, quick on his feet and lyrical in his speech, would do most of the talking in open court. Christine, extremely bright, detail-oriented, and academically focused, would prepare a myriad of motions and other written legal documents in response to the mounds of paperwork CNN constantly filed.*

But even John and Christine couldn't protect me from the legal maneuvering and attacks CNN would wage on me. Some of it was permitted by law.

One of the most invasive cheap shots CNN's lawyers took was to subpoena my personal obstetric/gynecological records from the hospital where I had given birth. A common intimidation trick by defense lawyers, it is usually meant to make a woman feel like giving up. Instead it only strengthened my belief that I was doing the right thing. After all, if they'd had any real evidence to use against me, they wouldn't be messing around with irrelevant minutiae.

*On July 9, 1999, John and Christine's law firm of Greene, Broillet, Taylor, Wheeler and Panish obtained the largest personal injury verdict in history—$4.9 billion against General Motors—in *Anderson v. General Motors*. The lead counsel on the case was Brian Panish. Christine Spagnoli acted as associate counsel.

Although most depositions last only a matter of hours, CNN insisted on deposing me for five days. Most of their questions were worded in an accusatory fashion, as if *I* were the one who had done something wrong. As torturous as it was, the ordeal could have been a lot worse. The lawyer merely *read* the questions to me in a dronelike, pedestrian manner. As a result, there were times when she seemed less like a tough opponent and more like a bothersome gnat.

Once, when I walked onto campus at Pepperdine Law School, where I had begun teaching law school, two professors, two deans, and one administrator told me, "Patti, I just filled out a questionnaire asking about your work here and requesting I turn over anything in writing from or about you." I was lucky. My past was squeaky clean. If a woman has the slightest bit of perceived controversy in her past, the corporate defense lawyers will tear her apart.

Yet even my innocuous background didn't stop CNN from trying to insinuate otherwise. They presented me with a résumé I had submitted in applying for my CNN job. The résumé had a date that was one year off. I had provided the network with other paperwork that listed the correct year, but CNN accused me of lying on my résumé. CNN's lawyers also went after what they believed to be a similar date discrepancy on my previous contract with KCOP, a local television station in Los Angeles where I had worked prior to CNN. I telephoned my former boss, who offered to testify on my behalf to explain the discrepancy.

CNN was also allowed to characterize me in any way they saw fit. The network's lawyers likened my lawsuit to an extortion plot. They claimed my newswriting ability was mediocre and my on-air presence boring despite the rave reviews I had received while working there. They characterized my male replacement as being tremendously more qualified than I, even though I had been at CNN longer, and insisted that I was simply a "junior female employee" replaced by a "more senior and able employee." Their lawyers also claimed that CNN's action in replacing me was something done "in the *entertainment* industry every day." I often wondered how some of CNN's award-winning journalists would feel knowing that CNN regarded them as "entertainers."

More disturbing, however, were the numerous phone calls I received throughout the lawsuit that turned out to be bogus "survey companies." One claimed to be an insurance company inquiring how many insurance claims or lawsuits I'd filed in my life. (One road of defense in discrimination claims is to show that the person complaining has a history of filing nuisance lawsuits. Fortunately, I didn't.) Another caller claiming to represent my telephone company asked whether I had a second line in the house and whether I was online and/or using a fax machine. I did have a second line, but when I called the phone company to verify the legitimacy of the survey, they knew nothing about it. They did point out that they, as my phone company, generally know how many lines a person has in their home. At times, men would sit in plain sedans at the park directly across from my house. Once I called the police and watched as a dispatched officer approached the car. The officer later told me he thought the stranger was a private investigator who, like any other person, has a right to be in a public park. Although we never were able to verify whether the surveillance and phone calls stemmed from the litigation, all of it stopped when the lawsuit ended.

What gave me strength in the face of everything was knowing that I wasn't the only woman at CNN to suffer this kind of treatment. Employees at CNN had begun contacting me to share their experiences. Some told me they had recently filled out a CNN in-house questionnaire as part of a "diversity study" the network was conducting. They said the survey had asked whether they'd ever experienced discrimination on the job. Although CNN had guaranteed anonymity to the employees who filled it out, many chose to come forward to testify about what they had written.

We subpoenaed the diversity study, but CNN refused to turn it over. In a heated hearing, John and Christine asked the judge to order CNN to do so, but the network still refused. Instead, CNN's lawyers accused me of just looking for a payoff, insisting I had no facts to support my "loser of a case."

John then interjected that if CNN really thought my case was such a loser, why had the network sent *four* lawyers down to the courtroom that day?

The judge ordered the survey turned over. She also allowed my lawyers to amend and broaden our original complaint, which would entitle us to the diversity study and other similar evidence we needed.

Instead, CNN asked a higher court to direct the judge to change her ruling.

Six months later, the California Court of Appeal rejected CNN's request, and CNN was forced to turn over not only the survey but the salaries of all CNN correspondents. It was a major turning point in my case.

Despite the legal upswing in my case, my name was fast becoming mud in the broadcast industry. Unless and until a woman publicly proves her case, most employers tend to write her off as a "problem employee." At broadcast industry cocktail parties, I'd often overheard men in management float the idea that a woman who had recently filed a complaint was just a bad seed that their company simply had to pay off. It's a reality that any woman filing a complaint must consider.

But media executives began to take note of my case as CNN women started coming forward to testify about their own experiences at the network. Shockingly, CNN's lawyers had arranged for Dave Farmer, their boss, to sit just a few feet from them as they gave their depositions under oath. They were forced to speak in front of the man they were complaining about—the supervisor they would have to report to the next morning. What upset one woman in particular, however, was a comment Ted Turner, president of CNN, had made to her while visiting the Los Angeles bureau. "What is it you [women] are all bitching about?" he had asked.

Throughout my lawsuit, the outdated views espoused by some of the male management at CNN puzzled many outsiders. What they didn't understand is that in its start-up days, CNN had difficulty attracting experienced network executives. Some of the first-hired bosses had never risen very high in their prior jobs, or had been laid off early in their careers. And some had no network experience at all, coming directly from smaller local television stations in and around Georgia and the South. As CNN rose to prominence, these men rose with it—some bringing provincial and bigoted attitudes with them. They were still in place when I worked there.

Yet the women remained strong. Catheryn Reardon, just one year out of college at the time, testified how she had applied for a promotion on the assignment desk when she was eight months pregnant. Instead of an interview, she received what she termed a "family moral issues" lecture from our bureau chief on how mothers in his day and age didn't work. She was also told there would be no more work for her at CNN.

Lisa Britton and Merrill Horowitz, two videotape editors, testified that they had learned their male coworkers were making more money. Merrill said that when they had complained to CNN of sex discrimination, the vice president of the human resources department had reacted with anger that they had "snooped" by asking the men their salaries.

Lynda Nikula, a young up-and-comer, testified to watching a succession of less-experienced men being promoted over her.

Ellie Miller, the assignment desk manager who had been on duty the day I'd covered the Simi Valley riot, also came forward. Her startling beauty had prompted the male management to ignore her professional demeanor and determination and treat her like a bimbo up for grabs, rather than the summa cum laude graduate she was.

Veronica McGregor had the most to give us and the most to lose. A single mother and senior producer at the Los Angeles bureau, there was no denying her talent and capabilities, yet Dave Farmer and his team of male leaders had consistently treated her poorly, subjecting her to numerous insults and actions steeped in sex-based bias. She testified that when she had told Farmer she was pregnant, he had initially informed her that he couldn't guarantee she would have a job after her maternity leave. She also related that after lodging a complaint about the general way the bureau was being managed, she found a package of premenstrual medication left on her desk, with the word "Loser" scribbled across it. When she brought it to the bureau chief's attention, he refused to acknowledge that anyone in the bureau would do such a thing.

Men offered to testify as well. My former weekend assignment editor swore that there had never been any complaints about my work and that it was always well received by Atlanta. He also related that he was deeply concerned that a male coworker was being retaliated against for complaining about CNN's poor treatment of women.

Not surprisingly, some of my colleagues were not as eager to involve themselves. One woman, after giving both me and the investigator a lengthy complaint about the discrimination she'd encountered, managed to forget everything she'd said when it came time to repeat it in front of Dave Farmer and the CNN lawyers. Under oath, she colored her testimony with doubt and characterized her bosses in a more favorable light. Other potential witnesses refused to return my calls. One of my closest friends asked me not to involve her. Yet a certain degree of that was to be expected. In most cases, people are unwilling to risk their careers for a coworker.

Most marriages would have crumbled under the incredible pressure of this kind of lawsuit, but my husband, Jeff, managed to take it all in stride. An Emmy-winning television news photographer, Jeff once worked at CNN, where his easygoing, likable personality often prompted reporters to request him as their photographer. Jeff left that job, however, when a local television station in Los Angeles offered him more money. Once I asked him why he was being so patient with my foul moods and low attention span. "Because when I told people at my work we were going to have a baby," he said, "no one asked me whether I might go all 'goo-goo' on them." Jeff never complained about my loss of income during those two years, either. He just worked overtime.

As we approached trial, more than two years after I'd been fired, the judge pressed us to enter into mediation with CNN. For the first time, CNN began to talk about real solutions. Within a month, my case had settled. As part of the settlement, I agreed not to disclose the exact terms and provisions of the agreement, so I cannot share that part of my case with you.

I can tell you that afterward women from CNN around the world called or wrote to thank me for bringing the issue of gender discrimination at the network to light. Some reported getting raises; others said they were offered better opportunities for promotion, or that they became more highly regarded.

My bureau chief was removed from his position, and a woman was brought in to take his place. Some time later, Ed Turner was also reassigned, to what various newspapers defined as a "sidelines position" of "largely ceremonial" significance. His reassignment came shortly after CNN reached an out-of-court settlement for a discrimination complaint lodged against him by his administrative assistant of twelve years. Still, publicly, the network continues to laud him as being a "superb news executive" who's been "absolutely loyal" to CNN's upper management.

Shortly after the lawsuit ended, I started a scholarship at Pepperdine School of Law, where I now teach. It financially assists law students who do 50 percent or more of the active parenting of a minor child—students who must take real time away from their studies to "be there" for a child.

People often ask me if I was elated when my case ended. The answer is no. I liken it to a woman finally getting herself out of an abusive relationship. She's never happy the minute it ends; instead she feels beaten and worn down. She can then only *begin* the healing process.

For me it was a slow, steady climb up. Now, several years later, I've managed to get back to my life. But the truth is, the entire ordeal forever changed me in ways I never would have anticipated. Three things prompted that change. The first changed me inside as a person. The other two motivated me to write this book.

First, I learned that we, as women, are really not as isolated in our employment problems as we often feel. In the year I was fired, a shocking 30 million women experienced sex discrimination on the job, according to the United States Department of Labor's *Glass Ceiling Report.* In fact, the report showed that one out of four working women believe that "being a woman/sexism" is the biggest obstacle they have to overcome in the workplace.

And it's not only women who work outside the home who are acutely aware of this problem. Throughout my lawsuit, I began to gather regularly with a small group of women for support and encouragement. One was an accountant. Another worked in her husband's plumbing shop. One was a lawyer, another an editor at a parenting magazine. And two were stay-at-home moms. Initially, I thought none of them would *truly* be able to relate to what I was going through. Yet not a single woman in my group was surprised to learn of what had happened to me. Instead, they each shared similar experiences with me. They opened my eyes to the knowledge that women everywhere have bonds that bridge all socioeconomic backgrounds—and that even the most traditional woman knows what it means to be discriminated against, whether it's just a subtle comment made in passing with a man in authority or a husband's insistence that she's not capable of organizing the household finances.

Ever since my lawsuit garnered national media attention, women from around the country have tracked me down to speak with me and to share their experiences. Some are professionals. Some are laborers. Some are illegal immigrants. Some are well-known, highly paid corporate executives. They are in their late sixties and in their teens. I came to realize that no matter how successful a woman is, no matter how rich or poor, no matter how much power she does or doesn't hold, no matter her political inclinations—she has at *some* time been singled out in the workplace and treated unfairly.

The second thing I discovered is that a tremendous void exists with regard to information and assistance for women who encounter discrimination.

Why isn't there more visible help for us? When I was fired, I had no idea where to turn for information. I desperately needed a list of options on how to respond each time I met with gender-biased remarks or actions, and I needed to know the consequences of each response I made. Yet most of the books I found addressed only social behaviors in the workplace—teaching corporate strategies and tactics to help women fit in to what has historically been a male-friendly environment. Although the books were valuable in some respects, they didn't give me the answers I needed. Many, too, addressed only women in executive positions, ignoring the great masses of women in the workplace.

Those few books that did address sex discrimination dealt only with the very narrow issue of sexual harassment. Harassment (sex for promotion, unwanted sexual advances, etc.) is only one area in which women need answers. What about pay disparities, women's lack of promotions as compared to their male coworkers, the assignment of lesser job duties to women, pregnancy, and implicit beliefs about women's ability to do their jobs? Ironically, the only books that addressed the full range of discrimination issues were written for *employers.* The cover of one such book boasts that the book will teach managers how to "set up a paper trail to defuse discrimination claims" and also "how to use performance reviews" to avoid such claims. Another book promises to teach an employer how to make "legally defensible decisions" in dealing with employee problems.

The third and final thing I realized is that women start at an enormous disadvantage. Most women are unaware that employers spend millions of dollars a year protecting and educating themselves and their managers. Did you know that in most companies high-level supervisors and management personnel are:

- sent to management training seminars on discrimination
- offered immediate legal consultation whenever a potential problem arises
- given armfuls of literature on how to carefully document workplace scenarios
- taught what items to include in an employee's file that will help protect the company should that employee ever complain of discrimination
- taught how to word employment agreements to shield an employer from being held responsible if a woman is ever fired for any reason, even one involving discrimination
- instructed how to keep track of day-to-day information that would be useful to the company should an employee ever lodge a complaint

Employees, on the other hand, are usually invited to a short company meeting, or are provided a pamphlet, informing them they don't have to put up with sex discrimination and instructing them to report any such discrimination to the company's human resources department or to a government agency. Often this information is provided not because a company really cares but because it's required by law.

Although there are some protections in place to prevent sex discrimination, most women don't know what they are. Some women are unaware of their own company's policy, or are unable to find out. Others are afraid of retaliation. In many cases, the facts fall into a gray area that precludes women from being able to tell whether their situation even constitutes discrimination, let alone know how to handle it.

Where are our seminars? Where are our armfuls of information? Who teaches us how to make day-to-day decisions that will affect our future? Who instructs us on how to posture in advance? Who tells us what every employee should document, whether she is having a problem with sex discrimination or not? And who teaches us how to proceed if we do face a discrimination problem? Where do we go and to whom do we turn? Where are our guidebooks?

This is one.

PART ONE

EVALUATING YOUR JOB

1.

Why Things Are the Way They Are: A Look Backward

"Something better than his dog; a little dearer than his horse."
—Alfred Lord Tennyson,
describing a woman in *Locksley Hall* (1842)

It wasn't so long ago that women were regarded as property. They were owned by their husbands. And because a husband was legally responsible for his wife's behavior, the law gave him the authority to discipline her. If a man's dog bit someone, *he* would be responsible. If his horse kicked a passerby, *he* would have to make reparations. Similarly, if his wife harmed someone, ran up debts, lied, cheated, or stole, *he* would have to correct the situation. So in order to allow a man to properly train his dog, his horse, and his wife, the law permitted him to beat them. Not a lot. Just enough for them to understand what was expected of them.[1]

The notion that women are somehow not fully capable of taking care of themselves and that men are better suited for responsibility has diminished greatly in our society, but not completely. Remnants of this notion are embedded in our everyday life, and nowhere does it manifest itself more than in the workplace.

Think about it. In general, women make less money, have more menial duties, and hold fewer managerial positions.[2] The majority of women answer to male bosses. Even if their immediate supervisor happens to be a woman, chances are that at the very top of the hierarchy is a man.[3]

Those women who *do* venture up the work ladder learn something very quickly: They are in an environment that for centuries has been developed and patterned to accommodate a traditional male lifestyle.

I once sat in on a corporate meeting of a Fortune 500 company. Two of the people scheduled to be at the meeting called to say they would be late. One, a male executive, called from his car to say he was stuck behind a four-car accident on a Los Angeles freeway. Not a single person batted an eye when he announced he would be an hour late. After all, traffic in L.A. was something to which they could all relate. One of the men at the table said that he used to commute on the same freeway but had taken to using side streets because of the constant congestion. Several others nodded their heads in agreement, noting how miserable that particular freeway was.

Minutes later a second employee, a woman and the only female besides myself who was scheduled to be present, called to say that she, too, would be an hour late. Her four-year-old son had suddenly become ill and she wanted to drop him at the doctor, where her baby-sitter was waiting. I watched as more than one set of eyebrows were raised at the table. One board member murmured to the woman's supervisor, "This isn't the first time she's had to take off because of her kid. You might want to mention in her next performance review that she needs to get her priorities straight. Have her clarify them for you."

I realized that, most likely, the men at the table had never personally experienced having to take time away from work to care for a child. Traditionally, men have had wives who assumed the day-to-day child-rearing responsibilities, so the workplace was never forced to respond to those kinds of needs. Even today, studies show that when two parents work, it is usually the mother who assumes the role of primary caregiver, doing duty as a worker both inside and outside of the home.[4]

Although the men at this meeting didn't seem particularly malicious in their criticism of the woman, they obviously just couldn't identify with her predicament—at least not in the same way they could with the man who was stuck in traffic. As a result, they viewed her as being delinquent, less serious about her job, and probably less productive for the company.

The workplace tends to tolerate, even subsidize, certain needs of male workers. I've seen corporate executives treat employees with alcohol problems (statistically an overwhelmingly male problem[5]) like long-lost brothers. "Sure, go into rehab. We'll be here waiting for you when you get out." The same empathy and understanding is usually nowhere to be found when a woman wants to, say, go on maternity leave.

It would be unreasonable and irrational for us as women to expect our employers to accommodate and subsidize our *every* need. We all have to make certain sacrifices for our jobs. We need to show commitment and give the time and effort they require. Yet at the same time, women must typically mold themselves to a greater degree than do men in order to "fit" into the workplace, simply because the female lifestyle is not as well tolerated. Since the demands that women make are not the "norm" in the workplace, we are much more vulnerable to being labeled as "undependable," "less serious," "not on target," "not a team player," even "uncooperative" and "irresponsible."[6]

How do women deal with all this?

For the most part, they mask their needs. For instance, studies show that many women tell their employers that they themselves are sick when they have to stay home to care for an ill child. They feel they are less likely to get criticized.[7] They simply cover up . . . mask . . . lie . . . play the game. Call it what you will. Women just don't bring their cards to the table.[8]

But the real answer lies elsewhere.

Rather than have women adjust themselves and their behaviors to fit into a workplace designed to accommodate their male colleagues, the ultimate solution lies in adjusting the workplace to include and accommodate women to the same degree that it does men.

So far the transition has been less than graceful. The workplace is bulging and stretching in directions no one would have anticipated, and it's creating pressure and strain on us all.

Supervisors are confused and angry that the rules they learned and were made to follow while coming up through the ranks are no longer in place. From their perspective, women aren't playing by the rules. They are cheaters.

From women's perspectives, employers are intolerant of their needs and, at times, discriminatory in their actions. Many women don't fully understand the dynamics of how and why the workplace has evolved to serve men so well and women so inadequately. Instead, they just *sense* that they are not being treated fairly.

When women object to this treatment, employers see themselves as victims of frivolous workplace complaints that are hard to document and even harder to defend. They feel attacked and react by taking on a defensive posture, utilizing a variety of mechanisms and legal weapons to ensure that if a problem ever does arise, employees will already have the legal deck stacked against them. This before-the-fact strategy is called "preventative labor counseling." Employers spent 60 billion dollars training 54 million people in 1998[9]—and much of that training involved preventative labor counseling.

This response would be reasonable if employers were truly protecting themselves against only false or frivolous complaints. But unfortunately, these devices also protect employers against any woman who has a legitimate complaint of sex discrimination.

Most disheartening is the tone used in some of those programs. Trainers take a ruthless approach to sex discrimination complaints as compared to other types of discrimination claims. For instance, when instructing employers on how to confront race discrimination, they speak about the importance of making judgments that are fair and consistent with the law and with notions of equality—judgments that are in the best interest of the person complaining. With sex discrimination issues, however, many trainers instruct employers to declare war. Attack the accuser. See what she's made of. Check out every angle and look for holes in her story, patterns of inconsistency, time frames that don't match, and colleagues who rebut what she claims. Many employers seem to have no qualms about doubting or discrediting the woman, and they truly believe their main obligation in assessing her complaint is to minimize their own liability.

For example, look at how charges of sexual harassment are dealt with in our courts. When a woman complains of harassment, employers and their lawyers often opt for the "nuts and sluts" defense. She's either a nut, with no basis for her complaint, or a slut, someone who asked for it and/or enjoyed it. Their attack on her character and credibility is relentless.

Why? I can only speculate that perhaps men believe the workplace need not accommodate women. After all, if the male worker is the "norm," then female needs are deviant.

Even some women managers buy into the male definition of what a "normal worker" should be. It's what they learned coming up in the ranks. Some of those women feel that since *they* had to play by those rules, then why shouldn't others?

The chances that you, as a woman, will experience some sort of sex discrimination during your career are greater than one in two.[10] It's just good business to prepare in advance for what will probably be. This book begins with the day you apply for a job.

2.

Looking for a Job

Job Recruiting

HELP WANTED (IF YOU'RE THE RIGHT SEX)

Shortly after my second child was born, I placed the following ad in a newspaper:

> Help Wanted. Child care in my home. Must drive, have experience and excellent local references.

I was surprised when a gruff male voice inquired on the phone whether my children were girls or boys. "Girls," I answered. "Oh, good," he muttered, "I like girls." Then he said, "I drive, I have experience and local references. When can I come by for an interview?" A *man* in my house caring for my two little girls? Feeding and clothing them as I was getting ready for work? It didn't feel right. Was I being sexist? Just as I was wondering how to respond, the voice chuckled and teased, "This is your brother-in-law, and I just wanted you to know what a sexist pig you are."

He had a good point. Just when *can* an employer legally tell you that a position should be filled only by a man or a woman?

The answer is rarely, and only under specific conditions and circumstances.

Few employers will actually advertise that a job is open only to men. The Equal Employment Opportunity Commission (EEOC) has taken the stance that the mere placement of such an advertisement violates the law, whereas some courts hold that it's the actual hiring that does so. In some states, newspapers that have separate columns, "Help Wanted—Male" and "Help Wanted—Female," can be found liable for discrimination.[1]

The basic rule is that any advertisement that can be expected to produce a disproportionate number of applicants of one sex is illegal. That means no specific wording, such as "stewardess" rather than flight attendant or "policeman" rather than police officer.

Laboring over word choice may seem like an innocuous thing, even a waste of time and effort. But words *are* important. They directly affect how we think and feel about issues.

I walked into my daughter's preschool one day and saw a sign that read, "Fireman Tim will be speaking to the children today about fire safety." I asked the teacher if she would consider changing the wording to "Fire*fighter* Tim." She immediately did so, just as Fireman Tim walked in the door and asked what she was doing. When she told him, he shook his head and said, "Oh, so we have to be politically correct now? Do you really think it makes any difference?" "Of course," I replied, but I could see the look of exasperation and disbelief on his face. So I asked, "If the job were a fire*woman*, do you think you would have applied?"

Later that day, when my daughter came home from school, she told me a firefighter had come to her classroom. I was glad that her first exposure to the career had not saddled her with preconceived notions based on gender semantics.

WORD OF MOUTH

Some employers don't use advertising to fill positions. Ruth N. lives in a small town where there aren't a lot of job openings. She recalls her difficulty finding a job this way:

> *I kept trying to apply for a traveling salesperson job selling office products to businesses. Everybody in town knew what a choice job it was. So I'd call every few months, but each time there was an opening, it would already have been filled by word of mouth through someone in the company. And I noticed that all the sales force was male, but the guy in the hiring department there told me it was just coincidence—that they didn't really have a policy either way. It was just that the workers already there found out about the opening first and told their friends to apply.*

Coincidence or not, the practice is illegal. Any recruiting technique that results in gender imbalance is against the law. In addition, an employer must prevent practices that *perpetuate* any present imbalance.

Word-of-mouth recruiting tends to do just that. So does giving jobs to former employees, close friends, and relatives of the existing workforce. If those practices result in imbalance, they're against the law.

EXCEPTIONS THAT ALLOW EMPLOYERS TO HIRE ONE SEX

There are two narrow exceptions to the rule that prohibits an employer from hiring one sex over the other.

One is small companies with fewer than fifteen employees. They are not bound by the federal laws that prohibit discrimination. This is because Congress did not want to burden small enterprises with costly litigation that might drive them out of business. Congress was also concerned about intruding into small family-run businesses, many of which have only relatives as employees. In addition, most states have antidiscrimination laws, some of which apply to businesses with *fewer* than fifteen employees. See Table I to determine how many people your employer must hire before being bound by your state's antidiscrimination laws.

An employer also has the right to seek job applicants of only one sex under the "bona fide occupational qualification" exception, or BFOQ. The employer must be able to show that the sex of the applicant is "reasonably necessary to the normal operation of that particular business or enterprise." This is a very narrow exception, and courts are continually construing it even more narrowly. Exceptions that would fall into this category would be along the lines of *Playboy* magazine looking for a model, a casting director looking for an actor to play a male or female role, and perhaps an artificial insemination clinic looking for a sperm donor.

For a more detailed explanation of BFOQ, see chapter 15, "Civil Rights Laws."

(Incidentally, one very successful edition of *Playboy* magazine had a man on its cover, dressed and made up like a woman. Venerated stage actress Dame Judith Anderson played Hamlet in tights and a blond wig at Carnegie Hall. And Mary Martin was a most convincing Peter Pan. However, I've yet to hear of a female sperm donor.)

JOB DESCRIPTIONS

It may surprise you to learn that employers write job descriptions with more in mind than just attracting applicants. A job description can give your boss leverage should you ever lodge a discrimination complaint.

"The smart manager writes every job description with the presumption that it will be used in court," says one prominent employment lawyer. "The more detailed a job description is—the more it specifically lists required qualifications and responsibilities—the less likely an employer will be held accountable for an arbitrary or discriminating decision." Also, armed with a detailed job description, an employer can easily point to legitimate failings on your part in not meeting the job's requirements.

The job description is a legal tool that notifies the employee of all her obligations yet remains conspicuously silent with respect to any obligations the employer might have. Job descriptions can be published in local newspapers, posted on company premises, listed on the Internet, or incorporated into company flyers and similar type publications. They will usually list all the education, work experience, and knowledge you're required to have, yet say nothing about how often you can anticipate raises and promotions, what your hours and working conditions will be, and whatever else you might receive from your employer in return. Some don't even list the salary you will earn. In other words, all the accountability and responsibility is given to you and virtually none to your prospective employer.

What can you do about this? Since you aren't really in a position to rewrite the job description, you must try to extract your prospective employer's reciprocal obligations in other ways.

Have a copy of the description with you when you inquire about or interview for a job. Ask questions such as "Am I going to be given periodic performance reviews?" Or "If I get good performance reviews, can I expect corresponding raises and promotions?" Or "If I do a good job, can I expect to continue working for you?" Take explicit notes of the answers you receive. Write the date and time of the conversation and the name of the person you spoke to.

Staple your notes to a copy of the job description and start a file. From this point on, I'm going to be advising you to place a lot of items in this file. Many will be things you never thought about keeping track of before. But know this: Your employer has a file on you. And the first thing your employer will put into it is a copy of the job description.

Job Applications and Interviews

Each and every question on your job application is carefully calculated to elicit promises and revelations from you that employers might use against you should you ever complain of discrimination. In fact, most application forms are drawn up by lawyers, many of whom subscribe to the notion that an employer should always hire with an eye toward firing.

I attended a lecture for employers titled "'Liar, Liar' How to Avoid Being Set Up for Litigation in Pre-Employment Interviews and Pre-Termination Discussions." The entire premise of this lecture was that employees walk in the door trying to trap an employer into a lawsuit. I was amazed at this presumption, considering that few job applicants, if any, know the legal implications of all that is said and done during the application process. If people *did* have that kind of expertise, the playing field would at least be equal. The truth is that *employers* are usually the only ones who fully understand these legal rights and repercussions. As a group, they tend to have more money to pay for consultants and legal advice. Ironically, in many cases it's the employer who, under the guise of avoiding being set up, is actually doing the ambushing.

Make a copy of your completed application. If the employer won't allow you to take the application home to fill out, then ask the employer to make a copy for you. Most employers won't mind. If the employer doesn't have a copy machine, then copy it yourself before you hand it in.

Place it in your file.

TELL THE TRUTH, THE WHOLE TRUTH, AND NOTHING BUT THE TRUTH.

When you fill out your job application, it's crucial that you be exact in answering each question. Any untruthful statement gives your employer a weighty tool to use against you should you ever complain of discrimination.

Look carefully at your job application to see whether it has an "acknowledgment" or "certification"—a one- or two-sentence statement, usually at the end of the application, where you certify that if you've listed anything untruthful or omitted something substantial, you can be disciplined or fired at any time.

Here's a sample of such a statement:

> I hereby affirm that the foregoing information is true and complete. I further understand that any false information or omissions will be grounds for a refusal to hire me or immediate discharge if hired.

Often when employers want to terminate a person they believe to be a problem employee, they prefer not to go on record with the real reason for dismissal because it may lead to a dispute or even a lawsuit.

Instead, employers will go back to your application, searching for a single misstatement or omission on your part. If they find one, they may then use it as a pretext to fire you. They can use these legitimate and seemingly unquestionable grounds, even if their real motive is discriminatory. Of course, you can always try to prove that the reasons they fired you are discriminatory, but because they now have this documented reason, it will be extremely difficult, if not impossible, for you to prove otherwise.

Why give them this tool? Tell the truth.

Your employer can also use your lie to prevent you from ever bringing a discrimination lawsuit. In that instance, an employer admits the discrimination took place but then asks the court to throw out your case because you do not have "clean hands." Courts rationalize that since you broke the law (lying) you cannot now ask the court to punish your employer for breaking the law (discriminating). Some courts will completely bar you from filing your discrimination claim. Other courts will allow you to file your claim, then limit what you can receive if you are successful.

Still, experts estimate that 15 to 25 percent of all résumés include at least one major fabrication.[2] The most common item people lie about is educational background, often inventing academic degrees or listing their GPA or class standing as higher than it really was. People also tend to misrepresent prior positions, adding more responsibility than they actually had, or inflating their salaries. Or they omit a job that failed to work out.

Does this mean you have to list every job you ever had? A good rule to follow is to list every job that is substantial or relevant to the job for which you're applying. By substantial I mean any job that has played a major role in your career. For instance, if you worked your way through college as a gas station attendant and fast-food clerk, it's probably not relevant to the career you now have as an astrophysicist. But you might want to include a line somewhere on the application like "I held several jobs in college [gas station attendant, fast-food clerk, etc.] that I have not listed but that can be provided upon request." On the other hand, if you're applying for a position as manager at a fast-food restaurant, then your early experience in that field is relevant and should be included. A job might also be considered substantial if you held it for a significant amount of time. For instance, maybe you held the same job throughout college. Or perhaps your résumé would show a large time gap if you don't list a certain job or jobs. In that case, you should include them, regardless of whether they were in your chosen field.

Employers are advised to request written, detailed information on job applications, because the more detailed it is, the more you can be held accountable for any discrepancy. Typically, they are well within their rights to ask for your full name; any prior names; addresses going back ten years; academic and professional degrees and educational institutions; prior employment, including dates, office locations, names of supervisors, and reasons for leaving;

prior criminal convictions; and any civil judgments or ongoing civil proceedings against you.

POLYGRAPH TESTING

Most employers are not allowed to request or require you to take a polygraph test as a precondition of employment. For a full discussion of polygraph testing, see chapter 11, "Invading Your Workplace Privacy."

WHAT IF YOU'VE ALREADY LIED?

What can you do if you've already lied? Not much. There are two defense strategies you can try to use, but they are difficult. Moreover, they won't completely absolve you, since you'll retain the stigma of having lied. Judges and juries will assume that since you lied about one thing you're apt to lie about another, and your testimony will be suspect.

If possible, find out how your employer has reacted in the past to other employees who have lied on their résumés or job applications. If your employer has chosen not to discipline or fire them, then it would be unfair for your employer to do so now with you. Your employer's policy must be uniformly enforced. Any exceptions would be inconsistent, discriminatory behavior toward you. Unfortunately, this kind of information usually can be brought to light only under subpoena. Otherwise, employers aren't likely to disclose it.

Also, what did you lie about? Your wrongdoing must have been of such severity that you would have been immediately fired had they found out about it. If your lie concerned a minor detail, and one that probably would have been overlooked when hiring you, then it cannot later be used to limit your discrimination claim.[3] The problem is that you and your employer are unlikely to agree on what is minor. Your employer will insist your lie was substantial; you will insist it was insignificant; and the two of you will inevitably wind up in court arguing about it.

MAKING COMMITMENTS

When Ellen applied for a position as a buyer at a major department store, she was asked the following questions on her job application: "Can you be available to work any hours?" "Are you willing to travel?" "Can you work overtime?" Wanting to be viewed as an eager and dedicated applicant, Ellen immediately checked "Yes" to all the questions. "I regret that to this day," says Ellen, who was hired and then fired eight months later when she informed her supervisor that she would need to leave work by 6 P.M. each day to pick up her son. "Other employees were asked to work late into the evening and refused. They weren't fired. They fired me because I'd told them I was available to work any hours on my job application."

According to the department store, Ellen was not living up to the commitments she had made on her job application. They were right.

How does this apply to you? Many women have child care responsibilities that employers are reluctant to tolerate. An employer cannot fire you solely because you have parental responsibilities, but *can* fire you if you misrepresent yourself. If an employer gets fed up with a woman whose family responsibilities take her away from her work, the employer might look to her job application and ask, "Did she inform us of these obligations prior to being hired?"

The next logical question is why would an employer hire you in the first place if you indicate on a job application that you are *not* available to work extra hours? The solution is to take a middle ground. Make sure you disclose any *significant* unavailability you might have, and don't bother with the rest.

When you do disclose your unavailability, try to do it in a positive, graceful way. For instance, in reply to the question "Can you work any hours, including overtime?" don't respond with "My children come first!" Instead try "Yes, I will be available and willing to work any overtime the company needs. I would like some notice when the overtime is required so I can make arrangements for child care." You've put your employer on notice of your responsibilities, you have not made any promises you can't keep, and yet you've indicated a willingness to work the overtime the company needs.

THE QUESTIONS THEY SHOULDN'T ASK, BUT DO

I've heard more than one attorney advise employers that the ideal employee is a "bachelor orphan"—a man with no wife or children, and no elderly parents to care for. (Elder care is regarded as the next big burden on the workplace, and is expected to outdo the child care dilemma as baby boomers hit retirement and lean on their children for personal care. The responsibility is expected to fall disproportionately on women.[4]) With a look toward the future, a bachelor orphan seems an ideal choice for a company that doesn't want the onus of dealing with the human needs most of us have.

Of course, no employer would openly use this criterion, but what's to stop them from quietly preferring the applicant with the fewest outside responsibilities or intrusions? Management consultants should be teaching employers how to hire in a nondiscriminatory fashion. Instead, some are teaching employers how to discriminate without getting caught.

Some courts say that an employer may *ask* any questions in an interview; it's only the discriminatory *hiring* that violates the law. Others say that merely *asking* questions that elicit restricted information is against the law.

Whenever an employer asks about restricted information, the law *presumes* the employer uses that information in the hiring decision. It's then extremely difficult for an employer to prove otherwise. A smart employer will not ask about things that cannot be legally used as part of the hiring process. But some employers can't resist.

One way employers ferret out restricted information is to ask questions in a roundabout way. For example, they are unable to ask your marital status, so instead they may ask you to list all former names. You then list your maiden name and/or any names from former marriages, thus giving them information about your current and past marital status. Since men don't usually change their names in marriage, this is not an issue with them.

At one employer seminar I attended, everyone was given a list of questions touted as "lawful counterparts to otherwise impermissible questions."

Here's a detailed look at what information is typically considered restricted during job interviews:

Name.

As already mentioned, they can ask your name and they can also ask for any other names you've used in the past. This is allowable since they may need to access your records in order to verify your work history. They are *not* allowed to inquire specifically as to your "maiden name" or whether you are to be called "Miss," "Mrs.," or "Ms." When you list your former names, you are not required to explain them. The changes could have stemmed from an adoption, or perhaps a stage name.

Age.

Age discrimination is not sex discrimination, yet it is a type of discrimination that women face significantly more than men because our culture emphasizes youth and attractiveness in women to a greater degree than it does in men. Consequently, it's common for employers to unlawfully use a female applicant's age as a criterion in the hiring process. They are not allowed to ask your age or date of birth, or request a birth certificate. They also may not ask for the years you completed elementary or high school, because that can be a roundabout way of calculating your age. If you attended college, an employer would be reasonable in asking when you completed it, since that would presumably be the year in which you started your career. Still, a college graduation date is not necessarily indicative of your age, because people attend college at varying ages.

After you're hired, an employer can ask for proof that you are a minimum age, which may be a prerequisite for the job. For instance, if you're applying for a job as a cocktail server, it is lawful for the employer to require proof of age—*after* you are hired—to make sure that you are old enough to serve liquor. Or if your job requires driving, the employer may require your driving records, which show your age.

Gender.

A question asking your sex should not be listed on a job application, nor should you put it on your résumé. Of course, your gender will be readily apparent to your interviewer, but the point is that when employers shuffle through a pile of résumés in order to decide on the best candidate, they shouldn't be looking at gender. They also can't request a photograph of you until *after* you've been hired.

Marital Status.

Your marital status is none of their business. Some employers have stereotypical notions about how a woman will perform on the job based on her marital status. One common belief is that married women will be less flexible because of family responsibilities. (By contrast, some employers believe that a married man will be more dependable because he has the stability of a family!)

An employer cannot consider your marital status when hiring you, whether you are single, married, divorced, or widowed. They cannot ask the name or address of a spouse, or how your spouse feels about your working.

Pregnancy.

An employer cannot ask if you are pregnant, or whether you plan to get pregnant. An employer can ask only whether you can do the job as of that moment. As long as your pregnancy does not prevent you from doing your job, or pose any risk to your coworkers, you are entitled to work.

Children.

Your responsibilities as a mother are also none of your employer's business, unless those responsibilities will prevent you from doing your job. Some employers love to inquire about family responsibilities of women; many of the same employers pretty much ignore the issue when interviewing men.

When Janis M., a quality-control chemist, applied for a promotion, her boss didn't want to give her the job. Says Janis:

> *He had decided that I was young and I was a woman and was probably going to get pregnant. We went out to lunch, and after he drank three martinis, he said, "This job requires a lot of travel and a lot of time away from your husband." Then he asked me whether I had children. I told him, "No." Then I shared with him that I couldn't have children. He said, "Oh wow, so it doesn't matter if you're gone traveling! So you're not going to ever have children so you'll never have the whole hospital thing?" I said, "Yeah." He said, "In that light, this would be a good deal." I said, "Yeah." So then he says, "Well, okay. I think this would probably work."*
>
> *I was happy to get the job, but I thought, What a jerk. A couple of years later, my husband and I adopted a child.*

Your employer has no right to ask the number and ages of your children, where they reside, your provisions for child care, your plans for pregnancy, your means of birth control, or any other personal facts about your family.

Some employers evade accusations of discriminatory hiring by asking the same question of both male and female applicants. Still, the questions really shouldn't be asked at all.

Past Claims of Sex Discrimination.
Sometimes a prospective employer will inquire whether you've ever lodged a discrimination complaint with a past employer. This is highly inappropriate. If an employer asks you this question, I suggest you ask why the employer wants to know. Employers who refuse to hire you because you've filed a discrimination claim in the past are themselves guilty of discrimination. The law is very explicit in this regard.

Membership in Organizations.
It's reasonable for an employer to ask whether you belong to any job-related organizations, clubs, professional societies, and other associations. You do not, however, have to disclose the identity of any of them if they would give your employer information about your race, religion, color, national origin, ancestry, sex, or age. For instance, if you belong to the National Organization of Minority Women in Business, you may choose to omit that on your application. It will not be considered an "omission" on your part. It's your choice.

Other Questions.
There are a host of other inappropriate questions that involve race, religion, disabilities, and other information that could lead to discriminatory hiring. I've listed only those that pertain to sex discrimination.

HOW SHOULD YOU RESPOND TO ILLEGAL QUESTIONS?

I wish I could give you the perfect responses to each question that shouldn't be asked, but I can't. Every situation must be looked at individually. Obviously, you should not always run from the interview straight to the nearest EEOC to file a complaint (although there may be times when that is recommended). What I *can* tell you, however, are some things to think about when deciding how to respond.

Is the illegal question indicative of the tone of the entire interview? Or was it simply one question asked in ignorance?

Did you get the impression that your answer to this question is something the interviewer will be seriously taking into consideration when deciding whether to hire you? Or do you think the unlawful inquiry was merely something said in passing that ultimately won't affect the decision at all?

Is there somebody at the company whom you met or interviewed with you could go to and ask why the interviewer posed the question(s)? Perhaps it can be explained away, or perhaps the interviewer will be corrected by someone who knows better, and perhaps they may just give you the job in an effort to show you that they really *are* a fair-minded organization after all.

Do you know whether any other job applicants have been asked the same thing?

Only you can determine how much of an objection you want to lodge at this early stage. Maybe you just want to try to clear it up with the company's human resources department by lodging an internal complaint. Or maybe you prefer not to work for an employer like that anyway.

BACKGROUND INVESTIGATIONS

It is not uncommon for employers to conduct background investigations on prospective employees. Background investigations probe beyond verifying past employment, dates, schools attended, and degrees received. Typically, they include information about your character, reputation, personal characteristics, and mode of living. They are usually based on personal interviews with your neighbors, associates, friends, and past or current employers and coworkers.

Background investigations are acceptable, with some limits.

The employer must notify you at least three days prior to conducting the investigation and inform you that you have a right to know the nature and scope of the investigation. If you request a copy of the results, your employer must provide it within five days of receiving your request.[5]

Your employer may also request a credit report to examine your credit standing, capacity, and worthiness. This is reasonable in light of the fact that employees are often entrusted with company funds. For example, fast-food workers handle a substantial amount of money on a daily basis. An administrative assistant often has access to company financial data. A salesperson may use corporate credit cards to travel on company business.

However, employers have to give you written notice that they intend to run a credit check, and they must obtain your signature authorizing them to do so. They must also inform you if their failure to hire you was due to the credit report.

Once collected, financial records must be kept confidential by your employer. Otherwise it's an invasion of your privacy.

Most important, all these investigations must be consistent. Your employer must be conducting them on *all* applicants, not just one group—for example, one sex or race of people. Your employer must also be consistent with the type and depth of background checks being done. If you feel you are being investigated more than other candidates for a position, then find out what standard procedure is. If possible, ask other workers to what degree *their* backgrounds were probed. Compile a list with the information. Look for a pattern—for example, were women investigated more than men? Place the list in your file. It's a lot easier gathering this information now rather than months or even years from now, because some of your coworkers may no longer be working there, they may have forgotten the information you need, or they may be less willing to cooperate later.

WHAT KINDS OF INFORMATION *SHOULD* THEY BE SEEKING?

The only inquiries an employer may legally make are those that relate to answering the question "Can you do the job?" Interview questions should probe your general knowledge and qualifications, your work experience, your weaknesses, your abilities to work with others, and your problem-solving skills. A good interviewer will ask you specific questions about your former job to determine whether you were a competent and productive employee. Typical acceptable questions range from "Why are you seeking a new job?" to "Tell me about a typical day at your old job."

In most cases, information about your personal life is irrelevant. The only exception might be a security-sensitive position (law-enforcement officer, FBI agent, military officer, etc.); the personal lives of candidates for these jobs are routinely investigated.

REQUESTING PERFORMANCE REVIEWS FROM YOUR PAST EMPLOYERS

Prospective employers may ask you to sign a statement or release on your application that allows them to obtain your performance reviews from previous employer(s). Past employers are becoming increasingly reluctant to give candid references for fear of being sued for slander. As a result, many former employers release only dates of employment, job title, and salary, with no comment about the quality of your work.

For your new employer, a look at your performance reviews may be the only verifiable and unbiased source of information about you.

During interviews, prospective employers may ask whether you received regular performance reviews. If you say you did, they may ask you to describe the reviews in great detail. It is important that you describe them accurately, because when you finish, they may ask for permission to obtain copies of the actual reviews directly from your former employers.

What does this have to do with discrimination? Often when a woman complains of discrimination, the company will start a slow and deliberate process of peppering her file with poor performance reviews until a "legitimate" reason to fire her exists.

Sometimes, building up the file is a calculated move on an employer's part. A boss may decide that because of your unwillingness to overlook what he perceives as a small transgression—one-time or occasional sexual harassment, for example—he will not cut you any slack at all. He will cease to overlook minor flaws in your performance, even though he typically does so for other employees.

Most of the time, however, the retaliation is not that deliberate. Instead, an employee complaint causes a manager to become resentful or to dislike the employee. Little things that never bothered the manager before become amplified. Then the irritated boss has nothing favorable to say when performance review time comes around.

Either way, you end up with a bad performance review.

Then, when you try to find a new job, it will come back to haunt you. It's crucial you understand the importance of keeping your employee file accurate and free of any criticisms that stem from discrimination and/or retaliation. In chapter 12, you will learn about performance reviews and how to make sure your reviews are valid and unbiased.

Job Testing and Criteria

A foolish consistency is the hobgoblin of little minds.

—Ralph Waldo Emerson

Sometimes employers give tests for job eligibility that make no sense at all. Or they insist on enforcing certain criteria that have no relation to your capability to perform the job. In many cases, when asked why such tests and criteria are used, employers reply, "Well, that's the way we've always done it."

The way they've always done it may be against the law.

Fire departments, for example, have recently been forced to revise their height and weight requirements because they disproportionately rule out women. Formerly, many fire departments had height and weight minimums of around 5'6" and 140 pounds. More men qualified than women simply because men are generally taller and weigh more.

If a rule excludes women in this fashion, then the employer must prove that the requirements have "a manifest relationship to the employment in question."[6] Fire departments were subsequently unable to prove that the height and weight minimums correlated to a person's doing a better job as a firefighter.

Employers must use instead other selection devices that "serve the employer's legitimate interest in efficient and trustworthy workmanship."[7] As a result, many fire departments now have strength and agility tests in place of height and weight requirements. Applicants must demonstrate that they can hold a blasting fire hose, climb a fire ladder, scale structures, and are strong enough to carry potential fire victims. A lot of women under 5'6" or 140 pounds have shown they can do so.

Some courts have applied an 80 percent rule. If the selection rate for any race, sex, or ethnic group is less than 80 percent of the group with the highest rate of hire, then the hiring process is considered discriminatory.

But there is no uniform rule. You need to determine whether an employer is hiring in proportion to the available workforce. If not, why not? And is the test being given really an accurate indicator of your ability to do the job?

3.

You're Hired

Employee Handbooks and Manuals

"Welcome to the company!" reads the opening line of the employee handbook you're given the first day of work. "This booklet will assist you in learning all about your new job."

At first glance, it may appear that your company is extending you a warm and hearty welcome by offering helpful information to get you started in your new position.

You might be surprised to learn, however, that the manual is actually a carefully drafted maze of legal tactics, loopholes, and mechanisms affording your employer as many rights as legally possible. It also deprives you of some of your own. In most cases, it was written not by your boss or a company employee but by an employment attorney or human resources consultant.

The handbook is by far the single most important piece of paper you will encounter on the job. It may be in the form of a book, it may be a ringed binder, or it may be just a few photocopied pages. Some address only company policies. Others may outline specific company operations and procedures. It may define the specific duties and responsibilities of the job for which you've been hired, or outline everything from proper workplace demeanor to maternity leave. Whatever its form or content, it's imperative you read each and every line.

Should you ever have to bring a discrimination claim, the handbook could quite possibly be the determining factor in your success or failure.

On her first day of work at a major motion picture company, Camelia, a public relations consultant, was handed a three-inch stack of paperwork and instructed to read it. Included in the stack was the company manual. Her new work schedule was extremely hectic, so she merely leafed through the paperwork and never bothered to read the manual.

Six months later, when my boss told me I was "dressing like a man" too much and that I should abandon my designer pantsuits and start wearing short skirts (like his secretary), I started a very loud argument with him about it. If I'd read the handbook, I would have known that I should have reported the incident to a specific person listed there. I also would have known that our screaming match was in violation of company policy of "proper business behavior," and that I was still in a one-year probation period in which I could be fired for any reason or for no reason. Most important, though, I would have known that our company dress code did not require skirts. It says pantsuits are allowed as long as they are business pantsuits. So my boss was wrong. But I found out all that too late, because I quit after my boss gave me a poor performance review, criticizing me for arguing with him.

Each topic in your handbook is carefully written with the specific purpose of holding you to a multitude of responsibilities. For you to understand fully all that your manual signifies, you must first become privy to some basic legal concepts.

At-Will Employment

Beware of any phrase or language that seems to promise permanent employment. It may give rise to an employee thinking they have a right to their job.

—Employment lawyer advising employers at a management seminar

Employers are instructed to "purge" the handbook of anything that could be legally construed as offering you job security; anything that implies a promise of permanent employment. Instead, most employers strive to classify you as an "at-will" employee.

It simply means that they can fire you at will—at any time—without good reason.

Although there are exceptions, your at-will status often shields your employer should you ever complain of discrimination.

If you are ever fired for reasons that suggest discrimination, you must first prove you had a right to your job. If you can't establish that, you have no valid claim. In fact, your employer will not even be required to come up with a good reason for firing you, since with no promise of continued employment, they can fire you at any time without cause. Your discrimination claim will then be extremely difficult, if not impossible, to prove.

Most employers are advised to include in the company handbook a clause similar to this one:

> Employment with our company is at will, and either the company or the employee has the right to end the relationship at any time, with or without notice, for any reason or no reason.

EACH STATE IS DIFFERENT

Each state has its own laws that designate which employees are at will and which aren't. Some states, like Georgia, heavily favor employers, proclaiming that every employee is at will. Other states, like California, bend over backward to find any reason to construe an employee as permanent and not at will.

Some states *presume* employees are at will, but then allow you to prove otherwise in court. Others *presume* you are permanent unless your employer can prove you are at will.

Montana passed a law that *all* employees have a right to their jobs and no one is at will! But if you're fired in Montana, the same law also prevents you from collecting large amounts of money; you are entitled only to get your job back.

The laws of your state can greatly influence the outcome of a complaint you might have. For a state-by-state look at at-will status, see Table II.

Regardless of whether your state assumes you are an at-will or a permanent employee, there are certain exceptions that override any state's presumptions.

BUT ARE YOU *REALLY* AT WILL?

There are many legal exceptions that prevent your employer from imposing at-will status on you. You can influence some of those factors yourself, and it's crucial you begin doing so from your first day on the job.

Following is a list of exceptions. Take note of those that might apply to you, then do all you can to make sure you can continue to be regarded as a permanent employee throughout your employment.

Statutory (Those Created by Law).

At-will employees can be terminated at any time for no reason, or for any reason . . . *unless that reason is a discriminatory one!* Our laws prohibit discrimination, and no employer can use someone's at-will status to circumvent these laws and discriminate against an employee.

There are federal antidiscrimination laws (which apply to all states), and state laws that apply only to your particular state.

Still, as an at-will employee, you'll have a tougher time proving your discrimination claim than a permanent employee would. Employers don't have to offer valid reasons for firing at-will employees, since at-will employees can be fired for no reason. Your employer need only show that it wasn't done for a discriminatory reason, whereas if you were a permanent employee, your boss would have to come up with a valid reason for having fired you. And if he or she can't do so, then it automatically points to discrimination.

In addition, attorneys are reluctant to take discrimination cases that involve at-will employees, because they immediately recognize the added difficulty of proving these cases in court.

One management seminar I attended was titled "How to Make Employee Claims Unattractive to Plaintiffs' Attorneys." It instructed managers how to constantly reemphasize employee's at-will status to the point where few, if any, attorneys would take the case. In effect, they were being taught how to sabotage an employee's chances of ever finding a good attorney.

Common Law.

Common-law exceptions are those that violate the underlying principles and beliefs of our country. We have certain public policies that we as a society adhere to, and no employer can force you to violate those policies.

One policy is that no employee should be forced to commit an illegal act. This might apply to an employee who refuses to comply with a workplace rule that is discriminatory.

In that case, an employer would be violating not only an actual law but also our *common law principle* that people should not be forced to choose between committing an illegal act and getting fired for not obeying their boss.

Another common law principle is that employees should not be punished for exercising their rights and responsibilities as citizens. For instance, an employee who wants to exercise her legal right to go on maternity leave or jury duty should not be penalized. An employee who reports discrimination or testifies for a coworker who has filed a discrimination complaint should not be retaliated against. Otherwise, that employee is being forced to choose between giving up her rights and responsibilities, and getting fired for exercising them.

There is another public policy that we as a society adhere to: that in business one should exercise good faith and fair dealing. If an employer hired you for a job and told you that you would be treated fairly, when all along he knew women are treated unfairly at that workplace, then he did not enter into the employment relationship in good faith, nor with the intention of dealing fairly with you.

The bottom line is that discriminatory actions toward you violate our country's common law regardless of whether you are at will or not.

Contractual Limitations.

Did you sign an actual contract that states you are an at-will employee? If you did, it will be difficult, if not impossible, to prove otherwise. This is because the contract was written especially for you, and is an express understanding between you and your employer.

Or you might have an oral contract. Did they verbally guarantee something to you? For Ginnie Waters, a San Francisco radio talk-show host, a verbal guarantee from her boss that she would be there "longer than he would" and that there was "nothing to worry about" in terms of her future was enough to convince a jury that she had an oral contract and was not an at-will employee. "They said they weren't *firing* me, but rather they were canceling my show and that they had the right to do that." In fact, the radio station had fired her while she was on maternity leave, claiming she had no right to her job. The jury disagreed and awarded her $89,500.

Think about what was said to you during your job interview. Human resources professionals are instructed to steer clear of any comments about job longevity that could be construed as oral contracts. Did they make any assurances that if you perform your job well, you can expect promotions and raises? These kinds of statements are binding remarks that can constitute oral contracts. Did you rely on what your job interviewer told you when you made your decision to accept the job?

It's important that you write down everything that was said and put it in your file.

Take note of who said it. Was it a person who had the authority to hire and fire? That would include upper management, your immediate boss, or even a human resources person.

Also, when were these comments made? If they were made *before* you took the job, you can perhaps show that you relied on the promises in accepting the position. Nevertheless, comments made *after* you've been working there can also serve to change your at-will status to permanent, although not as effectively.

It's also better if the comments were made to you personally, rather than during a general meeting where they were spoken to all employees present. Otherwise, the comments are apt to be regarded as broad statements made in passing rather than actual promises intended specifically for you.

Implied Contract of Permanent Employment.

An *implied* contract also can change your status from at-will to permanent employee. This comes about when your employer makes certain representations to you that *imply* you have a long-term right to your job. For instance, "I'm hiring you as my sales manager. I want you to conduct inventory next year in February, and then the following year in June and then the following year in

September." A person might reasonably conclude that the boss expects you to be around for a while. You might have an *implied* contract that you are a permanent employee—at least for the next three years.

Implied contracts can be established either verbally, as in the above example, or in writing.

The manual I was given while at CNN had an introductory message in it from the then president, Burt Reinhardt, that read:

> As you begin your employment at CNN and CNN Headline News, I want to extend a welcome from those of us already here. We are happy to have you on our team, and we wish you the very best of success and satisfaction in your work. Our company will conduct employee relations in such a manner as to merit the confidence and trust of all employees—fair, consistent and equal treatment, the opportunity for advancement, and a chance to contribute to successful operations. . . . We look forward to growing together.

Not only did they assure me that the opportunity for continued advancement existed, but they implied that as the company grew, they intended that I grow with it. Unfortunately, when my pregnant belly grew as well, they weren't quite as happy to have me on their "team" and assure me "success and satisfaction" in my work.

The CNN handbook has since been amended. Gone are the introductory assurances implying job security. In their place is a conspicuously blank page. Most likely, your employer has purged your handbook as well.

Look through your manual for disclaimers that resemble these:

- This manual is not an employment contract.
- This is not a contract of permanent employment, and the company reserves the right to modify or amend any personnel policy at any time without notice.
- This policy does not in any way affect our right to termi-

nate an employee for any reason, at any time, nor does it affect your right to leave at any time.

- This handbook is not intended to be a binding employment contract but only a general source of information.

Such disclaimers are typically placed in a prominent part of the manual. They use clear, simple language and are usually in bold print so that your employer will have an easy time proving that you saw it, read it, and understood it.

Some employers will have you sign an acknowledgment that you have received and read the entire manual and are therefore responsible for knowing its contents.

Yet even if your employer uses these disclaimer tactics to prevent your manual from being construed as an implied contract of permanent employment, a court may still rule that it is, in fact, just that. Courts look at the *totality of circumstances* in determining whether a manual is an implied contract, and your employer's disclaimer is but one piece of the whole picture.

In addition to the manual, courts will consider an employer's *actual* policies and practices. For instance, have you received regular raises and promotions? Have you received commendations? Have you worked there for a long time? In your particular industry, are people usually hired as permanent, rather than at-will, employees?

All of these factors and more will add to your argument that you are a permanent employee. See Table II for a list of states that do not recognize implied contracts from a manual or from any other unintended action by an employer.

Implied Contract of Just Cause.

Most of us have been brought up to believe that if we work hard and do a good job, an employer cannot arbitrarily fire us. We believe that an employer needs a good reason to terminate employment—a legal "just cause."

Just cause includes things like tardiness, not showing up for work, and not doing your job properly.

Look in your manual for phrases similar to this one:

This manual makes no promises to dismiss only for just cause.

By including this declaration, your employer is attempting to retain the right to make arbitrary, biased decisions and not have to answer to you for them. The good news is that the law doesn't allow your employer to just whisk away your rights by simply inserting a statement like this. The statement is just one factor among many that courts will consider when analyzing whether you can be fired without just cause.

If your manual implies that you will be retained as long as you perform up to certain standards, then there is an assumption that you can be fired only for just cause. Does your manual lay out a plan for regular performance reviews? And if so, does it explain how you can expect to get promoted or disciplined based upon those performance reviews? All this could imply that your job is dependent on your performance, not on arbitrary decisions by your boss.

Does your manual mention that the company looks forward to a long and productive working relationship with you? If so, it implies that you will have just that. And if the manual states there is a probationary period at the beginning of your employment, this implies that when the probationary period is over, you have become a *permanent* employee.

Longevity of Service.

If you've been with the same employer for a number of years, courts are apt to ignore all the disclaimers, the letters, and the handbooks. They will look at the length and success of your service, and regard you as a permanent employee.

What constitutes a "long-term" employee? There is no magic

number of years. Some courts require a minimum of five years. Other courts have ruled even fewer years are enough, especially when coupled with good performance reviews, raises, promotions, or even the absence of criticism of your work.

FULL TIME VS. PART TIME FOR AT-WILL STATUS

Being a full-time or part-time worker doesn't matter when determining whether you are an at-will employee. There are part-time workers who are permanent employees, and even full-time workers who are at will.

Other Issues with the Handbook

WHEN YOUR EMPLOYER MAKES CHANGES IN THE MANUAL

When an employer updates your manual, the general rule is that the changes do apply to you, but there are some exceptions.

Unbeknownst to me, CNN had revised its handbook after I'd started working there. Whereas the old handbook did not specifically address sex discrimination and harassment problems, the new one had definitive provisions and procedures for reporting it.

Was I responsible for following these new procedures?

Absolutely not.

CNN had made a crucial error—a common one among employers. The network had updated its manual but failed to notify me, an existing employee. I had no way of knowing that procedures had changed. CNN could not hold me accountable for the information.

If your employer never notified you of a change in the handbook, then you are not responsible for following the new rules.

In most instances, an employer will have you sign a statement that you have received and read a new handbook. It will read something like:

> I acknowledge that I have received a copy of the 1999 edition of the company employee handbook. I understand that this edition of

> the handbook supersedes all previous descriptions of policies, procedures, and employee benefits.

Sometimes, even when your employer does this, you *still* are not necessarily bound by the new manual. If the old handbook guaranteed you a pay raise every year, but the new handbook specifies only every two years, then your old rule should remain intact since it was the understanding you had when you took the job. Your employer cannot change what they promised simply by changing the manual.

"NO OTHER REPRESENTATION" CLAUSES

Your handbook will probably also include a statement similar to this:

> This handbook incorporates all prior discussions and understandings between employer and employee. The terms of the relationship cannot be altered except in writing from a member of the executive board of the company.

This is so you cannot rely on anything your boss tells you if it contradicts the handbook. Suppose you get hired in June and at the job interview your boss says, "All new employees are supposed to be on a probationary period for one year. During that time I can fire them without cause. But in my twenty years of working here, I've never done that, so you can ignore the probationary period."

You can't.

Remember: The handbook *represents all prior discussions and understandings* between you and cannot be altered *except in writing.*

Immediately upon receiving your employee manual, read it! If anything contradicts what you were told, write a note to the person you spoke to, your immediate boss, or to the human resources director. It doesn't have to be a formal letter. In fact, a short, friendly handwritten note is probably best, since it won't make their antennae go up, and perhaps you can solve the problem amicably.

> Dear ________
>
> While reading the company's handbook, I noticed it said I would be on probation for a year. But in my job interview, you told me I could ignore that. Could you please brief me on this?

Try to get the person who made you this promise to reassure you in writing that it still stands.

"ANY INCONSISTENCY" CLAUSES

> If there is any inconsistency between the handbook and actual practice, the handbook governs.

Companies like to put this phrase in manuals to avoid being held to "unwritten rules" that sometimes govern the workplace. That way they are not responsible for any unwritten discriminatory rules promulgated by middle management. Or at least they think they're not responsible. This phrase isn't always effective. It may prove helpful to an employer when the discrimination is an isolated incident, but if the company's typical practice toward employees is different from the way the manual reads, then the employer will be bound by those past practices rather than by procedures as described in the manual.

For instance, a manual might say that all women are to be afforded a three-month maternity leave and that any woman who takes more than three months will be fired. But suppose that it's standard procedure in the company to allow women to take four months. When you take a four-month leave, can they fire you for breaking the three-month rule? Which rule governs? If the company truly *does* have a different practice, then you are not unreasonable in following the customary practice rather than the written rule.

COMPANY POLICIES

Your manual will also outline general policies for things like tardiness and sick leave. It is your job to know these policies—and to what extent they are being consistently applied.

A company rule might state that any employee who has been tardy more than three times in one month will be fired. Maybe your boss has been anxiously searching for a reason to fire you ever since you rebuffed his sexual advances. On your third tardy day, he fires you and claims he has a right to do so under company rules. Other employees, however, who have been late three times in one month have not been fired.

Ordinarily your boss would have a right to fire you, but in this case he is using your tardiness as a pretext for what is really a discriminatory firing. Does your boss uniformly discipline everybody who violates this rule, or does he or she tend to overlook the problem in others? A company rule must be applied fairly and consistently to all employees before it can be used against you.

ARBITRATION CLAUSES

Your manual may state that you agree to settle any dispute with your employer by "binding arbitration." This is a process that is deeply prejudicial against employees.

The good news is that even if your employer includes this statement in your employee manual, it probably won't be enough to force you to agree to mandatory arbitration.

It's crucial that you have a good understanding of the arbitration process and all its repercussions. For a full explanation, see chapter 18, "If All Else Fails . . . See You in Court."

"EMPLOYEES MUST READ" CLAUSES

Your employer may also promulgate a rule that all employees are *required* to read the manual. If you do not read it, you are breaking yet another company rule. Moreover, if you are asked to sign an acknowledgment that you *have* read the manual, and then don't, you are technically lying to the company! If you ever file a discrimination complaint, you will be asked questions like these:

- Why didn't you follow the procedures listed here for complaining about discrimination?
- Did you read the employee manual that was given to you? Were you instructed to read the manual?
- Do you see right here in the manual where it specifically says it's your responsibility to read it? Why didn't you read it?

Or:

- Why did you sign this paper acknowledging that you read the manual if, in fact, you didn't? Do you always swear to things that are untrue?

Don't wait until you have a problem to find out what the proper solution and procedures are. By then it may be too late.

Letters of Understanding

When you are hired, you may receive a letter offering you the job and outlining what the job entails as well as your employee status. Like the employee handbook, it can be construed as a contract in determining whether your employee status is permanent or at will.

Look for statements like "We look forward to a long, pleasant, and mutually satisfactory relationship with you." This, taken in conjunction with other employer behaviors, may very well imply that you have a right to expect not to be fired arbitrarily.

On the other hand, the letter may specifically state that you are an at-will employee.

If you are already a permanent employee, a letter of this kind cannot be used to downgrade your status to at will. Therefore, if it's sent *after* you've been hired, it's ineffective. But if it's sent *before* you accept the job, your employer can show that at-will status was part of the original offer and you accepted it on those terms.

Independent Contractors

Many employers often prefer it if you are not an employee at all but rather an independent contractor.

In order for an employer to be accountable for discrimination, you must first be an *employee*. Since independent contractors are not employees, but rather people who work for themselves and hire out their professional services, companies who use their services are not responsible for any discrimination independent contractors encounter.

Lisa B. worked as an independent contractor in her job as a hairstylist for an upscale Beverly Hills salon.

> *I paid for my own hairbrushes and blow dryers. I brought in all my equipment. I rented a chair in the salon, which included the use of their receptionist to schedule my appointments. The salon did the bookkeeping and I paid them a percentage of my profits. One day, the salon owner decided to "improve" the salon image by having only men styling hair. So he told me at the end of the month he wasn't going to renew my chair rental. I tried to complain to the EEOC, but they told me since I wasn't an employee, the laws didn't apply to me.*

At one management conference I attended, advisers touted independent contractors as a "creative solution" for reducing employee benefits and "avoiding the discomfort and potential liability associated with managing workforces." In fact, they even titled an entire seminar "The Ideal 'Employee'—Does Your Work but Doesn't Work for You." Just think: an employer who is no employer at all—who wants all the advantages of your skills and efforts but refuses to afford you the benefits that the law provides for employees. Under the smoke screen of your independent contractor status, this employer retains the right to hire and fire arbitrarily—and maybe even discriminatorily.

I should point out that independent contractor status is not necessarily a bad thing. There are instances where it may be the best type of employment for your particular situation. Some people prefer making their own hours and being in business for themselves. Independent contractors are usually paid slightly more than employees to make up for the fact that they do not receive medical insurance, workers' compensation, or other employee benefits.

What's deplorable, however, is when workers are forced to take this status without knowing everything they are giving up—such as their right to file a discrimination claim. Most likely your employer is acutely aware of these implications, but an employer has no duty to tell you about them.

It's certainly okay to accept independent contractor status, but know what you are gaining and what you are giving up. Then decide if it's worth it.

Also know that your employer labeling you as an independent contractor is not enough, legally, to make you one. In fact, even if *you* label yourself an independent contractor, the law may still not recognize you as one.

Instead, a court will determine your status by looking at many different factors, the most weighty of which is the *right to control.* Does the organization have the right to control your method, manner, and time to complete a job? If so, then you are really an employee. Independent contractors are typically given only an assignment and a time frame in which to complete it. They usually don't report back until the job is complete. Employees, however, usually have set hours and are under the supervision of a manager who instructs them how to complete their work.

For instance, let's say you work out of your home, sewing dresses. A boutique hires you to sew a custom dress, which you agree to deliver in one week. They will then pay you a flat fee for the dress, regardless of how many hours it takes you to sew it. You are probably an independent contractor. The boutique does not control how and when you sew the dress or the method you use to sew it. They just want the finished product, and they want you to use your professional sewing expertise to complete it. If you are an employee at a sewing factory, however, you would probably work specific hours and have a boss periodically inspect your work and your productivity level.

One woman I know does bookkeeping for a local auto mechanic. Her job is to keep track of all their income and expenses. She usually works out of her home, but sometimes she works out of the mechanic's office in order to access his customer files and accounts payable. She enters the data into his computer, and at tax time she presents the completed books to the mechanic, who then takes them to his accountant. She is an independent contractor, since the mechanic doesn't tell her what hours to work or how to do the books, only to have them ready by tax time.

Here are some factors to consider in determining whether you are an independent contractor or an employee:

- the extent of control that the organization can exercise over the details of your work—the most important factor
- whether you engage in a distinct occupation or business. Independent contractors are usually brought on to complete a single job in an area where they have expertise
- whether this particular occupation is typically done under

the direction of an employer or by a specialist without supervision

- whether the skill required is typically done by a person of independent contractor status
- whether the employer or the worker supplies the tools and instruments used. Typically, an employee will use company property, whereas independent contractors have their own.
- length of time for which the person is employed. An employee tends to be long-term, whereas an independent contractor is typically brought on to complete a single project, then moves on to other projects or clients.
- method of payment: Employees are paid weekly or biweekly and employee taxes are taken out of their paychecks. Independent contractors are paid when the job is complete, or sometimes in increments throughout the job. No taxes are withheld. Instead, the independent contractor submits a bill and the organization pays it as they would any other bill for services rendered.
- whether the work is part of the regular business of the employer. In the case of the mechanic's bookkeeper, she is using a skill that is unrelated to working on cars. If she were one of his mechanics, he would have a tougher time proving she is an independent contractor.
- the intention of the parties. As I mentioned before, your employer labeling you an independent contractor, or even you labeling yourself as such, is not alone enough to make you one, but it is one factor among many the courts will consider. If, however, the majority of other factors indicate you are really an *employee*, then the courts will ignore your self-fashioned label of independent contractor.
- whether you are actually in business. Do you have a business name and a business license?

- whether you are permitted to do the same type of work for other companies. Independent contractors often have many clients.
- whether you may delegate the work to another. An independent contractor agrees to have a certain amount of work completed but is free to delegate or hire others to do it for her.
- whether you have employees of your own
- whether you are required to make a capital investment. Independent contractors sometimes must invest their own funds to get a job done.
- whether the work affords you an opportunity for profit or loss depending on your abilities

It's crucial that you document any of these factors that apply to you. Keep all written records and write down any remarks made that indicate your employee status.

In my own case, I had to scramble to gather evidence on this issue. CNN's lawyer told one hearing officer that CNN expected the entire matter to be resolved shortly in light of the fact that I was an independent contractor and not entitled to any employee rights or benefits. I was stunned at such a blatant mischaracterization. I had to search through four years of pay stubs that showed employee taxes had been taken out. Other things I gave my lawyer to prove that I was an employee included the following: paperwork that showed I participated in the Turner Broadcasting *Employee* Stock Purchase Plan; my employee ID card; my employee press passes; CNN employee phone lists; memos between me and my bureau chief in which I requested vacation days (independent contractors make their own schedules); receipts for office machines and hotel rooms I had obtained through Turner Broadcasting at "employee-only" discount rates.

This is the type of documentation you should put into your file. You don't have to keep absolutely everything—just enough to show your employee status.

Temporary and Leased Employees

Another way employers evade having a person classified as an employee is by using temporary workers. But sometimes employers call people "temps" who are really permanent employees.

As with the independent contractor test, the issue is the *right to control.* Does the employer exercise significant control over your work and your working environment? Who supervises your daily activities—the temp agency that sent you or the organization using your services? Who has the authority to hire and fire you? Who issues your work assignments and operating instructions? Who controls how and when you are paid and decides whether you receive raises and benefits? If the temp agency has relinquished most of this control to the company using your services, then you are a *dual* employee. As a result, both organizations are bound by the discrimination laws.

This is many employers' worst fear, since their entire purpose in using temps is to avoid having to furnish rights and benefits to their workers.

Office workers are the most common example of dual employees. Though initially hired by a temp agency, they often work for outside employers for extremely long periods of time, eventually becoming so absorbed into the workplace that they are hardly distinguishable from regular company employees. When that happens, a temp has evolved into an employee. As such, she can hold both the temp agency *and* the outside employer liable for discrimination.

Some courts say that if you have worked at a place for one year on a substantially full-time basis, you automatically become a permanent employee. But that's only a rough guideline. Look at all the factors listed above to determine your true status.

Employment Agreements

Employment agreements are contracts signed by you and your employer. Usually, but not always, they are used for higher-paid professionals. Many people are surprised to learn that in most cases you have more job security without one.

One lawyer advised employers to offer written contracts because "they make hiring and firing much easier."

If there is no contract, then you are either presumed to be a permanent employee or you are given the opportunity to show that you fit into one of the exceptions to at-will status.

Shortly after my lawsuit ended, CNN offered a written contract to one of the women who had testified for me. The contract stated that at the end of three years, CNN could either end their employment relationship or renew the contract, and at thirteen-week intervals CNN could terminate her for no reason at all. In addition, it said that should she ever file a lawsuit against CNN, she would do so in the state of Georgia and that only Georgia laws would apply.

Under the contract, fighting a discrimination battle would be a logistical nightmare for her. It would mean hiring an attorney two thousand miles away, plus paying for phone calls and travel expenses. Not to mention the fact that a Georgia jury would most likely be more favorably disposed to their hometown CNN than to an out-of-state litigious California female.

Most important, however, is the fact that Georgia affords few rights to employees, while offering many to employers. Unlike most states, Georgia has no state discrimination laws that regulate private employers. Residents there must rely only on the federal law. (For a look at which states have discrimination laws, see Table I.)

CNN offered this woman a raise at the same time they offered the contract. Prior to signing the contract, she had an absolute right to her job under California law. She had worked there for eight years and was a permanent employee. She could not be fired without proof of just cause. And if she ever had a discrimination problem, she could file in California, where the courts and the laws tend to favor employees.

As one labor lawyer put it, contracts allow employers to "side-step" usual employer obligations and can be "valuable deterrents to discrimination claims."

Be careful what you sign. The bone they throw you may be just that.

PART TWO

IN THE WORKPLACE DAY TO DAY

The law of nature destines and qualifies the female sex for the bearing and nurture of children of our race and for the custody of the homes of the world and their maintenance in love and honor. And all life-long callings of women, inconsistent with these radical and sacred duties of their sex . . . are departures from the order of nature; and when voluntary, treason against it.

—Wisconsin State Supreme Court,
in denying Lavinia Goodell the right to practice law,
In re Goodell, 1875

At the turn of the century, women weren't allowed to work in mines, because, according to our courts, it might "coarsen their gentle natures." They couldn't work as messengers, because Western Union was afraid there would be no gentlemen available to open their doors. Women couldn't sell liquor unless their father or husband owned the drinking establishment, because they might be subjected to unsavory men who would threaten their innocence. Nor could women operate elevators, read meters, drive taxis, or carry the mail.[1]

But most important, a woman could not disguise herself as a man to obtain one of these jobs, or she could be sent to jail.

Our history is filled with gender discrimination based not on malicious attitudes but on concerns for protecting the "weaker sex."[2]

Even today, our workplace remains littered with fragments of these archaic beliefs.

"It's for your own good," says a boss who tells a woman she isn't eligible for a job that requires heavy lifting.

"It's for your own good," says an employer who refuses to allow a woman of child-bearing age to work in a nuclear power plant.

"It's for your own good," says a boss who prefers a woman not to work the night shift because there's no security in the parking lot.

"It's for your own good," says a supervisor who insists a pregnant employee quit so she can stay home to take care of the child.

Each one of these examples was from a real court case. And in each one, the boss lost.

While at CNN, I was once assigned to report a story about how the National Endowment for the Arts (NEA) had withdrawn funding from a male performance artist because of complaints that in part of the act he was naked. Others, however, argued that the revocation of funding was a dangerous form of censorship. In my story, I showed part of the naked performer's act so viewers could judge for themselves the degree of artistic endeavor. After all, it was *their* public funds at issue, and the dilemma struck at the very heart of their constitutional rights.

My photographer shot the performer from several hundred feet away to avoid showing anything explicit. The stage lights were dim and the performer was turned away from us so that only his buttocks showed—hardly recognizable since his entire body filled up only about one-twentieth of the television screen.

Nevertheless, the instant my story aired, one of the male managers at CNN Center in Atlanta called the Los Angeles bureau, furious over the shot. He thought a man's butt had no business being on the air and ordered my videotape editor to take it out before the story was aired again.

Several months later, I was assigned a story in Palm Springs, California, about a new law prohibiting girls from wearing G-string "thong" bikinis on public streets. The ordinance had passed just before spring break, and now news reporters were flocking to the desert resort town to see whether college coeds would obey the new rule.

I cringed when I saw the video my photographer had shot. Almost every picture included women wearing the forbidden thong bathing suits—bronzed butts in full view. For a moment I breathed a sigh of relief when I thought I saw one usable shot of a woman in a *regular* bikini. But then I realized she was holding up a T-shirt that said "Just do me!" across the front. As I watched, the woman looked into our camera lens and mouthed the words "Just do me" as she pointed to her chest.

I called CNN Center in Atlanta. "We're in big trouble with this piece. We've got no usable video." I described what we had. "Sounds great," came the reply. "Use it. We want to see it. That's what the story's about, Patti. We need to show our viewers exactly what's being outlawed here."

We used it all, even the "Just Do Me" lady. Seconds after my story aired, my CNN computer terminal began to light up with messages from within the network, including one from my supervising producer. "Great video, Paniccia," read one. "Great T and A!" said another. "Absolutely loved your story!"

The point is that most of the time men don't even recognize the fact that the workplace is governed by *their* norms, *their* tastes, *their* sensibilities, *their* ideas of what's interesting or acceptable. It just sort of happens. And women often get caught in the middle.

Yet just because a certain behavior is part of our societal norms, does that make it right or acceptable? In this instance, there was no specific person trying to be maliciously sexist or discriminatory toward me. In fact, the series of decisions was made by several people. Instead, the incident stemmed from an established mind-set, one that permeates most workplaces, especially those that have historically been governed by men. The workplace merely reflects and nourishes the interests and concerns of those who control it.

Incidentally, a few weeks after the NEA story, I was assigned to cover the twentieth anniversary of the movie *The Rocky Horror Picture Show.* Imagine my confusion. Since my story was entirely about the movie, it was necessary to use at least a few seconds of the main scene, even though it showed actor Tim Curry wearing a corset, garter belt, and black fishnet stockings while seductively dancing to "I'm a Sweet Transvestite from Transsexual Transylvania." Was his an acceptable or unacceptable butt? I wondered.

No doubt you will or already have encountered situations at work that gnaw at your sense of what's fair. This part of the book will help you identify those issues and properly analyze them so you can determine whether your employer's behavior is violating the law.

And, by the way, I *did* use Tim Curry's butt.

4.

Sexual Harassment

One of the biggest mistakes women make is not doing their homework. They come marching into my office saying, "I've been sexually harassed and I want this guy fired!" when they haven't been harassed at all. Maybe what he did was inappropriate, unprofessional, or in bad taste, or maybe it was rude and insulting, but that doesn't necessarily make it sexual harassment. Women should learn what sexual harassment is before they start making accusations and demands to their employers. —Jane R., human resources manager

When I surveyed employers and human resource workers, they overwhelmingly said the biggest mistake women make is not taking the time to learn both the law of sexual harassment and the company's own sexual harassment policy. I can fully understand an employer's wanting employees to know their own company policy, but frankly I was a little surprised to hear that some human resources people expected women to know the intricacies of sexual harassment law. Some lawyers don't even know that. I wondered where they thought women would learn this information—certainly not in a company pamphlet on workplace rights, which typically offers only broad, generalized definitions of sexual harassment. I wondered how many of the human resources managers knew the law themselves before they started their highly specialized careers focusing on these issues.

Fair or not, it's absolutely crucial that you know how to determine from the beginning whether what's happening to you is sexual harassment.

For one thing, from the minute you begin to complain, whether they make it known to you or not, your employer will be using these legal definitions of sexual harassment to judge the severity of your complaint. If you are able to do the same, you will know how to respond to their questions, and perhaps even defuse the situation at its inception, before it can lead to serious problems in your career. You'll also be able to adequately judge whether your employer has responded properly to your complaint.

The main source of confusion is that nobody seems to know exactly what sexual harassment is and at what point a woman is justified in complaining about it.

Would you be unreasonable in objecting if your supervisor brushed up against you? What if he did so because he was in a crowded elevator? What if he had a reputation for doing just that to women in crowded elevators?

Or what if your boss regularly gives you a wink and a smile that you interpret as being suggestive? What if you later learn that he does that to everybody at work, male and female, as a friendly gesture? What if he sometimes teases you about your love life but truly has no idea he's embarrassing you? What if he makes occasional comments, either positive or negative, about your body? What if he thinks he's being friendly and cute?

In 1998, nearly 16,000 women claimed they had been sexually harassed on the job.[3] Just what definition were they using?

Unfortunately, even our courts don't have a short definitive sentence or two that specifies exactly what sexual harassment is. Justice Sandra Day O'Connor, the first woman appointed to the United States Supreme Court, ruled that the test "is not, and by its nature cannot be, a mathematically precise test."[4] Instead, she instructs us to consider myriad factors, no single one of which is determinative. It is the "totality of circumstances test."

Two Types of Sexual Harassment

Let's start by figuring out which of the two categories (maybe both) your own situation fits into—*quid pro quo* or *hostile working environment.*

QUID PRO QUO

Of the two types, *quid pro quo* is the easiest to understand and recognize. Don't let the Latin scare you. All it means is "this for that." For example, an employer says, "You give me sex, I'll give you a promotion." Or "I'll give you a raise." Or even "I'll give you a job." For an action to qualify as quid pro quo harassment:

1. Your supervisor must request sex or other physical contact of a sexual nature from you.
2. Your submission or rejection of that request is either:
   a. a term or condition of your continued employment, or
   b. the basis for employment decisions that affect you.
3. This is happening to you *because of* your sex—that is, because you are a woman.

Your boss can either be explicit by making a frank request, or he can hint around.

You can prove it in several ways, including your own statements, his statements, anything written he might have given you, or statements of fellow workers who had a similar experience with him. In other words, you can use anything that lends more impact to the validity of your claim.

You have to show that actual job benefits were lost or about to be lost if you didn't submit to his sexual advances. Job benefits means things like promotions, pay raises, opportunities for advancement, choice of assignments, overtime opportunities, and pension benefits.

HOSTILE ENVIRONMENT

I always think of *hostile environment* sexual harassment as the "they make you feel bad" type. In a hostile environment, there is no offer of exchanging sexual favors for work-related benefits. You don't even have to lose tangible benefits. Instead, "the workplace is permeated with discriminatory intimidation, ridicule and insult that is sufficiently severe or pervasive to alter the conditions of the victim's employment and create an abusive working environment."[5]

We must interpret this definition by asking:

1. What kinds of behavior constitute "discriminatory intimidation, ridicule and insult"?
2. How bad do things have to be for you before they are considered "sufficiently severe or pervasive"?
3. What changes constitute "altering the conditions of employment"?

First Question: What Kinds of Behavior Constitute "Discriminatory Intimidation, Ridicule and Insult"?

When Shelly S. started work as a medical assistant in a doctor's office, she was informed by a senior nurse that the doctor preferred the employees to stay on the premises during lunch in order to save time. As a courtesy for staying onsite, the doctor supplied the food. "The senior nurse told me he would occasionally come into the lunchroom and join us and that sometimes he would talk about whatever porn film he had most recently bought. She told me, 'Just listen to him and humor him. It's no big deal.'" So Shelly did just that. Now, years later, she confesses to being mortified that she never objected to the doctor's relentless and sometimes graphic depictions. "I didn't even realize it was sexual harassment," she says. "After all, he wasn't touching me or asking for sexual favors. I still don't really know how you tell when your boss is crossing over the line."

Sexual harassment encompasses a broad assortment of behaviors, including both words and actions. It occurs when a workplace is permeated with ridicule, offensive remarks, insulting sex jokes, aggressive sexual behavior, and/or intimidating comments. It might include asking for dates, bragging about sexual exploits, or making comments regarding your appearance or anatomy.

It can also include gestures, such as suggestive eye contact and mouth movements, or even touching oneself, especially if the touching is in a sexually sensitive area of the body. It can entail posting or circulating sexually oriented posters, cartoons, or pictures. Or it can be a demeaning job assignment.

Sexual harassment can include touching you, but a boss doesn't *have* to touch you to cross over the line. In one case, the harassment consisted of the giving of inappropriate gifts, even though the giver wasn't present when the gifts were received.

Unlike quid pro quo, the hostile environment type of sexual harassment need not be sexual, only sex-based. For instance, one woman listened day after day while her boss ranted and raved about how women were just "a bunch of dumb cows" and ill-suited for the workplace. His behavior constituted sexual harassment, even though the man never talked of anything sexual in nature, nor implied in any way that he wanted to have sex with any of the "dumb cows." In that light, words and actions can also include epithets, slurs, negative stereotyping, threatening and intimidating remarks or acts, and written or graphic material that denigrates or shows hostility or aversion toward a woman or women in general.

Second Question: How Bad Do Things Have to Be?

For behavior to be considered "sufficiently severe or pervasive":

- the average reasonable woman must consider the environment hostile or abusive, and,
- you, as an individual, must find it hostile or abusive.

The first prong of this test is meant to weed out women who are overly sensitive and who interpret just about everything as offensive and harassing. For instance, if one morning your boss remarks, "Say, that's a short dress you're wearing," and his comment sends you reeling in tears straight to the women's rest room and then to your lawyer's office, you're probably overreacting. The great majority of women, or the *average reasonable woman,* would probably not find the work environment hostile or abusive over that one remark, so even if you do, you have not suffered harassment. If, on the other hand, your boss says, "That's a short dress you're wearing. I'd sure like to see what's underneath. Would you mind lifting it up for me?" the average reasonable woman probably would be deeply offended.

The second prong, that *you* as an individual must find the workplace hostile or abusive, is meant to exclude women who aren't bothered by the kinds of things that would bother most women. If you're the type who'd trivialize the incident, saying, "Aw, heck. My boss is full of beans. I just ignored him and went ahead and did my job," you haven't been harassed. Your performance on the job has not been affected.

For centuries, we used an "average reasonable *man*" standard to determine whether people's behaviors were reasonable under the law. But now with sexual harassment, our courts have begun to recognize that most men cannot fully understand what it means or how it feels to be harassed. So they've inserted a new average reasonable *woman* standard, saying, "Conduct that many men consider unobjectionable may offend many women. . . .We adopt the perspective of a reasonable woman primarily because we believe that a sex-blind reasonable person standard tends to be male-biased and tends to systematically ignore the experiences of women."[6] Congratulations, ladies. This is a great stride forward for you, although it is little known by the general public.

Third Question: What Changes Constitute "Altering Conditions of Employment and Creating a Hostile or Abusive Working Environment"?

Your situation at work must be so bad that it becomes difficult, if not impossible, to do your job. Unlike quid pro quo harassment, you needn't show that tangible productivity has declined as a result of the harassment, although that *could* be a factor. Instead, we look at the totality of circumstances, which might include:

- the frequency of the discriminatory conduct. Was it one isolated instance, a repeated daily pattern, or somewhere in between?
- the severity of the conduct. Was it a joke in bad taste, or a graphic and explicit description of a sexual encounter?
- whether it was physically threatening or humiliating, or just a mere offensive utterance. For instance, in the case of *Harris v. Forklift,* Teresa Harris's boss had the bizarre habit of ordering her to fetch coins from his pants pockets. He also would throw objects down on the floor, near his feet, and ask her to pick them up. This would be considered physically threatening or humiliating. On the other hand, if the entire basis of your complaint is that your supervisor once uttered some sexist comment that offended you, it probably would be a "mere offensive utterance" and not

serious enough to affect the conditions of your employment to a sufficient degree.

- whether it reasonably interferes with your job performance, or whether you're able to continue working and concentrating
- whether it affected your psychological well-being. Were you mentally harmed from this ordeal? And if so, to what degree? In Teresa Harris's case, her former employer tried to argue that since she had not incurred severe psychological damage, she was not sexually harassed. But the Supreme Court disagreed, saying a woman needn't undergo a nervous breakdown before she can prove discrimination. In fact, the very purpose of the discrimination laws is to protect women before the harassment reaches the point of causing a nervous breakdown.[7] Like those listed above, psychological harm is but a single factor, and not a necessary one, to prove your claim. Nevertheless, if you have been psychologically harmed, bring that information forward, as it contributes to the weightiness of your claim.

Crucial Facts and Misconceptions

WHAT IF HE DIDN'T *MEAN* TO OFFEND YOU?

"I was just joking" is no excuse on your employer's part. The motive of the person doing the harassing is irrelevant.

The reason sexual harassment creates more than its share of controversy is that men and women can vary greatly in their perspectives of what is offensive or insulting, yet liability for sexual harassment is based only on a woman's perspective—whether a reasonable woman would interpret it as a hostile working environment, not whether a reasonable man intended it as such. In many cases, the harasser knows full well that he is harassing, but other cases involve misperception and miscommunication, where a boss is stupidly unaware that his behavior is offensive and discriminatory. He can be found guilty nonetheless. "Well-intentioned compliments by coworkers or supervisors can form the basis of . . . sexual harassment . . . if a reasonable victim of the same sex . . . would consider the comments sufficiently severe or pervasive." Adopting the victim's perspective ensures that courts will not "sustain ingrained notions of reasonable behavior fashioned by the offenders."[8]

THE "NUTS AND SLUTS" DEFENSE

Be prepared. You will be questioned as if you were the one doing something wrong. In most cases, employers will seldom, if ever, admit that the harassment has occurred. They may try to fix it, and they may even remove the person harassing you from his position, but they will never, *ever* admit that it occurred. Why? Because if they do, they are exposed to liability on two fronts. One, you could then sue them and would have no trouble proving that the harassment occurred (since they openly admitted to you that it did). And two, the harasser could then challenge the company's conclusion that he was guilty of harassing you, and sue for wrongly disciplining him and for ruining his career. Instead, companies try to solve these problems quietly without drawing any conclusions about either side (or at least not letting you know if they do).

Here's when knowing the definition of sexual harassment comes in handy—you will be better able to understand your employer's reaction to your complaint. Remember the two-prong test? In order for employers to show there was no sexual harassment (and absolve themselves of responsibility), they must show that at least *one* of those prongs isn't present. How do they do that? They'll begin by attacking your credibility with the "nuts and sluts" approach.

They can show that other reasonable women in your workplace experienced the same behavior and didn't find it hostile or abusive. They can say that you simply overreacted, that you are, for all intents and purposes, a nut. You are a confused individual, incapable of correctly judging social behaviors. You see danger and aggression where there is none. You are paranoid. You incorrectly perceive what is going on around you. You are reacting hysterically and blame your own workplace failures on discrimination.

Or they can show that you, as an individual, didn't really perceive the workplace as hostile or abusive. You are a liar—and maybe a vindictive one at that. None of this really bothered you as much as you say it did. You are an exaggerator. Or, most impactfully, you encouraged this behavior. You asked for it. *You* are a "slut."

YOUR WORKPLACE BEHAVIOR

Did you "consent" to this? If an employer can show that you did, then there's no sexual harassment. What types of behaviors on your part can be construed as consent? Can your employer consider the way you dress and carry yourself? You bet. Here's why:

In determining consent, the law asks one basic question: Were the advances "welcome" or "unwelcome" on your part?

Again we look at the totality of circumstances, such as the nature of the sexual advances and the circumstances under which they were made.[9] That might include asking whether you engaged in sexually provocative speech or dress, sexual horseplay, foul language, friendly association with the alleged harasser, or suggestive gift-giving, and whether you failed to report incidents of harassment to superiors.

You never know when you might encounter sexual harassment on the job, so for your own protection, even if you are not having a problem, keep a professional demeanor with everyone in the workplace, without exception. Even if you have close friends whom you trust implicitly, don't behave any differently with them at work than you would if your boss were present. Even your friends can be subpoenaed and asked to describe anything you may have said or done.

As for dress, am I saying never wear a miniskirt to work? Absolutely not. There are miniskirts and there are *mini*skirts. Is yours leopard skin with a slit up to your crotch? Dress the way you want, but be prepared to have your appearance used against you if your attire can be considered provocative.

Such clothing won't necessarily absolve your harasser of his misconduct, but a court or jury will consider your sexy apparel in deciding whether his sexual aggression toward you was "welcome" or "unwelcome."

Your employer will most likely be acutely aware of all this, and even though they probably won't ask you to your face, "Did you provoke this?" most HR managers are instructed to quietly document it in order to minimize their risk should things not turn out satisfactorily for all involved.

WHAT IF YOU SAID YES TO SEX?

This is an area where many people get confused, even employers. If you said yes to sex, it doesn't necessarily mean it was "welcome" behavior by you. Voluntariness on your part does not necessarily mean welcomeness. Often women say yes to sex because they truly believe there is no other choice. They believe they must agree to protect their job, or to prevent their boss from retaliating. So even though your actual participation in sexual intercourse was *voluntary* in the sense that it was not against your will, it may have been *unwelcome.*[10]

Still, should your situation ever escalate into a court case, your jurors may find your actions difficult to understand. They may tend to blame you.

If at all possible, just say no from the very beginning to everything that is improper and unwelcome. If for some reason you are unable to do that, then at the very least make sure you tell your harasser that your sexual involvement is not something you have chosen or welcomed. At the very least, inform someone else at the company that this entire situation is unwelcome by you.

Finally, if you said yes because you truly wanted to engage in sex with this person, then it's not sexual harassment.

WHEN A COWORKER IS HAVING A RELATIONSHIP WITH YOUR BOSS AND RECEIVING SPECIAL FAVORS THAT YOU'RE NOT

Is *her* sexual harassment *yours*? After all, you are suffering because of it.

If the relationship is consensual, there is nothing you can do about it because the situation doesn't constitute sexual harassment. Both men and women under this boss are suffering because of his behavior. You are not being singled out because of your sex.[11]

If his relationship with her is nonconsensual, however, it may be considered sexual harassment against you as well as her. This could be proved by a statement from the woman with whom he's having a relationship. In this instance, the law will consider whether this relationship is an isolated episode or standard procedure in your workplace. If he has a history of giving workplace favors to women who have sex with him, then his sexual practices have displaced ordinary business routines and prevented you from being evaluated on your merit.

SAME-SEX HARASSMENT

What if your employer is a woman? Could her actions be considered sexual harassment? Yes. Either she is sexually interested in you, or she acts in a demeaning, insulting manner to the women who work for her. Either motivation constitutes sexual harassment as long as it fits into the two-pronged criteria.[12]

What to Do About It

HOW TO COMPLAIN

Chances are your employer will not take an aggressive, hostile stance with you the very first day you complain. Most employers would prefer, as you should, to fix the problem quickly and internally. For them it means better employee productivity and less exposure to liability. For you it means less disruption in your life and a chance to continue with the goals you had in mind when you started your job.

But if your employer is unable or unwilling to fix the problem, and you are forced to complain to an outside agency or lawyer, your employer's tone will quickly change.

Suddenly, everything you ever said and did in the workplace, including every word you spoke or wrote in lodging your initial internal complaint, will be called into question and used against you in an attempt to discredit you and your story. Shirley Y. learned the hard way how this could happen:

> *When the human resources manager took my complaint, she asked me what I now know were loaded questions. She asked them as if she were really concerned about me. I remember once she even reached over and put her hand on my shoulder as if she were offering support. She said, "It's terrible to see you so upset. Is there anything else going on in your life that's upsetting you?" I searched my mind trying to come up with something and halfheartedly suggested, "Well, my husband has been really busy at work lately, so I haven't really felt like I wanted to bother him with all this." It was a stupid thing to say. Later, after I quit because they never fixed the problem and just allowed my supervisor to continue harassing me, I hired a lawyer. The company claimed I was having marital problems that made me overly sensitive—that my personal life was somehow skewing my judgment so that I wasn't reacting reasonably. It's amazing. They even quoted my own statements, but they exaggerated them and took them out of context.*

Know what your employer is listening for. Get it straight from the beginning, because, as you will learn in chapter 13, "Lodging a Complaint with Your Employer," an employer's main purpose in documenting your complaint is not necessarily to help you but rather to assess risk, minimize liability, and correct the problem—in that order. You need to put yourself first, because most employers won't.

WHEN TO COMPLAIN

Says Martha U., a telephone operator:

> *I sat there and listened to Chuck harass and embarrass me every single day . . . day after day. I never officially complained, but I knew for a fact my boss had overheard Chuck on more than one occasion. Three months into it, I had to go on medical leave because I just couldn't take it anymore, but the company refused to pay my salary, or even my medical and counseling bills. I thought they should, since they were responsible, but they actually claimed that since they had known nothing about it, that they had no way of preventing it. My supervisor, when he was questioned, said he was unaware of any problem. Why would he admit to knowing about a problem in his department that he hadn't solved? I had to fight and fight . . . even hire a lawyer. I never would have had this problem if I'd lodged a single complaint against Chuck.*

Your employer may seem to continually look the other way when a supervisor is harassing a woman. Often, though, the management really *is* that insulated from day-to-day workplace problems. In some unfortunate cases they just don't *want* to know, because as long as an employer is not apprised of the problem, their legal responsibility is still in question. (See chapter 10, "Just Who Is Doing the Discriminating?", which discusses holding employers responsible when they knew or should have known of discrimination.)

That's why it's crucial you either document or complain the first time it happens. Then, no matter how much they like this guy, he, and not you, has become a problem to the company. The management can be both fined and sued, not to mention have their image tarnished, if they continue to tolerate, and thus condone, a discriminatory workplace.

CREATIVE SOLUTIONS OF THE NONLEGAL TYPE

Often women are in a predicament where they fear the retaliation of complaining more than the harassment itself. Or maybe they have complained, but their employer does little or nothing about it.

Doreen, an officer in the armed forces (she prefers I not mention which branch), had her own reasons for not complaining:

I didn't complain because of the hassle—the "you said, she said" that goes on. Also, I thought approaching him would have no effect, and you don't want to be known as a complainer—a troublemaker. You throw eggs on the wall, you get spattered. It's better to choose which battles to fight.

When a same-rank married officer increasingly insisted on holding her hand and giving her hugs and kisses, the working relationship became extremely uncomfortable for her.

I probably didn't handle this very well, but my solution was that I made him so mad at me that he didn't want to harass me anymore. He was my supply officer, and when some computers came in without all the attachments, I sent him a memo listing what was missing, and I purposefully sent a copy of the memo to our commanding officer, who then forwarded it on to him with a note saying, "What happened to all the little computer pieces!?" The supply officer was furious with me after that and just left me alone. He called me every name in the book, and I ceased having a sexual harassment problem. Of course, I had the other problem of having him furious with me, but it wasn't as bad as the harassment problem. I also sent him a copy of the sexual harassment policy—of course, unsigned.

Sometimes women are forced to choose between options, none of which are perfect answers. They are placed in the position of risking their own reputations and jeopardizing the goodwill they receive from coworkers to correct problems that they never should have been made to face in the first place. It can be a lose-lose situation. Doreen is extremely smart and capable, and she was able to pull it off. But be careful. It's not always the best solution for everyone.

For Natalie, an extremely attractive woman, her job as a printing shop assistant came to a quick end:

> *My boss gave me a pair of panties and said, "I hope one day you'll model these for me." Then he pulled a wad of pesos from his pocket and said he was going to Mexico. He kept bugging me, "Oh come on, baby, go with me for the weekend." I'd had just about enough. I was just so angry that I turned on the loudspeaker and allowed his voice to go out over it. And then I announced, "Dan Brown has just come into my office and propositioned me." He thought I was crazy. I just quit.*

You walk a fine line when you use alternative methods to solve your problems, clever as they may be. It's best to use the mechanisms that are in place for you. I realize it can be difficult to lodge a complaint. I know how it feels—the fear of antagonizing your boss and jeopardizing your livelihood. Yet I still advise you to lodge a formal complaint when it comes to sexual harassment. Otherwise, all the repercussions I've discussed in this chapter may come back to haunt you.

5.

Receiving Less Pay and Fewer Benefits

I went in for my annual review and I was expecting a merit raise because I had worked so hard the past year and done so much for the company. Instead I was asked why I thought I needed a raise. "After all," [said the company's vice president,] "your husband works here and we just gave him a huge promotion with a raise, so why do you need one now?" I realized at that moment that even if I managed to talk him into giving me a raise, my future with that company was hopeless. With attitudes like that, I might as well stay home and collect my husband's salary.

—Martha S., researcher

Women have never earned as much as men. Even today, for every dollar men earn, women earn only 76 cents. This is so even in occupations where women traditionally outnumber men.[1] Female nurses earn 10 percent less than male nurses; female office managers earn 34 percent less than male managers; and female elementary school teachers earn 14 percent less than male elementary school teachers.[2] Despite the fact that women account for 46 percent of the U.S. workforce, less than 2 percent of top wage earners at Fortune 500 companies are women.[3]

Women face this wage disparity from the time they begin their careers. Female graduates of the top twenty U.S. business schools earn 12 percent less than their male counterparts their first year out of school.[4]

This problem stems from an underlying notion some employers hold that men are the breadwinners in our society. They have families to support and are more serious workers. As such, they're entitled to more serious pay.

Even in companies where these beliefs have been significantly purged, men may *still* be paid more simply because such a system typically perpetuates itself. For example, even if a man has the same amount of education and prior experience as a woman, chances are he will be offered more money when he *starts* his job because employers usually match past salaries when making offers. And since men generally make more money than women, their previous salaries are higher. Once a woman starts at a lower salary, it's nearly impossible for her to catch up.[5] The practice is called *red circled wages.*[6]

What if you learn that all or most of your male coworkers are making more money than you? Is there any acceptable reason for this disparity? There are a lot of gray areas when it comes to pay, because traditionally a person's salary is based on an employer's notion of that person's worth or value to the company.

Still, there are some rules to which your employer must adhere.

Equal Pay Act

The Equal Pay Act forbids an employer from paying men more than women solely because of their sex. In order for the Equal Pay Act to apply to your situation, you must be able to show that the work you do is *substantially equal* to that of your male counterpart. Your job must require *the same degree of skill, effort, and re-*

sponsibility, and it must be performed in the *same establishment* and under *similar working conditions*. All these factors must be present before you have the right to demand equal pay. Let's examine them one by one.

SAME ESTABLISHMENT

You and your male counterpart must work at the *same establishment* for you to have a basis for comparing salaries and demanding equal pay. Although this may seem an obvious determination to make, it isn't.

For instance, what if you both work as salespeople at Sears? Must you both be working at the *same* Sears store for you to demand equal pay?

Or what if you *do* work at the same store, but he works in Tools and you work in Intimate Apparel? Can you claim you both work for the same establishment and deserve equal pay? That's what happened in a real case. Sears employed men in its sporting goods and hardware departments and women in its clothing departments. Employees in sporting goods and hardware received higher pay. As a result, men were paid more than women. Sears tried to argue that the various departments should not be compared since the salespeople sold vastly different items, which justified paying different amounts. The courts disagreed.[7]

Different departments in stores are generally regarded by the courts as being part of a single establishment, for the purposes of comparing salaries.

In some instances, different stores in the same chain are held to be the same establishment. For example, if you work for a college or university, your salary should be equal with that of other employees who do your job throughout the entire campus, not just with those in your own building or department. Or if you work as a file clerk for a city, your salary should be equal to that of other city file clerks in locations throughout the entire city.

The question you should ask is whether your employer has a

centralized personnel system that oversees all these departments. Are people hired and fired through the same personnel system? Are all the employee records kept there? Do employees frequently transfer between departments and different locations? Do the company rules and regulations emanate from this central office? If your answer to most of these questions is yes, then most likely every department or location under the umbrella of this central office is considered a single establishment for the purpose of comparing salaries under the Equal Pay Act.

EQUAL WORK

Once you have determined that your male counterparts work in the same establishment as you, then you must decide whether you do *equal work.*

This would apply to people who have or have had the exact same job title as you, or jobs that are roughly equal to yours. Under the Equal Pay Act, equal work need not be exactly equal, only *substantially* equal.

For example, airlines used to pay female "stewardesses" less than male "in-flight pursers," claiming that the two jobs were not equal work. One airline claimed pursers had the extra duty of lifting heavy beverage racks onboard, which justified a higher rate of pay. Another said pursers were better able to stow heavy carry-on baggage for passengers, and that the pursers policed the cabin and lavatories. One airline declared that pursers made more money because they had the extra duties on flights to Hawaii of answering passenger questions about the islands and of wearing "Aloha" shirts!

But the courts said these so-called extra duties were insignificant and that the stewardesses and pursers were doing *substantially* equal work.

Make a list of your duties and your male coworkers'. If possible, obtain a job description of both positions. Notice which duties are the same and which are different. Then ask yourself if these extra tasks constitute a considerable part of his job, or if the two of you actually are performing *substantially* the same work.

Courts have ruled that jobs that are "very much alike," "closely related," and "virtually identical" are substantially equal.

Don't let differing titles steer you away. Sometimes they are merely artificial classifications. For instance, if you are a maid and your male counterpart is a janitor, you are probably doing the same work. One employer pointed out that janitors were required to exert slightly greater physical effort, but the courts held that there wasn't enough difference between the two jobs to justify a difference in pay.

Employers don't necessarily institute these classifications solely to circumvent the law. In many cases, the categorizations exist simply because they are remnants of the roles that men and women have traditionally played in our culture.

EQUAL SKILL, EFFORT, AND RESPONSIBILITY

If your male coworker is in a job that requires more experience, training, education, or ability than your job does, then his job requires more skill and your employer is justified in paying him more money.

Similarly, there's nothing to prevent an employer from paying more money for a job that requires more effort—that is, more physical or mental exertion. Are your male coworkers required to spend more time on the job, exert more brainpower, or face more physical challenges? If so, you cannot demand equal pay. The extra effort must be a *significant* amount, unlike the maid/janitor situation, where the janitor's extra effort was only *slightly* greater and not enough to justify higher pay.

Finally, an employer can pay a person a higher salary if his job requires more responsibility. Does your male counterpart have a greater degree of accountability for his decisions and work product? Does he supervise more people?

Comparing executive or professional positions can become

very difficult. Employers successfully argue that each job should be evaluated individually, without comparisons, thus creating a gray area. Professors with similar qualifications in academic institutions are usually held to have substantially equal jobs if they work in the same department, regardless of whether they teach the same subject. But it is more difficult to compare the jobs of professors who work in different departments.

Similarly, school athletic coaches are sometimes compared even though they teach different sports, or teach the same sport to both boys and girls, but not if they teach different sports to boys and girls—that is, you can't compare the girls' tennis team with the boys' football team.

But take note, even if the job of boys' football coach were to require more skill, effort, and responsibility than the girls' tennis coach job (and thus justify higher pay), an employer would still be violating the Equal Pay Act by restricting the football job to men and the tennis coach job to women. Women in that case are not being given an opportunity to earn comparable pay, but instead are being shuttled into lower-paying jobs.

SIMILAR WORKING CONDITIONS

I love cooking with Corningware. The only problem is I just can't look at that familiar Corning logo without thinking about the women who worked there in the 1970s. Corning Glass Works thought it was okay to pay women at its factory less money than it paid men. Corning claimed the extra pay was compensation to employees who worked the night shift—who just happened to be all men. Historically, women at Corning had been prevented from working at night (they needed to be protected). The Supreme Court, however, ruled that the two jobs were the same—day or night. The two shifts were considered to be *similar working conditions.*

Nighttime differentials *are* sometimes allowable, but not if the people receiving those differentials happen to be all one sex.

EXCEPTIONS TO THE EQUAL PAY ACT

There are four exceptions to the Equal Pay Act—seniority, merit, quantity or quality of production, and "any other factor other than sex."

Seniority is fairly straightforward. Time on the job counts for something. If you've been on the job a year and your male counterpart has been there five years and you both do the same job, a difference in pay would be acceptable. Just make sure the difference is somewhat relative to the difference in seniority. And make sure that when you've been there five years, you're making more than the new guy.

Merit means your employer is allowed to award the best employees with raises. But you must make sure your employer is not arbitrarily and predominantly giving these merit raises to men. They should be based on objective criteria such as competency exams or letters of acknowledgment from supervisors, not on unbridled discretion. You, as a woman, must be given the same opportunities to obtain a reward or merit.

Quantity or quality of production simply means that employers can pay an employee more who produces more or produces a better-quality product. This exception reminds me of an old *I Love Lucy* show: Lucy and Ethel are working in a chocolate factory. Lucy's job is to take chocolates off a conveyor belt and put them in a box. The conveyor belt moves too fast for Lucy, however, and she is unable to stuff the boxes fast enough. Lucy tries to solve the problem by eating the extra chocolates. No doubt the factory owner would be reasonable in paying Lucy less money than other employees received simply because Lucy's *quantity of production* was very low and her *quality of production* was probably even lower. (The one box she did stuff didn't look very "neat," not to mention her consumption of company property.)

Quantity and quality of production is easy to verify. Just look at the numbers and make sure your higher-paid coworker is actually producing more and better. This type of compensation scheme is commonly used for salespeople who get paid on commission. In other occupations, it can manifest itself in a coworker's simply making a higher base salary than you do.

"Any other factor other than sex" is a catchall exception that means your employer can use any valid reason for paying one employee more than another, as long as that reason is not based on sex.

Consider the situation of Valerie M., a records management specialist:

> *I'd been working as a librarian in the records management department of a large construction firm for seven years when they hired Fred. He essentially had the same qualifications as I did when they hired him, but he had held a much higher-paying job prior to coming to our company. He told the interviewer he wouldn't take the job unless they met his past salary, so they did. I was so upset because I had been with the company all those years and I had worked my way up from the bottom to be head librarian. My pay raises had been constant, but not huge. Fred, who was only an assistant librarian, was brought on board making twice my salary.*

What happened to Valerie is disturbing and sad, but it's not necessarily sex discrimination. Fred wasn't paid more because he was a man. He was paid more because of "a factor other than sex." The company wanted to match his former salary.

This is the red circled wages problem, discussed earlier. The courts are split as to what degree an employer can base workers' salaries on their past pay levels. Some courts say the practice perpetuates discrimination, since statistically women make less money than men and almost always start at a lower rate of pay. Since it perpetuates discrimination, it violates the Equal Pay Act.

Other courts, however, allow employers to consider a worker's prior salary, but only if it's used in conjunction with other factors. And once a worker has proven herself on the job, an employer may not continue to use her salary history to justify paying her a lesser amount.

Employers are allowed to rely more heavily on a woman's previous pay if her former job was commission-based, since in that case her past income is more apt to be an accurate reflection of performance on the job.[8]

Typically, "any other factor than sex" might include an employee's prior experience or educational degrees; transferring an employee from a different department where he or she was making more money and allowing them to keep their salary; paying a trainee, a temp, or a part-time worker less than a full-time worker (provided there isn't an inordinate number of women in those lesser-paid positions); profitability (e.g., if a person is well known and can attract clients or notoriety to the employer's business, thus increasing the employer's "profitability"); an employer's subjective evaluation of an applicant gained from the job interview; and an employer's personal knowledge of an applicant's ability to do the job.

Finally, in complying with the Equal Pay Act, your boss cannot lower other workers' salaries in order to make things equal. Instead, an employer must *raise* those salaries that are lower.

Receiving Fewer Benefits

Under the Equal Pay Act, employers are not allowed to discriminate when "paying wages." But just exactly what does the term "paying wages" mean? Obviously it means your salary, but it also includes your benefits.

Typically, things like overtime, uniforms, travel, office accommodations, and other things of that nature qualify.

Medical and insurance benefits also fall into this category. In order to receive the same amount at retirement, women who worked for the City of Los Angeles Department of Water and Power (DWP) used to be required to pay more into their pension fund than did their male counterparts. The DWP pointed to mortality tables that showed that women live longer than men and would therefore require more monthly payouts. But the United States Supreme Court ruled that the City of Los Angeles was violating the law. Although an individual insurance company can charge you a different premium based on your sex, your employer cannot. Nor can an employer pay out a lesser amount for a woman's pension than for a man's.[9] Regardless of how much employers have to pay out to insurance companies, they cannot pass the cost on to you as an individual because of your sex.

What to Do if You Are Receiving Less Pay or Fewer Benefits

It would not be unreasonable for you to ask your employer's human resources department whether your pay and benefits are in line with others doing the same job. Don't expect to be told what everybody else is making, but do expect to be assured that either your pay is equal or that there are significant reasons for your being paid less. If you know or have reason to suspect that you are not getting equal pay, see chapter 13, "Lodging a Complaint with Your Employer."

6.

Less Desirable Assignments and Fewer Promotions

Just to let you know you are not alone out there, I have been a state worker (clerical-judiciary) for fourteen years, finally working my way up through the ranks to a senior position. I have passed all the required tests for promotion and still must sit and wait for the MAN to promote me. It does get on your nerves knowing that even a well-qualified, hardworking and dedicated employee will never be recognized because of the system. I am in no way a male basher, but unless you stick together as a unit and push to promote women, we will never get ahead in business.

—posted on an Internet bulletin board in response to an inquiry from another woman experiencing a similar problem

When Supreme Court Justice Sandra Day O'Connor graduated at the top of her class from Stanford Law School in 1952, the only position she was offered was that of legal secretary.[1]

Ever wonder why women are "beauticians" but men are "hairstylists"? More important, ever compare the two salaries? The job title "beautician" suggests a small shop and moderate pay. "Hairstylists" are often men at the very top of the profession, prestigiously coiffing the tresses of the rich and famous.

The same is true for maître d's—well-paid men who greet and pander to restaurant customers. The female equivalent is a low-paid hostess who maintains a scribbled list of hungry customers as they appear at the door.

Traditionally, women were "seamstresses" while men were higher-paid "tailors" usually sewing more expensive, high-quality clothing.

Women dominate the teaching field . . . when it comes to relatively low-paying elementary school jobs. The majority of lofty professorships, however, at top-paying universities are reserved for men. (Personally, I think a kindergarten teacher should make more money, considering what's at stake—not to mention what's involved in managing a roomful of five-year-olds!) Even at elementary and secondary schools, where women constitute 90 percent of the workforce, they account for only 10 percent of school superintendents.

What's wrong with this picture?

Why aren't women being promoted? Why aren't they getting better assignments? Why are they steered toward jobs and occupations that don't lead to upper management? Why are women hitting what experts call the "glass ceiling"?

In 1991, the U.S. Department of Labor under President Bush commissioned a study of opportunities for women and artificial barriers to their advancement. The "Glass Ceiling Commission" spent four years examining and analyzing randomly selected Fortune 500 Companies, releasing its startling conclusions in 1995. Despite the fact that women make up 46 percent of the total labor force, they account for only 3 to 5 percent of management positions. More important, in the Fortune 500 companies, women account for only 2 percent of senior-level management (executive vice president and above), and only one-half of 1 percent of our nation's CEOs.

The commission also identified "gender clustering" of women into support positions, such as personnel/human resources, communications, public relations, community and government relations, customer relations, and the support staff side of marketing and finance. These jobs are not considered "line" positions that typically feed into senior management posts. And workers in these fields are not typically assigned high-visibility special projects that might allow them to win recognition within the company—projects that might bring a large increase in revenue to the company, say, or generate an expansion.

Although 71 percent of female executives identified this glass ceiling, 73 percent of male executives did not believe it even existed! Instead, they attributed the shortage of women to the fact that women have been in the workplace in equal numbers for only two decades. As a result, said the male executives, women have not had a chance to advance to upper-management positions.

The Glass Ceiling Commission, however, determined this reasoning to be faulty. A 1993 study of the Stanford University Business School class of 1982 found that 16 percent of the men were CEOs, chairmen, or presidents of companies, compared to only 2 percent of the women graduates. Similar disparities existed for vice presidencies and directorships.[2]

The Commission concluded that the shortage of women resulted from bias, insensitivity, and incidents of sexual harassment.

Many companies were using headhunters that found candidates either by word of mouth or by networking, the Commission noted. This tended to maintain an "old boy network" and perpetuate an already unbalanced workforce.[3]

In addition, women had not been proportionately selected for screening and grooming procedures companies typically used for development of management candidates. This lack of early training and development opportunities significantly decreased women's chances of later promotion.

Finally, in companies in which mentoring was a significant factor in advancement, senior executives were more likely to help people like themselves—other males. Women, on the other hand, rarely have strong mentors. One woman described networking and mentoring like this: "[We] share strategies and information that is unavailable elsewhere. Those who are close to or through the glass ceiling tell others where the cracks are and what size hammer to bring."

What You Can Do About It

Your employer is not necessarily discriminating against you just because you didn't receive a promotion or job assignment that you wanted. If the lack of promotion is truly based on your lack of qualifications, then it's not discriminatory.

At the same time, an employer cannot deny you the experience you need for promotion, then refuse to promote you because you don't have the requisite experience.

Once, as a reporter, I went flying with the Navy's Blue Angels. I was upside down at just under the speed of sound when it occurred to me that no one had ever told me this was a career I could have chosen to pursue. Later, I asked my pilot why there weren't any women pilots in the Blue Angels. "None of them are qualified," he told me. "In order to fly for the Blues, you have to serve a tour of duty aboard an aircraft carrier—out to sea for six months. Women aren't allowed out to sea, so they don't have the proper experience." Nor would they ever have the chance to *obtain* the proper experience, regardless of how good a pilot they were.

This rule has since changed, but in many companies women are denied the chance to learn the skills they need in order to advance.

If you have recently been refused a promotion, you should first find out who has made the decision not to promote you. Ask that person to explain to you why you were passed over. This need not be a confrontational meeting. Instead, explain that you consider yourself on a fact-finding mission to improve your chances of promotion in the future. Solicit concrete explanations as to what it is you lack.

If it turns out that your male competition had fewer skills than you, there is a presumption of discrimination.

If your male competition had skills equal to yours, there exists a gray area.

Ask your employer what skill(s) or experience you need in order be chosen for the next promotion. If possible, make sure your subsequent acquisition of those skills gets mentioned in your next employee performance review.

If you do acquire these skills, reapply the next time there is an opening. If you do not get the job, ask your employer to explain why not. Again, document the explanation. Does it sound reasonable? If your employer has no credible explanation, there arises a presumption of discrimination.

It may be that the person who made the decision does not want to speak to you about it, but rather simply refers you to the human resources person in your company. This is okay, as long as the human resources person is able to give you an adequate explanation. If not, then lodge a discrimination complaint within the company.

Finally, an employer cannot maintain a separate line of progression for men and women desiring promotion. There must be only one seniority list, and it must include both males and females.

7.

Mommydom

The paramount destiny and mission of woman are to fulfill the noble and benign offices of wife and mother. This is the law of the Creator. And the rule of civil society must be adapted to the general constitution of things.

—United States Supreme Court, *Bradwell v. Illinois,* 1872, in denying Myra Bradwell the opportunity to practice law after she had taken and passed the bar exam. Eventually, Illinois began admitting women to the bar, but Myra Bradwell refused to reapply. Shortly before her death twenty-five years later, the Illinois Supreme Court, acting on her original application, admitted her.

The Supreme Court was actually trying to be kind to Myra Bradwell in instructing her on her proper path in life. The court was merely acting as a conduit for "the law of the Creator."

The notions upon which this case was decided are still with us. Despite an abundance of laws prohibiting discrimination based on pregnancy, maternity leave, and child care, many women in the workplace still face the stigma of "mommydom."

Mommydom is a word coined by Ed Turner, former executive vice president of news gathering at CNN, who used it in his memo to me questioning whether I might go all "goo-goo" on CNN after the birth of my baby and advising that I "quit thinking CNN and start considering Mommydom."

I'm not sure exactly which part of mommydom Ed was instructing me to consider, but since he insisted I do so, I will.

Mommydom comes about when a woman, after announcing to her employer that she's expecting a child, suddenly finds herself the recipient of subtle probing: Who will take care of the baby? How will you combine work and family? How good an employee will you be after the baby? Will you be willing to work as long and as hard?

Mommydom entails inquiries in the form of questions (sometimes seemingly innocuous), indirect comments, or maybe even little "jokes."

ATTORNEY FOR CNN: Your Honor . . . It's undisputed. Those remarks were in a joking memo . . . [Ed Turner] thought it was cute to say, hey, don't even think about CNN. Don't think about CNN if you go Mommydom on us. . . .

MR. TAYLOR FOR MS. PANICCIA: The "goo-goo ga-ga memo" was something they say was a joke. Fine, let them sell that to the jury. My client did not take that as a joke; and given the fact she was then terminated, neither did Mr. Turner.

Mommydom is wondering why when men announce they are going to be a father, no one questions their commitment to work or presumes they will be a lesser employee.

Mommydom is a young woman struggling with the issue of how to combine work and family, and wondering why men are not being faced with the same dilemma.

Mommydom is when a husband takes a day off work to tend to a sick child and his employer asks, "What's wrong with that guy? And what's wrong with his wife?"

Mommydom is announcing to your boss that you are pregnant and knowing that your career just went down the drain.

Mommydom (not to be confused with *motherhood*, which I cherish) stinks.

Here's a question that another mommy, Debi, recently pondered. It was posted on an Internet bulletin board under "Women Talk/Issues in the Workplace":

> *I have been a CPA for nearly twenty years and a mother for six years. Had three children in less than three years and worked full-time, including overtime during tax season, while I was pregnant. I was so damn tired. I didn't even want to get dressed some mornings during the third pregnancy. It was not the best time of my life. . . . Most people were in awe that I managed to handle everything I did. I have not lost any of my client base and even picked up a few more clients. The real difficulty I had was the attitude of my boss, [who] coined a new phrase that he used to describe me—Professional Mother. He started treating me so badly that I finally walked into his office and shut the door behind me. I told him that I would not be treated the way he was treating me. It got ugly. He had to get his partner in the office to restore the calm. I am still working there, but I could never trust my career to him. . . . So do you think working and having children is difficult due to physical and emotional demands . . . or do you think it is difficult because of the attitudes of men?*

Marital Status

In the eyes of the law the husband and wife were one person—the husband.

—Norma Basch, *In the Eyes of the Law: Women, Marriage, and Property in Nineteenth Century New York* (1982)

Discrimination based on marital status is not as common as it once was. Overt rules disallowing married women from working are no longer in place (although as recently as the 1980s, airlines would immediately terminate any flight attendant who got married[1]). Even so, sometimes an employer may have an unpublicized preference for hiring an unmarried woman.

It might be that the employer has a misconception about a married woman's viability on the job. Some people believe that a married female employee must always answer first to the needs of her husband and family, and as a result puts her job last. The employer may think that since you are married, you might someday have or already do have children. This means you are a distracted employee and may even bring your child-care problems to work. Your family, if you have one, will increase the employer's insurance premiums and expenses. What's more, you might suddenly quit your job should your husband get transferred.

Another reason an employer may prefer a single woman is a sexist or sexual attraction for women who are unmarried and "available."

Marital status discrimination is difficult to ascertain or verify. Sometimes it peeks through via cryptic remarks or even jokes, but often it manifests itself when an employer regards you as a less-favored employee than your unmarried counterparts. In that situation, you might never know that your marital status is being held against you.

The only way you can be sure that your ill treatment is truly linked to your marital status is if one of your supervisors makes a specific comment to you or about you in this regard, or if there is a distinct pattern in your workplace of single women being treated better than married women.

If you do hear a derogatory comment, write it down, and note who said it and who overheard it besides yourself.

If there is an obvious pattern of married women being treated poorly, then log the pattern. If possible, talk to the women involved and get their story. If your employer truly is exhibiting a "pattern and practice" of discrimination based on marital status, then it's illegal. At some point, you may want to lodge a complaint about it.

Pregnant on the Job

The physical well-being of woman becomes an object of public interest in order to preserve the strength and vigor of the race.

—United States Supreme Court, *Muller v. Oregon* (1908)

At the turn of the century, there were absolutely no workplace laws—no minimum-wage laws, no sanitation laws, and no workplace safety laws. They were prohibited because the Supreme Court ruled that the government should not be allowed to dictate to private employers how the workplace should be run.

But there was one giant exception—workplace laws that protected women. The Court allowed these laws because it believed that the government had a stake in the offspring that women bore—an interest in preserving "the strength and vigor of the race." Concern for offspring has been a traditional grounds for discrimination against women.[2] It has prompted protectionist laws that prevented pregnant women from earning a living.

These same concerns are sometimes manifested today.

Some people just can't refrain from voicing their opinions about what pregnant women should and shouldn't do. Their purpose is usually not malicious, and they may even be motivated by kindness. Some feel compelled to speak up for the sake of the baby. They may view it as a moral issue and believe it's their duty to make sure each fetus and each child has a happy and healthy environment. The problem is that only women are instructed or criticized on this issue. Fathers aren't penalized for not staying home with their babies.

That's sex discrimination.

There are only two situations in which an employer can reassign you or force you to go on mandatory leave when you announce you are pregnant. They are: (1) if your pregnancy renders you unable to do your job; and (2) if your pregnancy endangers the health and safety of others—this is called the "safety exception."

UNABLE TO DO YOUR JOB

Your employer must show that the particular skill your pregnancy is preventing you from doing relates to the "central mission" of your job or to the "essence of the business."[3] For instance, if you're a firefighter and your pregnancy renders you unable to adequately hold a blasting fire hose, then you are incapable of doing your job. Since fighting fires is the central mission of your job, your employer is justified in either reassigning you or placing you on mandatory leave.

On the other hand, if you are a schoolteacher, your pregnancy would most likely not interfere with the central mission of your job, so you have a right to work throughout your entire pregnancy.

This is so with most jobs.

In addition, the Pregnancy Discrimination Act declares that unless pregnant employees differ from others in their ability or inability to work, they must be treated the same as other employees.

THE SAFETY EXCEPTION

The second situation, called the "safety exception," occurs when your pregnancy jeopardizes the safety of others. For instance, in the firefighter example, even if you *are* able to lift a fire hose, your pregnancy might be causing you to do so at an extremely slow rate—to the point where it endangers the lives of other firefighters or fire victims. Since you are jeopardizing their safety, you can be reassigned or put on mandatory leave.

It is this safety exception that allows airlines to ground female flight attendants during the later stages of their pregnancies. Since a flight attendant's job is to ensure passenger safety, she must be able to open emergency exits and windows and quickly evacuate passengers. She must be one hundred percent physically able and strong, or lives will be jeopardized.

It's crucial to note, however, that the safety exception does not apply to *your* safety or to the safety of your fetus—only to the safety of third parties.

For instance, airlines may *not* ground a flight attendant for fear that she will be continually exposed to increased amounts of radiation in flight and thus harm the fetus (a risk that is a proven fact).[4] Nor can airlines ground a flight attendant out of concern that she may go into labor while onboard and be unable to secure the medical help she needs.

Only *you* are allowed to decide on the amount of risk to which you expose yourself and your baby. Your employer cannot force you to quit, or even reassign you to a different job, unless *you request it!*

I'm certainly not suggesting that you risk the health of your baby or yourself, but I am telling you that it is your decision and not your employer's.

If you choose not to expose your baby to proven workplace dangers, you have the right to be transferred to another position or, if one is not available, to go on leave.

Some employers are fearful that a working pregnant employee or her baby may someday sue them for having been exposed to harmful conditions. But fear of a lawsuit is not justification for an employer to prevent you from working throughout your pregnancy. Your employer must fully inform you of the risks you take, and the ultimate decision is up to you.

MANDATORY LEAVE OR TEMPORARY REASSIGNMENT

If you cannot do your job when you are pregnant, who decides whether your employer reassigns you or places you on unpaid leave until the baby is born?

It depends on the state in which you live. The federal Pregnancy Discrimination Act requires that pregnant workers be treated the same as or better than other temporarily disabled employees. Some states allow their regular disability rules to apply to pregnant workers. In that case, if your state allows employers to put temporarily disabled workers on mandatory leave, then the same applies to you. Other states have specific laws for pregnancy-disabled workers that disallow employers from placing pregnant workers on mandatory leave. Instead, those states require that employers reassign those workers at the same rate of pay. Usually these laws apply only to businesses that employ a certain minimum number of employees, ranging anywhere from five to fifty.

Your state human rights office can tell you exactly how your state deals with the issue of reassignment and mandatory leave. See Table III.

IF YOU CAN DO PART OF YOUR JOB BUT NOT ALL OF IT

Questions sometimes arise when a pregnant woman can do only part of her job—perform some tasks but not all. In that case, she can be reassigned only if those tasks she cannot perform relate to the central mission or essence of her job. For instance, if a teacher is required to carry heavy stacks of books from the library to the classroom and becomes unable to do this during her pregnancy, she *cannot* be reassigned. Carrying books simply does not relate to the essence or central mission of her job. A teacher can teach without carrying books.

INFERTILITY

An increasing number of women are requesting time off work or reduced schedules in order to receive medical treatment for infertility.

Some employers are reluctant to allow this since the employee is technically not "ill." Recently, however, the U.S. Supreme Court ruled in *Bragdon v. Abbott* that infertility is considered a "disability" under the Americans with Disabilities Act, commonly called ADA.[5] ADA defines a disability as a "physical or mental impairment that substantially limits a major life activity."[6] The Court in *Bragdon* concluded that one's ability to reproduce is considered a major life activity.[7] Therefore an employer is required to accommodate your efforts to become pregnant.

But there are some limitations. ADA applies only to employers of fifteen people or more. Plus, your employer is not required to accommodate you if it would be "unreasonable" to do so. Unreasonable is a term that's left open for courts to decide on a case-by-case basis. Past cases have held that unreasonable includes anything significantly difficult or expensive for an employer.

Also, your modified or part-time schedule must not be an open-ended arrangement where you work only when you are able. That, too, would be unreasonable.

This law is fairly new and still somewhat emerging. If you are facing this type of infertility issue in the workplace, I suggest you check with an attorney to see what the current state of the law is.

Maternity Leave

I once heard a very high ranking Los Angeles police officer complain that four of his officers had gone on maternity leave at the same time, and that as a result his other officers were not receiving the backup they needed. "It's just terrible," he moaned. "I'm so angry at these women. And so are the rest of my men. How else can you expect them to feel?"

"Angry at your chief!" I replied.

This was not an employee problem. It was an institutional one. The police department had no system for replacing female officers on maternity leave—thus the reduced workforce jeopardized the safety of the remaining officers and caused resentment among the troops.

Historically, police departments have not had to grapple with the fact that officers have babies. Today those institutions with a tradition of an all-male workforce, such as police and fire departments, or the U.S. military, seem to have the most difficulty with accommodating pregnant employees.

Once while covering a story for CNN at a federal courthouse in Orange County, California, I encountered a most bizarre reminder that many of our courthouses are still unaccommodating environments when it comes to pregnant women.

I was covering the trial of a banking executive being prosecuted for the failure of North America Savings and Loan, an Orange County–based thrift that had bilked taxpayers and investors out of $120 million.

During a break in the proceedings, I rushed to talk to one of the prosecutors CNN wanted me to interview. Since cameras aren't allowed in federal courthouses, I had to convince this lawyer to join me outside for the interview. As I ran down the hallway to catch her, she passed through a metal detector. I was hesitant to follow because I was five months pregnant and had recently read that although there's no data that a metal detector can harm a fetus, there's also no data that it can't. In order to be safe, the book had advised, avoid metal detectors and ask for a body search.

So I did.

"We can't do that," replied the federal marshal. His fellow marshal nodded in agreement. "I really don't mind," I said. "I need to get down the hallway to catch up with that lawyer." But he refused and insisted I walk through the metal detector, pregnant or not. I asked if there were any women marshals available, but there were none.

Then he offered me an astonishing alternative. He asked me to "prove" that I was pregnant. If I could, he would let me through. "Would you like a urine sample?" I retorted. Very seriously, he replied, "No, just lift up your blouse a little so I can see if you're pregnant." I was aghast. But then I watched the lawyer walking away from me down the hall . . . and I had just been told that CNN Executive Vice President Ed Turner, upon hearing of my pregnancy, had stated, "Another good reporter down the drain!" I pictured Ed at CNN Center in Atlanta asking, "Why didn't we get that interview?" Someone would reply, "Because Paniccia's pregnant and refused to go through the courthouse metal detector." In an instant, I lifted my blouse to just below my bra, exposing my pregnant belly. The marshal allowed me to pass.

I caught up with the lawyer, who agreed to talk to us. As I sat on the curb outside waiting for her, I began thinking about what had just happened. I had been so desperate. But now all I felt was shame. I had lifted my blouse in front of two federal marshals, my CNN field producer, and several other people waiting behind me to pass through the metal detector.

Slowly, my shame turned to anger as I realized that I never should have had to make such a stupid choice in the first place. This institution, like so many others, was simply not equipped to deal with pregnant women. And why hadn't there been any female federal marshals?

Later, I rode back to the bureau in silence interspersed with an occasional exasperated sigh over the fact that the lawyer had not even come outside for the interview as promised.

Weeks later, when ex-President Reagan came to Los Angeles to give a videotaped deposition for the upcoming Iran-contra trial of Admiral Poindexter, I would again face a federal marshal at the entrance to a courthouse. Only this time, security was even tighter because of Reagan's presence. My request for a body search was flatly denied. No metal detector, no access to the courthouse. Period.

Beaten, I chose the metal detector and joined my reporting competition in chasing Admiral Poindexter down the courthouse hallways.

The rest of the day (and later whenever I remembered the incident), I thought of a *Mary Poppins* song called "Sister Suffragette." There's a line that goes: "Though I adore men individually, we agree that as a group they're rather stupid." Unbeknownst to most men, some of the institutions they create and perpetuate are rather stupid—ill-equipped for and unconcerned about accommodating anyone other than themselves—whether it be maternity leave policies or a simple entrance procedure to a courthouse. Why should they accommodate pregnant women, anyway? After all, these institutions have for hundreds of years been operating just fine without them.

Here's what you need to know about what you are entitled to receive:

Maternity leave is your right, not your privilege. You shouldn't have to feel as if you are taking a "joyride" on the company's time.

Maternity leave is not for the purpose of spending time with your baby. People often confuse maternity leave with child-care leave. Maternity leave is a disability-type leave granted to allow you to medically recover from your pregnancy. That's why fathers and adoptive parents are not allowed to take maternity leave.

The 1993 Family and Medical Leave Act (FMLA), however, provides not only for maternity leave but for *child-care* leave as well. As a result, men and women, both adoptive and natural parents, are allowed to take time off to care for a child under FMLA. (FMLA is discussed later in this chapter. This section discusses only maternity leave.)

Your employer's policy toward granting leave to other temporarily disabled employees should be the same policy that applies to your maternity leave. That is, if your employer typically holds a job open for non–pregnancy-disabled employees, then the employer should do at least the same for you. Moreover, some states require employers to provide you with even *better* benefits than those offered to non–pregnancy-disabled employees. For instance, nonpregnancy leave time may comprise only a two-month period, but pregnancy leave may extend longer, usually to three months.

In addition, the amount of maternity leave your employer grants must be sufficient for recuperation from pregnancy. Our courts have held that two months is not enough. Three months is adequate, and very often four months is allowed if you've had a cesarean-section delivery or other medical complications.

Your state government may require employers to grant a minimum number of weeks for pregnancy disability. If you call your state human rights commission, they will tell you what your state-allowed leave time is.

HOW AND WHEN SHOULD YOU NOTIFY YOUR EMPLOYER

The law requires that you give "reasonable notice" to your employer of your intention to take a pregnancy leave. Reasonable notice depends on your particular occupation and circumstances. Some women prefer to wait until after the first trimester, when the greatest risk of miscarriage has passed.

If you know that your employer is depending on your presence during the time you will be on leave, or if you know your position will be extremely difficult for your boss to fill, it might be considered "unreasonable" not to give immediate notification. Michelle L. worked for a large health care provider. Her job was to convince large companies to sign up with her health care service by making dazzling boardroom presentations. Her boss depended on her knowledge and expertise in that area.

Consider what happened when she became pregnant:

We'd been trying for several years to woo one particular client. Finally I got a chance to make a presentation, but I had to wait until September when it was time for that company to make its health care renewal decisions. Shortly after the first of the year, my boss gave me this list of my so-called goals for the year, and at the very top was this September presentation. I wanted to die, because I knew I had just gotten pregnant and my baby was due in September. I knew I'd be on leave.

In a situation like that, it would be unreasonable not to immediately inform your supervisor of your pregnancy.

Your employer probably has a policy regarding pregnancy notification—a specified length of time that is "reasonable" in light of the particular business you are in. It may be printed in your employee handbook or in other literature your employer has given you. You can also ask somebody in the human resources department (except that this person's first response will probably be "Why? Are you pregnant?").

If your company *does* have a policy, then follow it. If you don't follow it, you have violated company policy, and that's grounds for disciplinary action or termination.

If your company does *not* have a policy, and there are no other compelling reasons, then notifying your boss when you are three months or four months pregnant is reasonable.

Also, the Family and Medical Leave Act has specific notice provisions that you must comply with if you want to be protected under that law.

MATERNITY LEAVE PAY

Your employer has to pay you during your leave only if other temporarily disabled employees at the company receive disability pay.

Find out what your workplace policy is for maternity leave pay and compare it to the pay for temporary disability leave. You must be paid that amount—or more, if your employer chooses.

Don't expect the amount you are paid to equal your full salary. Some employers will do this for you, but since it's not required, most won't.

If your employer either does not pay or pays only a partial amount, you may be entitled to state disability payments as well. Call your state disability office to find out. Each state is different. Typically, if your employer pays for only six of the twelve weeks you are on leave, the state pays you during the remaining six weeks. Usually the amount is less than your salary.

ACCRUING SENIORITY AND OTHER BENEFITS WHILE ON LEAVE

There is no hard-and-fast rule on this issue. It's up to your employer whether you will accrue vacation and sick time, and seniority or length-of-service credit for a company retirement plan.

Typically, whatever policy your employer has implemented for other disabled employees must also apply to you.

IF YOUR BOSS REASSIGNS YOU WHILE YOU'RE ON LEAVE

If specific positions are generally kept open for those on nonpregnancy leave, then your boss must do so for you on maternity leave. In addition, most state laws require an employer to reinstate you with the same pay at your same job, or to a job with equivalent pay, benefits, and other terms and conditions of employment. Your state human rights commission can tell you exactly what you are entitled to.

The bottom line is that your leave should not affect any of your job benefits and opportunities *in any way.* That includes a situation like the one Colleen O. encountered. A marketing manager for computer software, she took a three-month maternity leave when her son was born.

> *The year my son was born, I lost a great deal of money because the company changed the compensation structure for people in the marketing department. Our new compensation was based on the previous year's earnings and some other information. My previous year's earnings were lower than normal because of a three-month maternity leave. At the time, I was too naive and ignorant of my rights to contest it, so instead I just took what the company gave.*

Colleen had a right to protest this method of calculation, and to have her maternity leave not counted against her when determining her pay rate. Maternity leave often creates situations like this—ones that don't "fit into the boxes." It's up to you to see to it that your company makes the individual provisions necessary to keep you on equal footing with your coworkers.

In addition to being protected by your state law, you are entitled by the federal Family and Medical Leave Act to be reinstated to your same position or to a position equivalent to your old job in pay, benefits, and other terms and conditions.

DON'T COLLECT UNEMPLOYMENT WHILE ON MATERNITY LEAVE

If you are on maternity leave, don't try to collect unemployment.

Unemployment is for people who are *able* to work but cannot find a job. By going on maternity leave, you are swearing that you are *unable* to work because of your pregnancy disability. If you seek unemployment during your leave, you must swear that you are willing and able to work.

The two statements contradict each other, and employers are taught to use them against you. Here's how:

Sometimes a woman is discriminatorily fired in the midst of her maternity leave. Finding herself out of work, she then applies for unemployment compensation. She also files a discrimination complaint against her employer. Her employer, however, can claim that she was able to come back to work but didn't—legitimate grounds for firing her. The employer will prove this by flaunting her own signed statement from the unemployment office, in which she swore she was ready and willing to work.

Lawyers regularly advise employers immediately to check with any government agencies the woman might have contacted to see whether she has made any contradictory statements of this nature.

If you've been fired, wait until after your allowed maternity leave has finished before you apply for unemployment. If your state or your ex-employer offers pregnancy disability payments, try to continue collecting those until your allowed leave time is over.

WHEN IT'S TIME TO RETURN TO WORK

Prior to going on leave, you should have checked with either your employee manual or the human resources department to see what they expect of you when it's time to return to work. Some companies require that you call a week or so beforehand, others want written notice, and some just expect you to show up on a prearranged date.

Regardless of your employer's policy, I advise a courtesy call to your immediate supervisor and to any other supervisor who you think might appreciate being reminded. Just let them know what day you're coming back in case they want to anticipate or prepare a workload, and tell them you are looking forward to it. It will send them the clear message that you are serious about your job.

Child Care

This passage, published in the *Harvard Law Journal* in 1978, was written by Rena K. Uviller:

> Until the daily concerns of child rearing become the shared responsibility of both father and mother, there is little chance that women with children will achieve equality outside the home. . . . Not until men regularly are willing to leave the office early to attend to their children's needs will it be regarded as legitimate for women to do so. Only when acceptance as a "serious" producer in the working world does not preclude concurrent child care duties, when "working father" takes on the same connotation as "working mother," will employed women not be penalized for bearing children.[8]

I've never been very good at having babies, which makes it especially ironic that CNN thought I, of all people, would go all "goo-goo" on them—that is, become so distracted with caring for my infant that I'd be unable to do my job.

When I had my first child at age thirty-eight, I'd spent my entire life until that point oblivious to child rearing and its responsibilities. I'd spent my late teens and early adulthood in Hawaii, surfing on the north shore of Oahu and competing around the world on the women's pro surfing circuit. I'd worked part-time throughout college, put myself through law school, and then later taught at law school. I had been a television news reporter in Santa Barbara and Los Angeles; I'd met presidents and world leaders, modern-day saints and martyrs, murderers, debutantes, homeless people, political candidates and political refugees, movie stars and social activists. I'd visited their homes, their places of work, their trials, their private jets, their shanties, their churches, and at times their prison cells. I'd stood in the midst of fires, riots, and floods to cover the daily news.

But on the day my daughter was born, I didn't even know how to change a diaper, much less hold her in my arms to stop her from crying. I was the least likely person to go "goo-goo" on CNN. Nevertheless, I was unable to escape the prejudices and preconceived notions that some men possess. Did CNN think I would no longer be willing to travel on breaking stories because of my child-care responsibilities? Did they presume I would begin missing deadlines in order to get home to my baby?

Managing your child-care responsibilities concurrently with the demands of your job will be one of the most challenging endeavors you face. Even more challenging will be learning how to avoid others' preconceived notions of your worth as an employee *after* you become a mom.

Here are the rules.

"SEX-PLUS" DISCRIMINATION

An employer who discriminates not against *all* women, but only those with children, is still guilty of sex discrimination. It's called "sex-plus discrimination"—discrimination based on sex plus one other factor, in this case children.

If your employer has a separate set of rules with regard to women with children, it's against the law.[9]

ILLEGAL ASSUMPTIONS SOME EMPLOYERS MAKE

Most employers don't have rules that openly discriminate in this fashion. Some, however, do make broad assumptions about women with children.

Justice Ruth Bader Ginsburg tells the story of how, as a professor at Columbia Law School, she received constant phone calls from her son's school. Although she describes her son today as a "fine human being," she says that at the time he was a "spirited ten-year-old."

> *There were calls from the principal, almost monthly, requesting a meeting with me to discuss my lively child's most recent adventure. One afternoon, when I felt particularly weary, I responded: "This child has two parents. Please alternate calls for conferences." After that, although I observed no quick change in my son's behavior, the telephone calls came barely once a semester. There was more reluctance to take a father away from his work. There still is.*[10]

Studies show that in most families where both parents work, women often *do* assume most of the parenting responsibility.[11] Still, an employer cannot automatically presume that (1) this is necessarily so for you and your family, or (2) that you are somehow a less valuable employee because of it.[12]

An employer cannot deny you promotions, raises, or other job opportunities simply because you are a mother. If, on the other hand, your parenting is seriously interfering with your ability to do your job, your employer may have a right to discipline you. For instance, in most cases you have no right to be tardy more than other employees just because of your child(ren)'s needs.

Some states have specific laws that prohibit employers from firing or discriminating against employees who take time off from work to participate in activities at their child's school. In these cases, employees are required to give reasonable notice, and the employer may require the employee to use vacation time. The purpose of these laws is to make sure parents don't miss out on school plays, teacher conferences, graduations, and other events at the school. Call your state's human rights office to find out whether your state has such a law.[13]

FAMILY AND MEDICAL LEAVE

Under the 1993 Family and Medical Leave Act (FMLA) you are allowed to take time off to care for your child. You can take up to twelve weeks over a one-year period. Unlike maternity leave, where your employer is sometimes obliged to pay you, family care leave is unpaid.

The Family and Medical Leave Act is extremely complex, so it's crucial that you carefully read this section to fully understand how to ensure that you are continually protected by it. For the relevant text of FMLA, see Table IV.

Who Is Covered Under FMLA.

The Family and Medical Leave Act applies only to employers of fifty or more people.[14] Federal, state, city, and other public agencies are also covered by FMLA, regardless of whether they have fifty employees. So are elementary and secondary school agencies, both public and private.

You must have been an employee for at least twelve months (the twelve months need not be continuous) and you also must have worked for at least 1,250 hours within the past twelve months. Holiday time, vacation time, sick leave, and unpaid leave are not counted toward the 1,250 hours you must have worked.

You are entitled to leave under FMLA:

- to care for your newborn child, your newly adopted child, or your newly placed foster child; or
- if you have *a serious health condition* (including pregnancy); or
- if a family member has a *serious health condition.* A family

member includes your child, your spouse (not domestic partner), or your own parents (not in-laws).

A "serious health condition" exists when:

- you have to stay in the hospital overnight
- you are incapacitated for more than three consecutive days and receive medical treatment at least twice; or
- you are incapacitated for more than three consecutive days, must receive medical treatment once, and are put on continuing treatment, such as a prescription medicine or physical therapy
- you have a pregnancy-related illness, including morning sickness. (Unlike other illnesses, pregnancy-related illnesses do not require that you be ill for three consecutive days in order to qualify for family medical leave.)
- you must visit your doctor for prenatal care
- you or a family member have a chronic condition requiring long-term medical supervision
- you or a family member require multiple treatments, such as treatment for cancer

Duration of Leave.
You are normally entitled to a maximum of twelve weeks within a twelve-month period.

If you are a part-time worker, your leave is prorated. For instance, if you work twenty hours per week instead of forty (i.e., half time), then you are entitled to six weeks of leave time instead of twelve.

Calculating Your Leave Time.
It's up to your employer to determine how the twelve-month period is calculated.

Some employers use the calendar year, so that from each January to December you would be entitled to twelve weeks' leave. Other employers use a fixed year based on your hire anniversary date or the company's fiscal year. Some calculate the year by measuring forward from the first time you ever take a family medical leave.

Under these three models, you could conceivably take twelve weeks off for the last part of one year, then another twelve weeks for the first part of the next year.

Most employers, however, disallow this by calculating by a fourth method. They measure backward from the date the first FMLA leave begins. You must then wait another twelve months before being entitled to family medical leave.

Your employer must be consistent and apply the same method of calculating the eligibility year to every employee. If your employer decides to change the method, all employees must receive sixty days' notice.

Intermittent or Reduced Leave.

You don't have to take your leave all at once. For example, if throughout your pregnancy your morning sickness renders you unable to work the entire day, you can take mornings off for a couple of months until the sickness subsides. In that case, if you take off one hour per morning for ten days, you have then used up ten hours toward your twelve-week leave. This is called "reduced leave."

Or maybe you need only an occasional day or two when your morning sickness is particularly bad. This is called "intermittent leave."

In both cases, your employer will prorate your pay according to the amount of time you have missed. You can take intermittent or reduced leave without your employer's permission if an illness requires it.

If your leave is for the purpose of taking care of a newborn, or an adopted or foster child, you can take intermittent or reduced leave *only* if your employer agrees to it. You must then make a reasonable attempt to schedule your leave so as not to disrupt the business operations, and your employer may require you to transfer to an alternative position if it does (unless transferring is prohibited by your union). This includes being transferred to another location, and you can refuse only if the new location would adversely affect you in terms of time, distance, and cost. If you unjustifiably refuse to transfer, you will lose your protection under FMLA.

How to Request Leave and Give Proper Notice.
Under FMLA, you can give written or verbal notice of your intention to take leave, either in person, via telephone or telegraph, or even through a spokesperson. I recommend you always give FMLA notice in writing. Employers are advised by their attorneys to always give *their* notices in writing in order to "preserve the record." You, too, should preserve the record in case there is a dispute as to whether either side gave accurate and timely notice. Keep copies of everything you send and receive.

In your request, you must tell your employer the anticipated duration and timing of your leave.

You need give notice only once, regardless of whether your leave is to be taken continuously, intermittently, or on a reduced work schedule.

If your leave is clearly foreseeable (e.g., the birth of a baby or a scheduled operation) and you have no reasonable excuse to do otherwise, you must give your employer at least thirty days' notice. If your leave is unforeseeable (e.g., sudden adoption of a child, illness, or the premature birth of your baby), you need give notice only "as soon as practicable." Usually that means one to two business days after your learning of the need for leave, or whatever is reasonable under the circumstances.

If you don't comply with these notice requirements, you may lose your FMLA leave rights.

Required Medical Certification.
Your employer can require medical verification from your health care provider either within fifteen days or as soon as reasonably possible under the circumstances. Your employer can request that this certification contain any or all of the following: the date the illness began; the expected duration; a statement that you are unable to perform your job or that you are needed to take care of a spouse, child, or parent; and a description of the illness. (Some states, to protect the privacy of employees, disallow employers from requesting any specific description of the illness. In those cases, the only information they're allowed to receive is a statement from the doctor saying that your condition warrants leave.)

For intermittent leave, your employer can also require the dates and expected duration of the medical treatment.

Your employer has a right to request a second or third medical opinion. Some states, however, have laws that prevent an employer from seeking additional opinions in pregnancy cases.

Your employer can request recertification every thirty days. If you request an extension of your leave, if your circumstances change, or if your employer has a reasonable basis to doubt the validity of your certification, the employer can request recertification sooner than thirty days.

Your employer also has a right to request a "fitness for duty" certificate from your health care provider before allowing you to return to work.

How and When Your Employer Must Respond to Your Request.
When you notify your employer of your intention to go on leave, the employer must then provide you with information about your rights under FMLA. Your employer must tell you (either verbally or in writing) how your twelve-month eligibility year will be calculated; that your leave time will count against your twelve-week allotment; whatever medical certification requirements exist and what the consequences will be if you do not provide them; your

right and/or your employer's right to substitute paid leave; your obligation to make benefits premium payments during your leave and the procedures for doing so; your potential liability for premium payments if you do not return to work; whether you are designated to be a "key employee," and if so, how and when your reinstatement can be denied (key employee status is discussed later in this chapter); and whether you need a "fitness for duty" certificate before returning to work. Your employer must also tell you if you're entitled to leave under company policy or under other laws, such as a state FMLA or a state workers' compensation law (which usually applies to pregnancy), or the federal Americans with Disabilities Act (ADA).

Your employer must respond to your FMLA request within two business days. If you have not completed all the necessary medical certification, your employer must still respond within two days. In that case, your employer will often grant a preliminary approval. When you hand in the necessary medical certification, your employer can then make a final designation of your eligibility to take family and medical leave.

If your employer fails to get back to you within two days, you are deemed eligible for the leave, regardless of whether you would be eligible otherwise.

Using Vacation or Sick Time.

An employer has the right to require you to apply your paid sick leave, personal leave, or vacation time toward your family medical leave. For instance, if you have two weeks' vacation time due you, and you request twelve weeks off under FMLA, your employer can pay you for two of those weeks and delete your accrued vacation. This is an *option* on your employer's part, not a requirement of the law.

For instance, if someone tells your boss, "Jill's on vacation, but she's really at home taking care of her sick baby," then your boss has the option of counting your vacation days toward your family and medical leave.

Also, if *you* want to have your accrued vacation or sick days applied toward your family medical leave (so you can receive pay during your leave), you may elect to do so.

Retaining Benefits While on Leave.

During your FMLA leave, your health benefits must remain intact. You do not, however, accrue vacation, sick leave, or length-of-service credit.

However, if you take any paid leave, such as using up your vacation time, you will accrue these benefits.

When you return, your benefits must be restored to exactly what they were before you left, including life and health insurance, disability, sick leave, annual leave, seniority, educational benefits, and pensions.

Your pension and benefit plans must not treat your FMLA time as a break in service for the purpose of vesting or other participatory requirements.

Reinstatement.

You are entitled to be restored to the same or an equivalent position. An equivalent position is one that offers the same pay, duties, benefits, working conditions, hours, opportunities for advancement, and geographic location as your prior job.

After Julie H. gave birth to triplets, her boss expressed concern that she might not be able to do her job. Julie works as a commission sales representative for a large manufacturer, servicing commercial clients. Since her six-figure income was higher than her husband's, they decided *he* would stay home and take care of the triplets while she returned to work. Two weeks after she returned from her maternity leave, Julie's boss informed her that he was cutting her sales territory in half.

I told him, "I am the sole support of this family now and I can't give up that area. And I don't see the fairness of taking this away." I had raging hormones at the time. I was nursing three babies, and I remember him looking blankly at me and saying, "This has nothing to do with you or your pregnancy, and I want to make this clear." And I just cried.

Now the children are three years old and I've worked my sales up in my smaller territory so that my income is about what it was before. Just last month, my boss wanted to use me as an example at the company awards banquet. He wanted to say, "Look, we took all these things away from her and she dug in and she's gotten back to where she was two or three years ago." I told him I didn't want his award.

If Julie were to object to her boss's decision, she would have to prove the decision was made in response to her pregnancy. Her boss, however, would try to claim that the cutback fell into one of the allowable exceptions under FMLA. They are:

- if your job has been eliminated due to reasons unrelated to your FMLA leave; or
- if you are unable to perform essential functions of your job owing to your physical or mental condition; or
- if you are a "key employee."

Key Employees.

Key employees are salaried workers who are among the highest-paid 10 percent of employees in the company within seventy-five miles of the worksite. Your employer must notify you of your key employee status as soon as you request leave. Key employees aren't always denied reinstatement, but can be if:

- the employer determines that it's necessary to prevent *substantial and grievous economic injury* to the business; and
- the employer notifies you of the injury your reinstatement will cause as soon as the employer knows of it.

Temporary Workers.

If you are a temporary worker, you may still be covered. FMLA considers you a "joint" employee of both the temp agency and the place they send you to work. The temp agency is considered your "primary" employer, and is responsible for providing the leave. You must have worked for the agency for at least twelve months, during which time you must have worked a minimum of 1,250 hours. In addition, the agency must have at least fifty employees.

If the agency has fewer than fifty employees, your secondary employer may be responsible for granting you leave. If you've worked for the secondary employer for at least twelve months and 1,250 hours, the secondary employer has as least fifty employees, *and* the temp agency continues to provides workers to the secondary employer, then the secondary employer is obliged to grant you all FMLA benefits, including full leave and reinstatement to your former position.

Teachers Have Special Rules.

If you teach for an elementary or secondary school, regardless of whether it's public or private, your FMLA rules are slightly different. If your leave is scheduled to start or end during the last few weeks of the academic term, your employer can request that you not return until the next term. See Table IV, "Family and Medical Leave Act," Section 2618, for exact time limits on this option.

A Harsh Reality

Even with all these protections in place, mothers who work outside the home still face a large degree of intolerance from the working world.

To raise her two young sons, Deborah F., a deputy district attorney, opted for a temporary "job-sharing" program in her office, where she works half time.

It's not like we're cut any slack in terms of what we're expected to do when we're here. But some men act like we're taking a vacation on the county. We're only paid for the time we work, and we don't even receive benefits.

There are resentments from other women, too, who either can't do this for financial reasons, or maybe don't want to do it . . . but feel like they should want to do it. So it's not just coming from the men. That's the part that was surprising to me.

There's no doubt that we aren't taken as seriously in terms of a career path. If any one of us wants to come back to work full time, there's really a question whether we'd be in the place where we left off. It's clear that it's a derailment. Even if you're highly regarded, it's understood that you don't come back to the same position.

I don't know for sure where this idea comes from, but it's sort of the old notion that if you want to do a man's job, then do it. And men don't take maternity leave or child care leave.

The United States is the only industrialized nation in the world that does not provide paid leave for women when it comes to child care; some countries even provide paid leave for men. Given that fact, it's not surprising that women like Deborah continue to face intolerance and resentment.

A majority of women will tell you that their having children has meant sacrificing or jeopardizing their career in some way.

8.

"Sweet Young Things"

Women and Age Discrimination

Once while I was working at a small television station in Santa Barbara, California, I was interviewing a fifty-year-old cowboy in the Santa Ynez Valley. In the midst of my questions, the cowboy allowed his eyes to wander toward a cowgirl walking by. As she approached, he murmured to his friends, "Looks like she's been rode hard and put away wet." "Your horse?" I asked, having not seen the cowgirl at first. "Well, in a manner of speaking. At first I thought that broodmare was a filly," he said, pointing to the cowgirl, "but I was mistaken."

Women in our society are judged more harshly on their appearance than are men. Youth and attractiveness can open doors for a woman. Those same doors may slam shut later in life when she finds she needs more than a smile to get by. Sometimes, even when a woman *does* have more than a smile to offer (i.e., an education and work experience), she may still face men who would just as soon put her "out to pasture" than hire, promote, or appreciate her.

Television news is rife with examples. News directors and the viewing public seem to like female anchors young and pretty, and male anchors older and more "seasoned" looking. Some network execs, in order to avoid this type of criticism, like to point out that they now have a significant number of older women on the air. What they fail to note, however, is that most of those women are extremely attractive and youthful looking for their age. Only when the networks hire older women with wrinkly skin, pudgy bellies, blotchy complexions, thinning hair, and/or dreadful toupees (all attributes of some of the top male correspondents currently on the air) will things truly be equal. For now, growing old in the workplace, if you're a woman, is not a pretty sight.

HOW EMPLOYERS BREAK THE LAW

Employers who prefer younger women usually do so for one of two reasons:

Some believe older women have few skills to offer. Many of these women have spent a portion of their lives working in the home. The skills and experience they acquired there, however, are sometimes treated with arrogant disregard by employers.[1]

Sally J., age sixty-four, raised two children as a single parent, while working as a manager of medical and dental offices.

I made my last boss a millionaire in five years. Through the years as a household manager, I've accumulated a tremendous amount of knowledge. I invested his money, negotiated his bank loans, bought his insurance policies, bought and updated his computer system, hired his employees, did his accounting, and researched medical and retirement benefit plans for the office.

When her former employer merged with another office, Sally was "merged" out and then quickly learned the job market was no place for an older woman.

They can't get it through their heads that what you're bringing to them is a certain sense of maturity—business acumen that you've learned all these years. They just want something nice and fluffy up front.

In most occupations, older women have proportionately the lowest rate of hire and earn the lowest wages.[2] This is so even when their education and experience level is equal to that of their male and younger female counterparts.[3]

A second reason some employers prefer younger women on the job is sexual attraction.

Says Jean K., age thirty, a cashier:

I used to work at [a discount retail chain], and my boss used to like to hire cashiers who were young and attractive so he could watch them all day from behind the counter where he sat. I used to see a lot of older ladies come in and apply for a job. I'd see him pretend to be interested, but he never called them back. He always called the young ones.

As Jean points out, most bosses won't come right out and tell you they prefer younger women, so it can be difficult identifying age discrimination.

If you have fewer skills and less experience than a younger candidate who is promoted over you, your boss has a perfectly good reason. If you have equal skills and experience, however, it's perhaps a gray area as to why your boss chose her.

The Age Discrimination in Employment Act (ADEA) applies to employers of twenty or more people, and protects workers over the age of forty. ADEA also applies to overseas workers if they are employed by an American corporation, but it does not apply to the U.S. military.

Proof of age discrimination under ADEA is of two types: (1) a specific remark made by your employer indicating a preference for younger women or a distaste for older women, or (2) a clear "pattern and practice" by your employer whereby younger women are routinely given more and better employment benefits and opportunities than older women.

If either or both of these criteria apply where you work, you should begin keeping a detailed log of all the situations where they occur. Include a list of names, and, if possible, informally talk to the women involved. If you ever lodge a complaint (within your company, with the EEOC, with a state human resources agency, or in a court of law), you should present your lists and logs. Unfortunately, you may be unable to acquire a complete and accurate list, because most employers won't turn over this type of evidence unless you file a lawsuit and subpoena the information.

IF THE PERSON WHO TOOK YOUR JOB IS ALSO OVER FORTY

If the person who took your job is over forty, the ADEA still applies if the difference in your ages is "substantial." There is no set number of years that is considered substantial. Obviously, the greater the disparity in ages, the more likely the court is to find age discrimination. If you are close in age to your replacement, you will need other strong evidence to show there was age discrimination.

In fact, you could even be replaced by someone older than you and still prove age discrimination if your evidence is strong enough. As one court said: "Replacement by someone older would suggest no age discrimination but would not disprove it conclusively. The older replacement could have been hired, for example, to ward off a threatened discrimination suit."[4]

STATE LAWS

In addition to ADEA, some states have their own equivalent versions of ADEA. Depending on your state, the law may apply to employers of fewer than twenty people. See Table V.

Dress Codes and Looking Good

DATELINE: Fort Lauderdale, Florida. *American Bar Association Journal.* March 1995

Crystal Holjes of Pompano Beach, Florida, was representing a client in a Broward County courtroom when Circuit Court Judge Barry Goldstein told her she should leave immediately because he did not allow women appearing before him to wear shorts.

Holjes says she tried to explain she was wearing "culottes," which she describes as "half skirt, half shorts that are very dressy and come down almost to the knee." The judge responded by ordering her removed from the courtroom.

Armed deputies grabbed the 100-pound, five-foot, one-inch Holjes, pulled her over a bench for spectators and dragged her out of the courtroom.

Shackled in handcuffs, Holjes was charged with resisting arrest and put in a holding cell until fellow lawyers convinced another judge to release her.

We all have to adhere to certain grooming standards in the workplace, but how do we determine whether we're being held to a standard of good grooming or to an employer's sexist notion of how a woman should look?

Your employer is allowed to establish a reasonable workplace dress code. It's okay if that dress code imposes different requirements for women than it does for men, because standard business attire is different for men and women. For instance, an employer who requires men to wear ties doesn't have to require women to do the same. Similarly, an employer who allows women to wear earrings doesn't have to allow men to wear them.

Problems arise, however, when employers try to define what is "acceptable" business dress.

When I was working as a television news reporter at a Santa Barbara television station, the management there hired an image consultant. This expert on my personal appearance, makeup, and clothing informed me that maroon was *my* color, insisting I wear as much maroon clothing as possible. And while I was at it, I should apply more eye shadow and lipstick, preferably in shades of maroon.

A few years later, while I was working at a Los Angeles television station, another image guru was hired to instruct us reporters and anchors on how best to present ourselves. "Whatever you do, don't wear maroon," he warned. "It's terrible for you. It makes you look swarthy." All I could think about was my closet and makeup drawer at home, jam-packed with varying shades of maroon: Light maroon. Dark maroon. Medium maroon. Cranberry. Raspberry Pie. Tropical Maroon. Mellow Maroon. And my personal favorite, Marooned on Maroon.

The point is that not everybody seems to agree on what looks good or acceptable (or, in my case, not "swarthy"). These self-anointed appearance counselors probably had no basis for their analyses and recommendations other than their own personal opinions and tastes. Professional business attire is just a reflection of contemporary fashions. It's also a reflection of someone else's preconceived notions about how certain groups of people should look.

Viewed in that light, dress standards appear arbitrary and capricious. Why aren't men allowed to wear "women's jewelry," such as earrings? Why do women feel they must wear high-heeled shoes if they really want to get "dressed up"? Why must men keep their hair short? Why can't women wear pantsuits or culottes in some business settings? Does good grooming require that you wear makeup? If you wear too much makeup, is that bad grooming? If your skirt is too short, is that unprofessional? How short is too short? Does good grooming include having clean, white teeth? What if they're yellow and stained? What if your glasses are broken and bent? Where do you draw the line?

The law says that if your employer does impose a dress code, it must be applied evenly to both sexes. It cannot be stricter or more demeaning to women, nor can it be more stringently or harshly applied.

In one case, a bank required its female employees to wear uniforms and its male employees to dress in "appropriate business attire." A federal court ruled that the dress code was discriminatory because the women's rules were stricter than the men's. The bank had bowed to a stereotype and assumed that it needed to reduce competition among the women with respect to clothing, that women were less capable than men of selecting appropriate business attire.[5]

Similarly, if a dress code is demeaning to women, it's considered discriminatory under the law. This includes requiring women to dress as sex objects and wear sexually provocative clothing.

MORE STRINGENTLY OR HARSHLY APPLIED

Even though a dress code may appear fair and reasonable, sometimes women are subjected to more rigorous enforcement of the code than are men, and are given far more scrutiny concerning their compliance with it. Moreover, women's failure to abide by the dress code may be taken more seriously by an employer, because the employer may believe that women's appearance is more important than men's. Appearance may well be important in your occupation, but it should be no more important for women than it is for men.

IMMUTABILITY

One factor that can help you decide whether your employer has a right to criticize your appearance is whether the particular item your employer is asking you to alter is *immutable.* Can you change it, or is it part of your innate appearance? For instance, your wardrobe can easily be changed. So can a hairstyle or a hair length.

But what if your employer doesn't like the *type* of hair you have? What if it is thought to be too curly, too frizzy, or too straight? Is that something that's immutable? If not, at what cost of time and energy? Or what if your employer doesn't like your acne? Is that a matter of cleanliness and grooming, or is it just genes? What if your employer says your yellow teeth don't contribute to a good business "look"? Should you be required to alter the appearance of your teeth?

The more innate a characteristic is (the more difficult to alter or modify), the greater the chance that it is immutable under the law, and therefore any request to change it would probably be deemed discriminatory.

NO FAT CHICKS

DATELINE: Las Cruces, New Mexico. Reuters. August 22, 1996

Miss Universe, Venezuela's Alicia Machado, left New Mexico on Thursday, refusing to answer questions about her weight. . . . She came under intense scrutiny following reports she was given an ultimatum by Los Angeles–based Miss Universe, Inc., to drop 27 pounds in two weeks or risk losing her crown.

Organizers flatly denied ever threatening Machado but immediately put her under wraps and blocked access to her.

Is weight a mutable characteristic? Most people think it is, but some medical authorities view certain cases as a medical problem and thus an immutable physical characteristic. As such, your employer cannot demand that you change it, or factor it into your "professional business look."

In some cases, however, a weight requirement is allowable if it's necessary for safety and competency on the job. For instance, a weight requirement for a lifeguard might be deemed reasonable, since an obese lifeguard would not be as agile and swift-moving as a lean one.

It could also be argued that weight is a factor when the job requires beauty and aesthetics; this might apply to a beauty queen, a fashion model, a dancer, or possibly even an actor. The occupations that fall under this standard can be determined only on a case-by-case basis, because there is no hard-and-fast set of criteria. For instance, in the case of an actress, it must be asked if she was cast for her acting skills or for her svelte figure.

A well-known Washington news correspondent once informed me that she was told her contract would be renewed for only one year instead of two because she had not lost weight as the network had asked her to do. This extremely bright and savvy woman wondered what the size of her butt had to do with her ability to interview congressional leaders and analyze national policy issues. She responded by telling her supervisor that she would be glad to comply—as soon as the network asked some of its top male correspondents to lose weight as well. (She named two well-known reporters who are overweight and at times quite sloppy in their appearance. She, on the other hand, is always attractively groomed.)

The network, unable to dispute her claim that there were separate standards in place for men and women, eventually signed her to a long-term contract.

Even if weight requirements *are* allowable in your profession, make sure that they are not more restrictive for women than for men. For instance, some companies create and use weight charts that allow for a higher percentage of body fat on men than on women.

In some states, weight requirements are completely prohibited unless on-the-job safety considerations require them.

The bottom line is that we, as a society, are much more tolerant of overweight men than we are of overweight women. If your boss is asking you to lose weight, make sure that in addition to the "no fat chicks" rule there's a "no fat dudes" rule as well.

Not Sweet Enough

Now, why would a nice young lady like you want to go and throw kitty litter in the punch bowl?

—former Secretary of Education William Bennett, in response to a "difficult and inappropriate" question I asked him during a press conference

The question I asked Secretary of Education Bennett concerned President Reagan's budget. Bennett had just spent twenty minutes regaling his audience on the attributes of inner-city teacher Jaime Escalante and expounding on the importance of education. "If you are truly this concerned about education," I asked, "then why have you just proposed a three-billion-dollar cutback in education, the largest in history?"

The thought that my question might cause me to be regarded as "not nice" or "unladylike" surprised me. I've always been cordial and professional on the job. That doesn't mean my questions haven't been direct and probing.

Perhaps Bennett would have accused a man asking the question of being "ungentlemanly." I don't know. But I *do* know that sometimes women find that their workplace behavior is judged by standards different from men's.

When well-known criminal defense attorney Gerry Spence was asked to critique prosecutor Marcia Clarke's performance during the O. J. Simpson trial, he said, "I wouldn't want to go dancing with her." Dancing? Is that the criterion for judging a prosecutor? Was he watching Johnny Cochran's every move in order to determine whether Cochran, too, would be rotten company on a dance floor?

I know some businessmen who are quite gruff. They scowl at their staff, demand absolute perfection from everyone around them, and expect coworkers and subordinates to accommodate their every need. At the same time, they're heralded as go-getters, demanders of excellence, shrewd and savvy executives, and leaders of men. Not only are their "rudeness" and lack of social grace put up with, these men are treated with respect and deference. In short, nobody's ever called them "a bitch."

Ann Hopkins was an accountant at the Price Waterhouse accounting firm in 1983. When she became eligible to make partner, the company's overwhelmingly male management voted against it, despite the fact that she had garnered $25 million of business for the company (more than the sum produced by any other associate) and that her clients had expressed no problems with her. Instead, her male coworkers noted that although she was an "outstanding professional," she "lacked interpersonal skills" and was "overly aggressive," "unduly harsh," "difficult to work with," and "impatient with her staff." Moreover, they criticized her for being "too macho," saying that she "overcompensated for being a woman" and advising her to "take a course at charm school." They also noted that she occasionally used foul language.[6]

Hopkins sued Price Waterhouse and her case went to the Supreme Court, which noted that women at Price Waterhouse had been reviewed favorably if they "maintained their femininity" and unfavorably if "they were viewed as aggressive women's libbers." The court said some of the opinions had stemmed "from an impermissibly cabined view of the proper behavior of women."[7]

After a seven-year battle, the court ordered Price Waterhouse to rehire Ann Hopkins, make her a partner at a salary comparable to what her colleagues were making, pay her $371,000 in partial lost earnings, and pay her legal fees.

If you're getting complaints at work that you are being too assertive, aggressive, abrasive, pushy, domineering, outspoken, harsh, or difficult to get along with, then you need to step back and take a good look at both yourself and your workplace. You must determine whether these criticisms are accurate—whether there is a serious lack of people skills on your part—or whether they stem from a sexist view of how women are supposed to act. Are men who act the same way getting ahead in the workplace? Who are the women being advanced?

If you receive criticism that you feel stems from ill-conceived notions about how women should behave, I suggest you lodge a complaint with your human resources department or, if there isn't one, to your boss or your boss's boss. It's crucial that you immediately go on record as recognizing the criticism as sex-based.

If you ignore it at this stage, eventually the company will have a litany of bad reviews against you. If the company ever decides to deny you a promotion or a raise, to discipline you, or even fire you because of these complaints, you will have a much harder time proving they were sex-based than you will if you are on record complaining about them.

9.

You're Not in the Club: Where the Boys Bond

He has monopolized nearly all the profitable employments, and from those she is permitted to follow, she receives but a scant remuneration. He closes against her all the avenues to wealth and distinction which he considers most honorable to himself. As a teacher of theology, medicine, or law, she is not known.

—official statement of the Seneca Falls Convention, organized by Lucretia Mott and Elizabeth Cady Stanton and regarded as the beginning of the women's rights movement, New York, 1848

Sometimes, no matter how hard you try, you're just not in the club. That can be anything from a male-only club in which members transact important business, to an unspoken club—a group of men in the workplace who relate well to each other but regard you as an outsider.

Susan B., a bank vice president who loaned money to midsize businesses, found that she, too, was not in the club:

It was important for my bosses to meet my clients so that they'd know who I was lending all these hundreds of thousands of dollars to. One afternoon I arranged for an important client to play golf with me, my senior vice president, and my regional manager. Our bank had memberships in all the local country clubs because it was an important way to entertain clients. I booked at this particular club because I knew my senior vice president preferred it. But when we arrived, the club management informed me that women were allowed on the course only two days per week, and this wasn't one of them. My bosses and my client, well, they all just sort of stared at me, wondering what I would do. Not one of them suggested we go elsewhere. Finally, trying to sound cheerful, I said, "You go ahead and play. I'll go back to the office." I said that because I didn't want to make my client uncomfortable, even though I was uncomfortable and embarrassed. I didn't want to lose the account or anger my bosses.

It doesn't matter if the club is a golf course, a country club, a service organization, a bowling alley, a hunting lodge, or an athletic association. If you're not being allowed in and if men regularly conduct business there, then you're being discriminated against.

One of the most frequent comments I hear from women is "Why would I want to join a club with all men, anyway? Let them have their space." That's fine as long as all they're doing is taking up space. The reason some women *do* want to join is that they realize how much business is transacted in these informal settings. Clubs are often where salesmen garner important accounts, lawyers woo clients, bosses decide whom to promote, politicians pick whom to appoint, and business owners choose whom to purchase their supplies from. Clubs have the potential to make or break you in the workplace.

Partial Restrictions

Some clubs do admit women, but restrict them from making full use of the facilities. For instance, country clubs often restrict tee times for women to either certain times of the day or certain days of the week. Other clubs restrict areas of their restaurant facilities to men. These partial restrictions can be regarded as discriminatory as well.

Public Clubs

If a club is using public funds to operate, the club cannot prohibit you from joining or from making full use of the facilities. Public clubs are funded by taxes *you* pay. To disallow you from joining would be a direct violation of your constitutional rights.

This rule also applies to any private club that regularly meets on public property, such as in a city park, a school auditorium, or a county office building.

Private Clubs: Are They "Business Establishments"?

Private clubs are more difficult to desegregate. If you can show, however, that a private club is a "business establishment," it will fall under the purview of your state's public accommodations law, which prohibits discrimination by business establishments.

A wide variety of organizations, whether they are nonprofit organizations or not, have been deemed by our courts to be business establishments. They include country clubs, vacation clubs, beach clubs, athletic clubs, and others.

The following questions will help you determine whether a club is a business establishment:

Are the services it offers the type that are usually offered to the general public? For instance, can members just "drop by," or are there scheduled, structured meetings? Members dropping by indicates it's not a private club at all, but rather a public facility or place of amusement—and thus a business establishment.

Does it have a business purpose? If a club rents facilities to the public, it's considered to be a business. This criterion includes renting banquet rooms for weddings, parties, bar mitzvahs, and similar events. Also, a club can be construed as having a business purpose if it regularly transacts business with nonmembers—including business transacted in the club's restaurant, snack store, golf pro shop, or similar outlet.

First Amendment Concerns

Even if your club is deemed to be a business establishment (and thus subject to discrimination laws), it may still be allowed to restrict its membership to men. The First Amendment of the U.S. Constitution grants that right in some cases.

RIGHT-TO-ASSOCIATION EXCEPTION

The First Amendment allows us the "right to associate." This means the right to enter into and maintain certain private relationships without the government intruding. If a club truly is an intimate association, the government will not interfere and force it to desegregate. According to our courts, intimate relationships are "deep attachments and commitments to the necessarily few other individuals with whom one shares not only a special community of thoughts, experiences and beliefs but also distinctively personal aspects of one's life."[1]

In determining whether a club meets this criterion, the law looks at four things: the size of the club (the smaller it is, the more intimate); the club's purpose (whether its purpose is public in nature); how selective the club is in picking its members (the more selective a club is, the more intimate it's deemed to be, whereas if *any* man can join, then it's not considered a truly personal club); and whether outsiders are excluded from the intimate parts of the club meetings. (If they aren't, the club is, in effect, sending a message that it has no real need for privacy. As a result, the court won't afford it much.)

RELIGION EXCEPTION

The First Amendment also grants us freedom of religion. If your club is a religious one and your particular religion allows only one sex to participate in certain religious activities, then the government will not force the club to admit women.

FREE SPEECH EXCEPTION

The First Amendment guarantees us the right to free speech. For this reason, if a club can show that admitting women would somehow interfere with their right to speak freely, then the government will not force the club to admit women.

The type of speech that is most protected by the First Amendment is political speech, which includes discussion of political parties, candidates, ideologies, doctrines, et cetera. Our government is founded on the idea that we govern ourselves. Therefore, open political discourse is crucial to the functioning of our country and should be vigorously protected.

Other types of speech that deserve varying degrees of protection are social, economic, educational, and cultural discourse.

BALANCING TEST

Even if these First Amendment concerns (right to associate, freedom of religion, and free speech) are present, a court may still force a club to desegregate. A judge or jury will be asked to weigh these First Amendment rights against the state's interest in forcing desegregation. The decision as to which weighs more heavily is made by the courts on a case-by-case basis.

The IRS Is on Your Side

The Internal Revenue Service punishes any club that restricts its membership to men. Normally, club expenditures are tax-deductible as business expenses. Club members who feed and entertain clients there are allowed to deduct dues, business lunches, greens fees, and similar costs.

The IRS, however, prohibits anyone from taking these deductions if the club restricts its membership to one sex, or limits its services in any way, based on sex.

This recently passed tax law has inspired a significant number of clubs to see the value of admitting women.

If you know that a club excludes women, you should consider asking whether the club's fees are being deducted on tax returns by its members. If so, you might want to bring the matter to the attention of the club's board of directors. Surely, they wouldn't want you reporting this information to the IRS, in which case they might seriously consider changing their policy.

Liquor Licenses

One effective method for encouraging private clubs to open their doors to women—and used by several states, including Connecticut, New York, and New Jersey—is to revoke the liquor license of any club that restricts membership or membership privileges based on gender. As one club member put it, "We like alcohol more than we dislike female members." More important, club owners realize that their restaurant business would be seriously diminished if they couldn't serve alcohol, not to mention the fact that potential members might think twice about joining.

The Unspoken Club

Says Dinah H., a real estate agent:

> *I tried to specialize in listing bank repossessions . . . you know, selling homes that had been repossessed by the bank. It's easy money once the bank decides to give you the account, because you get a couple of new listings per week. And getting listings is one of the hardest parts of any real estate agent's job. But I found out very quickly that banks like to give those accounts to men. Banks are very conservative and they trust men to handle it properly. It's hard to pinpoint that it's discrimination, because they don't come out and say so, but it's as if they're all in the same club. They know and trust each other. Their wives shop together. They relate well to each other. You know . . . they're in the same club. And we're not.*

In Dinah's case, there is no actual club—just an unspoken bond that ties together men who share the same lifestyles and viewpoints on life. The bond serves to exclude others who don't fall into that category.

People like people who are like themselves. They relate well to them and feel as if they can trust them. Hiring and promoting people who come from different backgrounds and who hold different perspectives on life is considered to be "risky."

As a result, women and other minorities are sometimes seen as not being the "best candidate," especially if their lifestyle or workplace demeanor doesn't completely conform to the behavior patterns of the male business world. As one Fortune 500 CEO said, "What's important is comfort, chemistry, relationships, and collaborations. That's what makes a shop work. When we find minorities and women *who think like we do*, we snatch them up."[2]

This occurs at every level of employment.

Donna, a twenty-eight-year-old fast-food worker, describes her experience:

They had this thing at the bowling alley where every Thursday night the guys would all go drinking there together after work, including my boss. Then there was this assistant manager job open . . . and my boss gave it to one of his drinking buddies, this guy who'd been on the job a way shorter time than me. Then another job came up and he goes and gives it to another one of his bowling partners. When I asked my boss why I didn't get the job, he said because he knew the other guy better so he could trust him to do the job. Yeah, I guess you could say I wasn't in the club. I didn't really want to be. I shouldn't have to be. But I did want those jobs. I worked harder than all of those guys put together.

Donna was right in saying she didn't think she should have to hang out at the bowling alley to get a promotion.

If your qualifications are roughly the same as those of a male coworker's, your boss is somewhat free to choose him over you. Part of promoting, after all, is choosing employees with whom a boss feels comfortable. But there are instances when the "unspoken club" goes too far—when your boss's comfort level seems reserved for men only. If, over time, you see a *regular pattern and practice* of promotions and other work benefits being given predominantly to men, then lodge a "pattern and practice" complaint. Whether your boss realizes it or not, any pattern and practice of favoring men is against the law.

10.

Just Who Is Doing the Discriminating?

Is your employer responsible for all the discrimination you encounter on the job, or only discrimination carried out by your immediate supervisor? Obviously, if it's a CEO committing a discriminatory act, the company is responsible. But rarely are the lines so clear-cut. What if your boss is a low-level supervisor and the upper management knows nothing about it? What if he is a supervisor, but not *your* supervisor? What if he's a coworker? Or perhaps your boss is insisting you tolerate the sexual advances of an important client.

In the case of a female lifeguard subjected to sexual advances by her bosses, a court ruled that while the supervisors who committed the acts were liable, their employer, the City of Boca Raton, was not.

DATELINE: Boca Raton, Florida. Associated Press. March 22, 1998
[Former ocean lifeguard Beth Faragher] alleged that harassment was pervasive on the beach, under the control of Marine Safety Chief Bill

> Terry. She said Terry, on many occasions, touched her shoulders and waist, patted her thigh and slapped her on the rear end.
>
> She also accused supervisor David Silverman of making offensive comments and gestures, including asking her and other women to shower with him. He would bang on the shower door as the women huddled inside, she said. "We resorted to a herding type of behavior," Faragher explained. "We'd all go in there, lock the door and kind of protect each other."
>
> Faragher won $10,000 from Terry and Silverman . . . [but] the 11th U.S. Circuit Court of Appeals ruled the city could not be held liable because it did not know about the harassment.

There are two reasons why the lifeguards would want to hold the city responsible. One is that the city has more money than the individual supervisors and is better able to pay for whatever lost salary and compensation the women are entitled to receive. A second, more important reason is that if a company or entity is *not* held liable for the actions of its workers, the company has no incentive to encourage or force its workers to correct the problem. Unfortunately, in many cases only when sex discrimination problems begin diminishing company coffers are they regarded as serious issues in need of immediate attention.

This chapter will help you determine when the discrimination you encounter on the job is attributable to your employer. The standard was laid down by the United States Supreme Court after the lifeguard described in the newspaper story quoted above appealed the ruling. The city was found liable.

Your Supervisor

A supervisor is someone who has authority sufficient to affect your work opportunities.

Employers are always liable for supervisors' actions done

within the scope of their duties—that is, the company is responsible for any decision your supervisor makes if it's a matter that has been assigned to him because of the position he holds. This typically includes discriminatory decisions regarding pay raises, maternity leaves, promotions, employee benefits, and any other issue that the company has delegated to your boss.

SEXUAL HARASSMENT LIABILITY

Your employer is responsible for any quid pro quo–type sexual harassment—that is, when your supervisor asks for sexual favors in exchange for job opportunities. Since it's one of your boss's duties to set up criteria for your advancement on the job, then quid pro quo sexual harassment is done within the scope of those responsibilities.

Hostile environment–type sexual harassment, however, is governed by a different set of rules. The U.S. Supreme Court, in *Faragher v. City of Boca Raton*, ruled that an employer is automatically liable for the actions of its supervisors unless the employer proves:

- that the employer exercised reasonable care to prevent and correct promptly any sexually harassing behavior, and
- that the employee unreasonably failed to take advantage of any preventative or corrective opportunities provided by the employer or to avoid harm otherwise.[1]

The first condition usually means having an effective antidiscrimination policy in place, including appropriate training for all employees (especially supervisors) and an adequate complaint system.[2]

One of the women at the CNN Los Angeles bureau telephoned me shortly after my lawsuit was settled to say that CNN had sent a company lawyer around the network to lecture employees. The attorney had said that the network would not tolerate discrimination and encouraged them to report it. She asked me whether I thought CNN was changing. My response was a hopeful "Maybe."

The bottom line is this: If your company management tells you how much they abhor discrimination, just know that the only thing they abhor more is the liability they face if they don't have an effective policy in place. In many cases, newfound "sensitivity" toward women in the workplace is probably nothing more than management's attempt to better insulate themselves from future discrimination lawsuits.

The second condition in *Faragher* means that it's crucial you complain to your employer. Otherwise, your employer will probably be excused from responsibility. See chapter 13, "Lodging a Complaint with Your Employer."

A Supervisor, Not Your Own

If the person discriminating against you is a supervisor other than your own, the company may still be liable.

If this person is high-ranking or is above you in the direct chain of command, the company is liable.

If the supervisor is *not* above you in the chain of command, the company is liable if this person has the authority to affect your work opportunities.

This condition might also apply if the supervisor *unofficially* affects your work opportunities. For instance, in one case a supervisor convinced a fellow supervisor to fire a woman after she rebuked his sexual advances.[3]

If the supervisor is wholly unconnected to your department and you really don't believe he has the authority to influence your job, then the same rules are in effect as those that apply if the supervisor were a coworker.

Coworkers

For six months, Jenny, a telephone customer service representative, sat next to John for eight hours a day. At first she enjoyed his flirtatious remarks and obvious interest in her. But as time went on, his behavior became more and more aggressive. He began giving her notes complimenting her on her body parts. Some of the notes described how he fantasized about her naked, and graphically depicted what he wanted to do to her. He would often roll his chair back far enough so he could stare and watch her work. Finally, Jenny quit. She was too embarrassed to tell anyone why she was quitting because she felt as if she had led John on in the beginning, and that she was partly to blame for what happened. Jenny had a tough time getting a new job, because she was unable to clearly express why she had quit her old one.

This is not an unusual situation. In fact, more than half of all sexual harassment occurs between coworkers.[4] Was Jenny's employer responsible for her predicament? Probably not. If a coworker is doing the harassing, then an employer is responsible only if the employer *knows* or *should have known.* If Jenny had lodged a complaint, the company would have had to fix the situation or be held liable for sexual harassment.

A company is considered to know that discrimination took place if:

- you lodged a formal complaint
- you informally told your boss's supervisor (even if he or she laughed it off)
- any management person witnessed the harassment
- a fellow employee informed a management person

In some instances, a company may not have known but *should have known* that discrimination was likely to occur. This might be the case if:

- your employer did a background check on an employee before hiring him and learned that he'd treated women like this before
- your employer failed to do any background checking that would have brought to light the employee's propensity to behave in a discriminatory manner
- the person openly exhibited hostile, offensive, or insulting behavior toward women—for example, made nasty comments about women to fellow management staff
- management was aware of clues, such as graffiti or other offensive material on the premises
- your employer gave this person little or no training in sex discrimination issues
- other women in the company have lodged similar complaints about him in the past
- despite the fact that other women have lodged similar complaints about him, your company failed to discipline him or maybe even promoted him after that

In these instances, your company has chosen to ignore the warning signs, and as a result has put you in harm's way. Therefore, your employer is legally responsible for what has happened to you.

Customers or Third Parties

Linda G. was a clothing rep for a swimsuit manufacturer. Her job required her to attend trade shows to display her current line of swimwear for potential buyers. One such buyer, a particularly obnoxious man who worked for a very large department store, always sought Linda out. He would then ask questions like "Would you privately model this bikini for me?" or "Would you show me the skimpiest swimsuit you have, just so I can fantasize how you look in it?" At first Linda managed to defuse the jokes by changing the subject or even joking back. As time went on, however, the buyer's comments became more and more sexually explicit.

> *I didn't think it was sexual harassment, because he wasn't my boss. But I knew I didn't want to lose the account. One time my boss was there and witnessed it, but he just told me, "Mellow out. He represents one of our biggest clients. If we get our stuff in his store, every other store will want us. Just deal with it. It's not like he's touching you."*

Linda was fired after her boss reported to the company owner that she was "just too uptight." At the time, she was embarrassed to admit she was a casualty of sexual harassment.

> *I thought it was all my fault. People in the swimsuit business are cool. I figured I was uncool—uptight.*

If clients treat you in a manner that's sexually insulting and demeaning, and your employer knows or should have known about the treatment but did nothing to fix the situation, then your employer is responsible. Why? Because the law requires that an employer provide you with a workplace free of harassment, regardless of who is doing the harassing. This applies not only to customers but to any other third parties you are required to come into contact with on the job, including consultants and vendors.

11.

Invading Your Workplace Privacy

DATELINE: Los Angeles. *Los Angeles Times.* February 22, 1995
Chevron Corp. on Tuesday agreed to settle a lawsuit for $2.2 million by four women who accused the company of retaliating against them after they complained of sexual harassment. . . . When they complained, the company began monitoring their phone calls and e-mail, installed a surveillance camera outside the office of one woman, labeled the women as troublemakers and threatened the jobs of others who associated with them, according to the suit.

Chances are your employer is spying on you. According to a survey by the American Management Association, 45 percent of major U.S. companies engage in some form of employee surveillance. Moreover, up to 26 percent don't inform employees of the surveillance.[1]

With today's technology, employers can monitor your telephone calls and voice mail, videotape your movements in the workplace, track the exact location of your company vehicle, and account for every second you spend on your personal computer (including every stroke you make on the keyboard, every screen you view on your terminal, any Websites you access on the Internet, every file you use or create, and every piece of e-mail you send or receive).

Workplace monitoring is a critical issue when it comes to claims of discrimination, for several reasons. One is illustrated in the Chevron example above, where the employer used invasive technology to investigate women who had lodged sex discrimination complaints. It's crucial you know the boundaries your employer must adhere to when investigating you.

Another reason is that *you* might be able to use the information your employer gathers to help prove your discrimination claim. For example, Kristi Knox, a female correctional officer in Indiana, had a difficult time initially convincing others that her boss, Robert Stewart, was sexually harassing her. Eventually, though, she found evidence—right under her employer's nose. This is what the court had to say:

> Starting in December, 1991, Stewart began sending Knox electronic mail messages asking her for sex. He often propositioned Knox using acronyms; for example, he frequently asked her whether she wanted to have a HGTWM, which was later translated as a "horizontal good time with me." Stewart also repeatedly asked Knox out on dates, calling her on the telephone and leaving messages reminding her to check her e-mail. . . . Stewart initially denied any knowledge of why Knox would have filed a complaint against him, but his tune changed when he found out that the investigator had copies of the e-mails he had sent to Knox."[2]

Prison officials had been logging and storing all e-mail as a matter of standard bookkeeping, and Kristi Knox used it as evidence. It's crucial you know whether your employer is doing the same, especially in light of the fact that an estimated 20 percent of female computer users have received sexually harassing e-mail at some time.[3]

A third reason workplace monitoring is relevant to sex discrimination is that since your employer is monitoring the workplace, the employer can be expected to have known that a discrimination problem existed. It would be difficult in this situation for an employer to "play dumb" so as not be held accountable.

Most important, you should fully understand *right now* the type and extent of surveillance your employer is conducting and the kinds of information your employer is keeping about you. Should you ever encounter a discrimination problem, your complaint may be sabotaged or undermined by this surveillance data. For instance, when a woman complains of discriminatory treatment, employers often try to cover up their actions by offering fake reasons for why she was disciplined, demoted, or fired. Employers often look to their surveillance data banks, searching for seemingly legitimate grounds to justify their discriminatory actions against her. Say, for instance, the data shows that you've been spending a lot of time on the phone, or that you haven't been working at a fast enough pace.

This chapter discusses your privacy rights as an employee, the types of surveillance your employer has a right to implement, and in what instances your employer oversteps legal bounds.

Workplace Privacy Laws

Your privacy rights stem from a number of different places, including the U.S. Constitution, your state constitution, federal and state wiretapping statutes, and various court cases that interpret the specific extent of invasiveness that is allowed under the general principles of privacy.

When all these laws come into play, it very often leads to

confusion, even among lawyers. For that reason, I want to take you step-by-step through your workplace privacy rights.

It's important to note that in some instances, even when wiretap statutes *allow* for eavesdropping, the laws governing reasonable expectation of privacy forbid doing so.

Wiretap Statutes

There are two federal wiretap statutes, the 1968 Omnibus Crime Control and Safe Streets Act, and the Electronic Communications Privacy Act of 1986. Most states have their own wiretap laws as well, and state laws differ in the extent and depth of the privacy protection they offer.

LISTENING IN ON YOUR PHONE CONVERSATIONS, HIDDEN MICROPHONES, AND VIDEO SURVEILLANCE

The federal Omnibus Crime Control and Safe Streets Act[4] prohibits interception of wire and oral communications, such as telephones and microphones. However, there are three significant exceptions to this law, and many employers are tutored by employment defense lawyers on how to make their workplace fit into one of these exceptions, thus giving them the right to monitor you.

The first exception involves consent—yours. Your employer can listen in on or record your conversations if you grant permission. You can grant permission either in writing, verbally, or you can *imply* consent. Some courts will construe your implied consent, for instance, if your employer posts a notice that your calls are being monitored. If you see the notice and do nothing about it, your consent is taken for granted, or *implied.*

A second circumstance that allows eavesdropping is the *ordinary course of business* exception. This often occurs when a boss picks up an extension of an employee's phone line, allowing him or her to eavesdrop for numerous so-called business reasons, such as to improve customer service, to decrease theft of company property, or to stimulate worker productivity. It can also be used to make sure employees aren't using the phone for personal reasons. In that instance, once an employer determines that you are using the phone for personal reasons, the employer must then immediately hang up. Even though an employer has a right to investigate whether a call is personal, he or she does not have a right to *listen* to it—because it's personal.

Be careful, however, because not everyone agrees on what's personal. In one case, two hospital employees used an in-house telephone to complain to each other about their supervisors. A third employee recorded the conversation, played it for the supervisors, and the two other employees were fired. They sued, claiming invasion of privacy, but the court held that the call was *not* personal since it occurred during office hours, was between coworkers, and discussed supervisors in their official work capacities. Since it wasn't personal, the management had the right to listen in . . . and the right to fire them both![5]

The third and final exception that allows employers to listen to and record you is the *private communications systems* exception. Originally, this exception was for phone company repair people. As phone system providers, they occasionally need to listen in on calls to see whether their equipment is working properly. This exception, however, has been interpreted to include *any* phone system provider, including your employer. So if your workplace has an in-house phone system, your employer has a right to eavesdrop. In-house phone systems are becoming increasingly common in large companies.

Videotape surveillance is *not* forbidden by the wiretap laws if it is silent videotaping. If, however, the video has sound with it, then it's treated under this law the same as telephones and hidden microphones.

COMPUTER MONITORING AND E-MAIL

What degree of privacy can you expect in your computer or e-mail? Is it the same amount you would expect from a written letter or a telephone call?

Technology is available that allows your employer not only to monitor every keystroke you make on your computer but also how many keystrokes you type per minute, each time you turn your computer on and off, the time it takes you to complete a particular assignment, and the number of errors you make while completing it. In addition, there are programs that track how many times an employee visits a particular Website, log all computer programs launched, and then, at five-minute intervals, send the employer "snapshots" of what is on your computer screen.

The 1968 Omnibus Crime Control and Safe Streets Act (discussed above) originally protected only oral or wire communications. It didn't address electronic communications—that is, computers and e-mail. In 1986, Congress amended the law by passing the Electronic Communications Privacy Act, or ECPA.[6] This law prevents unauthorized *electronic* surveillance of *electronic* communications. As a result, the same rules that apply to telephone eavesdropping now apply to your computer and e-mail.

All three of the exceptions apply as well.

In the *consent* exception, your consent might be implied if your employer officially knows the password you use to log on to your computer. This might be the case if your employer assigns passwords or if you are required to disclose your password to your employer. If, however, you're allowed to choose your own password and keep it confidential, you have not given your implied consent.

The *ordinary course of business* exception also applies in that your boss is allowed to electronically monitor your computer for the same reasons he or she is allowed to listen to your telephone conversations.

The third exception, that of *communications system provider,* applies if your employer has an in-house or in-network computer system. In that case, your employer is deemed to be a communications system provider and has the right to monitor all communications within that system.

Finally, you should print out every piece of e-mail that refers to your job performance, explains or changes your job parameters, or exhibits any kind of discrimination. Put it in a file and save it. E-mail is as legitimate a communication as written memos and letters. In other words, employers are just as bound by what they send you via e-mail as they are had they sent it in a written memo.

After I sued CNN, the network began claiming that my work was inadequate and poor, despite the fact that all the feedback I'd ever been given on my performance had been very good. I'd never been given annual performance reviews. Instead, almost all of my job critiques were sent via e-mail. Fortunately, I had printed out my e-mail whenever it pertained to my work. Otherwise, I would have had no record at all of my work having been praised.

Also remember that e-mail messages don't necessarily disappear if you delete them. They stay in the system until they are actually written over. This may take a matter of months, or even years. That means that you or your employer can sometimes access e-mail even if it wasn't printed or stored.

VOICE MAIL

Your voice mail is also protected by ECPA. However, if the voice mail system is an in-house, company-owned system, your employer falls into the communications system provider exception and has a right to monitor it. If, however, you use an outside voice mail provider (such as the telephone company or e-mail company) then your employer does not have a right to access it.

If your employer officially has your voice mail password, then you may have implied your consent for your employer to access it.

PAGERS

Pagers are treated the same as voice mail for purposes of determining whether your employer has a right to access them.

"Reasonable Expectation of Privacy" Laws

Even though wiretap laws might *allow* an employer to monitor you, your employer may still be prohibited from doing so because of the *reasonable expectation of privacy* laws. These laws stem from your state constitution.

PRIVACY TEST

There is no one rule or rules that constitute the law on reasonable expectation of privacy. Instead, one general principle applies. It states: *If you, as an employee, have a reasonable expectation of privacy in an item or area to be searched, then your employer has no right to search it.* "Search" means not only conducting a physical search, but also listening in on conversations, electronically monitoring conversations, and accessing files, e-mail, or voice mail.

To determine whether your employer's snooping violates this general principle, ask the following five questions:

1. Do you have a reasonable expectation of privacy?
2. If so, have you or your employer done anything to diminish that expectation of privacy?
3. Does your employer have a legitimate and important interest in obtaining this otherwise private information about you?
4. If so, does your employer's interest outweigh the privacy interest involved?
5. Is your employer able to gather the information needed using less intrusive means?

First Question: Do You Have a Reasonable Expectation of Privacy?

It would be logical to assume that a person has a reasonable expectation of privacy where his or her person and private possessions are concerned. Most women have an expectation of privacy when it comes to their purses, so an employer would have to demonstrate that a particular suspicion prompted a search of the purse. For instance, an employer might have to prove there was a reasonable basis for believing you were stealing from the company or carrying drugs.

Normally, desks and lockers are searchable if your employer has furnished them for your use while you are working. Some courts have ruled that if an employee has *exclusive* or *primary* use of certain areas, such as an office, desk, file cabinet, or locker, then this exclusive or primary use creates a reasonable expectation of privacy; thus the areas are not searchable. It's simply a judgment call by you, your employer, a judge, or a jury.

If you want privacy, you must do everything you can to exhibit control over your work space. For instance, you might consider bringing your own personal lock for your desk or locker. That way you are sending a clear message that you have an expectation of privacy with respect to whatever it is that you've locked up.

Video Surveillance.

An increasing number of employers are installing video surveillance systems in the workplace. In many cases the video is for security reasons. For instance, banks videotape their lobbies to identify robbers. Convenience stores do the same. Department stores and drugstores often videotape customers so as to discourage shoplifting. Employees do not have a reasonable expectation of privacy in these types of public work areas. This is true even if the purpose of taping is to monitor the employee. For example, banks videotape not only to catch robbers but also to monitor their tellers, who handle huge amounts of money on a daily basis. A teller's work space is considered to be a public work area, and allows for no reasonable expectation of privacy.

The issue becomes murkier, however, when the video surveillance is in a less public area or when an employer does not disclose to employees that they are being monitored.

Nordstrom's department store installed a hidden camera in a back room to videotape the activities of its employees. Some of the employees became upset upon learning of the camera, because they regularly had used the room for engaging in personal conversations, changing clothes, and taking care of personal hygiene. They sued Nordstrom's for invasion of privacy, but a court ruled that they could not have had a reasonable expectation of privacy because there was no lock on the door to this room.[7]

In many cases, however, it's difficult for an employer to justify having video surveillance in an employee rest area, lounge, or similar places.

Moreover, if you are a union employee and there is a hidden surveillance camera at your place of work, your employer must have bargained with your union for the right to videotape you.

Second Question: Have You or Your Employer Done Anything to Diminish Your Expectation of Privacy?

If your employer notifies you that you are being monitored, then you no longer have a reasonable expectation of privacy. For example, if you know that your telephone calls are being recorded, then you cannot claim you had an expectation of privacy on the phone. Or if your employer has a posted policy that your computer files are to be shared with coworkers, you have no reasonable expectation of privacy with respect to your computer. And if a video surveillance camera is not hidden, but in plain view for all to see, there can be no expectation of privacy, since any reasonable person would deduce they are being videotaped.

The bottom line is that your employer can control your expectation of privacy by letting you know exactly how much privacy you can expect.

Sometimes your own behavior diminishes your reasonable expectation of privacy. For instance, if your boss assigns you a locker that you use regularly but never bother to lock, you are sending a message that you don't consider it to be a private place. Or maybe you regularly instruct coworkers that it's okay to rifle through your desk drawers in search of files. In cases such as these, your own behavior indicates that you don't have an expectation of privacy.

Strategies Your Employer Uses to Diminish Your Expectation of Privacy.

Employers are tutored to use a variety of tactics so as to reduce your expectation of privacy, and thus allow them the right to search all or most areas of your work space. Most of these tactics involve giving you some form of official or unofficial notice that you are being monitored or that you should not expect your use of company machines to be private.

Employment attorneys usually advise employers to put these notices in their employee handbooks or a similar publication, such as policy and procedures manuals.

Some lawyers encourage employers to have employees actually sign an acknowledgment form that reads something like:

> I acknowledge that the workplace is a public place and therefore have no reasonable expectation of privacy while on the job.

A broad statement like that can give your employer the green light to monitor or search just about every area of the workplace. Unfortunately, most workers have no idea of the implications of the statement.

Another way employers word this statement is the following:

> The use of all business machines and the transmissions sent or received on them may be monitored on an as-needed basis to ensure legitimate business use and proper utilization.

This statement not only notifies you that you can be punished for misusing company property, but it allows your employer to reduce your expectation of privacy. It also permits your employer to fall into the business use exception of the wiretap laws, thus ensuring that the employer's "eavesdropping" is not in violation of wiretap laws.

When it comes to voice mail, your employer will typically inform you that your voice mailbox is company property (and thus subject to search) and is to be used for business purposes (and thus is not subject to wiretap laws). This might be done with a statement such as the following:

> This system is provided to assist in the course of business within the company. All communications remain the property of the company.

Look for these statements in your handbook, in various other workplace publications, posted on workplace walls, or in the fine print of any forms you are asked to sign.

And look for them in one more place. One lawyer advises employers to make sure that every time an employee boots up a company computer, the following words appear on screen: *This computer may be monitored from time to time for business reasons.*

Third Question: Does Your Employer Have a Legitimate and Important Interest in Obtaining This Private Information About You?

Legitimate business reasons for monitoring or searching the workplace include workplace safety; crime, such as theft or sabotage; preventing alcohol and drug use; measuring worker performance; and needing access to your work files when you are absent.

If, however, your employer is conducting searches simply because he or she "wants to know," that's not enough justification and is a violation of the law.

Fourth Question: Does Your Employer's Interest Outweigh Your Privacy Interest?

Under the law, a person's privacy rights are weighed against your employer's purpose in monitoring or searching.

I know a woman who works as an administrative assistant for the federal Drug Enforcement Agency. She gets searched every morning on her way into the building. She goes through a metal detector, she shows identification, and sometimes she must open her purse. Yet this procedure is deemed reasonable considering what's at risk: the safety and identity of agents working undercover, and the prevention of infiltration into or sabotage of a critical branch of our nation's law-enforcement efforts. In fact, a court would most likely call this security procedure the "operational realities" of her workplace.

On the other hand, if an employer were videotaping the employee rest room simply to make sure employees keep it clean, the employer's interest would probably not outweigh that of the employee's.

Fifth Question: Can Your Employer Conduct the Investigation Using Any Less-Restrictive Means?

An employer may have a legitimate purpose in monitoring or investigating but be overzealous in carrying it out. For instance, are you getting a full-body pat down when a simple metal detector would do? Is your employer requiring that your *entire* desk be subject to a search for business files instead of allowing you at least one drawer for your personal belongings?

These, too, are judgment calls that a judge or jury would make in deciding whether your privacy was invaded.

IF YOUR PRIVACY *IS* INVADED

If your employer has implemented policies or procedures that you feel are invasive or unfair, you should immediately discuss the situation with your boss or your human resources department. If you don't feel the policy or procedure is justified, ask your employer to reconsider it. You may also want to point out that you think it's a violation of your privacy. Maybe you can suggest another procedure that achieves your employer's goal but is less intrusive.

Unfortunately, many employers are unreceptive to their workers' input on matters of this nature. Moreover, they may be unwilling to share with you the information you need to assess whether their motivations are recognized as legitimate under the law.

The situation can be extremely difficult and tension-ridden for all involved. Your employer's behavior in response to your concerns will probably dictate what your options are at this point. If the employer completely shuts you out, you have a last resort: a lawsuit. An employer who violates your right to privacy may be guilty of violating both the U.S. Constitution and your state constitution, as well as federal and state wiretap laws. The employer may also be liable for invasion of privacy, and intentional and/or negligent infliction of emotional distress.

Employers Must Keep Information About You Confidential

Whatever information your employer learns through monitoring and surveillance must be kept confidential and may be used only for the business purpose that originally justified it.

Similarly, an employer who readily shares your personal medical file with those who do not have a "business need to know" may be in violation of the Americans with Disabilities Act, as well as your individual right to privacy.

The Americans with Disabilities Act (commonly called ADA) applies to companies that employ twenty-five people or more. It requires employers to keep your medical information separate from your personnel file in order to protect your medical or disability privacy, something employers often fail to do because of carelessness or ignorance of the law. As a result, a supervisor or coworker who accesses your personnel file might learn private information about you, such as whether you've undergone a miscarriage, abortion, mastectomy, or other intimate medical procedure. (Typically, an employer collects this type of data to ascertain your right to a medical leave.)

A supervisor who's considering promoting you will often request your personnel file, and your past medical condition should not be a factor in his or her decision.

So it's a good idea to occasionally check your personnel file to make sure it's not carrying medical records.

Under the ADA, employers are allowed to share your medical file with only the following parties: a supervisor or manager who needs to make accommodations necessary for your medical condition or disability; first-aid and safety personnel who need to be prepared if you require emergency medical treatment; state workers' compensation agencies that are investigating claims; and insurance companies evaluating health coverage and treatment plans for an employer.

Individual states also have laws requiring employers to keep a worker's medical records private.

Sometimes employers ask workers to sign authorization forms allowing the employer to disclose medical information to *anybody*. You're not required under the law to sign such a form—that is, it would not be deemed unreasonable if you refused to sign the statement.

Your financial records are also protected. Sometimes employers run credit checks or gather other data on an employee, especially during the job interview stage. Although this is allowable under some circumstances, these records, once collected, must be kept confidential.

An employer who releases any of this type of information about you may be liable for invasion of privacy, slander, defamation, intentional infliction of emotional distress, and/or negligent infliction of emotional distress.

Different Rules for Public Employees

If you work for the government, a different set of rules applies when it comes to your privacy. The term *government*, for the purposes of this discussion, refers to any federal, state, county, city, or other governing body. It also means any public entity that uses taxpayer dollars to operate, such as public schools and local water districts.

The government as an employer is restrained by the privacy rights guaranteed you in the First, Fourth, and Fifth Amendments of the U.S. Constitution. These rights are evaluated under the same "reasonable expectation of privacy" standard (discussed earlier in this chapter) used for the private sector.

In addition, most records or files kept by the government are subject to inspection by the general public. The laws that guarantee this public access are called "public information acts" or "government in the sunshine" laws. They are based on the premise that all government business should be conducted in the open. As a result of these laws, some of your work product may be a matter of public record and therefore cannot be considered "private." Your employer should inform you which, if any, of your files are subject to public inspection. Usually, your personnel and medical files are exempted from this law and therefore are *not* a matter of public record. So are documents that stem from pending lawsuits, law-enforcement investigatory files, and any information where your privacy outweighs the public interest. This last exception is a catchall that can be unpredictable at times, and is decided by a court on a case-by-case basis.

Polygraph Testing

Employers are generally not allowed to ask or require employees to submit to polygraph tests. The Employee Polygraph Protection Act of 1988 (EPPA) prohibits employers from administering any mechanical or electrical testing—including tests using lie detectors, psychological stress evaluators, and voice stress analyzers—unless the employer has some specific knowledge that the employee has committed a crime.[8]

There are a few exceptions to this rule. Companies that provide security services, such as those that employ armored guards, security guards, or workers who install and design security systems, are allowed to administer polygraph tests. So are companies that manufacture, dispense, or distribute controlled substances.

Employees of federal, state, and local governments are not covered under the Employee Polygraph Protection Act. Neither are employees who work for government contractors if their jobs involve high-security work. These government and government-related employees *do* have some protection against being forced to take lie-detector tests: the Fourth Amendment prohibits the government from conducting unreasonable searches against individuals, and the Fifth Amendment gives citizens the right to refuse to answer questions if doing so might incriminate them.

For all other employers, there is only one very narrow exception that allows the administering of polygraph tests: when an employer has a reasonable suspicion that an employee is involved in a workplace theft or similar crime that is causing economic loss to the employer. In the case of theft, an employee must have had access to the missing property before an employer is justified in requiring a lie-detector test.

Before you can be forced to submit to a lie-detector test, you must be given forty-eight hours' notice and be provided with a copy of all questions that will be asked.

During the test, employers are not allowed to ask questions about your religious and political beliefs, racial opinions, sexual behavior, or labor union activities.

Some individual states have their own laws restricting polygraph testing.

Mail

It's a violation of federal law for anyone, including your employer, to open your mail. This is considered a serious offense, and courts recognize no reason that justifies it.

PART THREE

ENCOUNTERING CRITICISM AND DISCIPLINE

12.

Performance Reviews

There are moments in life when people forget their precious gifts as human beings, virtues that make them shine wherever they may be and whatever the difficulties; times when those who're always sure of themselves begin to hesitate, when potential geniuses look less than average, when something caves in and an otherwise tough and dynamic person melts into soft and motionless jelly jammed down by the walls of its container. They mean this when they say life is no bed of roses.

—Nelson Mandela

Dealing with bad performance reviews can be one of the most difficult and personally challenging things you encounter in your career. A bad review can cause you to question all that is good about yourself and your abilities. It can also devastate your self-esteem.

Originally designed to enhance communication and measure proficiency on the job, performance reviews have instead evolved into tools to assist employers in setting up paper trails that successfully insulate them against claims of discrimination.

Performance reviews are touted as being "key evidence that supports management decisions." Or, as one employment lawyer proclaimed, "Performance reviews, properly worded, will assist an employer should a decision to fire someone ever be challenged in court." Employers are taught how to augment your file with specific comments and criticisms so as to give them maximum leeway to discipline or terminate you.

No other workplace practice has more potential for abuse and manipulation by your employer.

At the same time, poor performance reviews can drastically affect your future career. Should you ever apply for a job elsewhere, your prospective employer may ask to see your past performance reviews.

This chapter will teach you how to read between the lines of your performance review and how to recognize when your employer is purposefully sprinkling your file with comments that may undermine your rights. You will understand what your employer is writing about you and why. More important, you will learn what you can do about it.

What Is a Performance Review?

Performance reviews are written evaluations of your work, usually done once or twice a year by an immediate supervisor. Typically, performance reviews analyze your efficiency and effectiveness on the job, specify areas in which you need to improve, and list goals you should strive to meet. They also evaluate whether you've met the goals listed on your last performance review.

Some bosses merely fill out "review forms," assigning scores in different areas, such as "ability to complete a project" or "willingness to take on responsibility." Other bosses write detailed comments about an employee's individual work.

Quite often, performance reviews determine whether you are entitled to a promotion or pay increase.

Are You Being Given a Fair Review?

For a performance review to successfully shield your employer from a discrimination claim, it must be a true and valid characterization of your work. A review that's inaccurately written or contrived can backfire against an employer. Not only will a shabbily constructed review *not* prevent discrimination claims, it can actually be used in your favor to help *prove* such a claim.

To satisfy yourself that your employer is giving you a fair and valid review, you should ask three questions: Is the grading system accurate? Is the performance review administered consistently? Is the review process objective?

IS THE GRADING SYSTEM ACCURATE?

Obtain a copy of the actual review criteria your supervisor uses. Carefully study the items on which you will be rated. Make sure these are factors that are truly relevant to your job performance.

One woman was rated poorly year after year for her unwillingness to travel out of town. She had answered a standard question on her original job application stating that, as a single mother of three, she was not available to travel. Not once in her five years on the job had she ever been *required* to travel. Yet each year at performance review time, her boss would go over her original application and ask a set of standard questions, including whether she was willing to travel. Each time she said no, and was marked down for it. On at least one occasion, she was lectured about how she shouldn't let her children interfere with her job. On all other issues she received excellent evaluations. In her case the criticism was not valid, since travel had not been specified as a component of the job.

You should be critiqued only in those areas that are necessary for effective job performance. Your evaluation must be focused on real aspects of your position, not derived from generalized criteria that don't fully apply to you.

Colleen O., a marketing director for a computer software company, was criticized for matters wholly unconnected to doing her job. Her boss reprimanded her for spending her lunch hours with her son at the company's day care center.

> *I had been so concerned about being perceived to be on the "mommy track" that after that I made a deliberate effort NOT to visit my son at the center during the day. Now that I'm older and wiser, I realize that I should have visited him as often as possible, since my superior's perception was molded more by his own biases than by my behavior.*

Make sure your review is focused on your job and not your lifestyle. Also, your review should be viewed with an eye toward your actual job description. Did the employer hire you for one thing and then judge you on another? If so, the review is invalid.

Finally, your employer should periodically audit the review system to verify its accuracy. Such an audit would detect whether the system is a true measure of a worker's performance or just an arbitrary assessment. An audit will also show whether men in your job group consistently rate higher than women. If they do, there is a likelihood that discrimination permeates the rating process. If your employer does not audit the system, take note of that fact; it can be used later to show that the entire grading system was invalid.

IS THE PERFORMANCE REVIEW ADMINISTERED CONSISTENTLY?

Your employer must be consistent in administering performance reviews. For instance, if your company has indicated that all employees will be reviewed annually but reviews only some employees or reviews employees only once in a while, the performance review system is invalid and cannot be used against you. If a company does not consistently follow its own procedures, any decision with regard to disciplining or terminating you may be considered arbitrary—and possibly discriminatory.

And if your employer completes performance reviews only for the purpose of firing employees, this also renders the review process invalid.

IS THE REVIEW PROCESS OBJECTIVE?

Performance reviews that allow a supervisor too much discretion may generate discriminatory evaluations. Reviews of this type are often successfully challenged in court.

Several factors can make a review too subjective. One is grading employees on vague traits and characteristics rather than actual job performance.

One of the women who testified for me in the CNN lawsuit said she had received an excellent review except for one "complaint." Her supervisor had written that she "could not get along" with two men at CNN who were in low-level managerial positions. It was no secret that both of these men treated women poorly. When she pressed him to explain what he meant by "couldn't get along," he said that she was "not nice enough." This woman pointed out that she had never been rude or unprofessional. She is a very bright, outspoken, and assertive woman—all attributes that are highly valued in the broadcast news field—but for showing these traits she was given the label "not nice" by a company manager.

Evaluations should not be based on attitude, demeanor, appearance, social behavior, or personality characteristics. Criticisms like "bad attitude," "not a team player," and "no one likes being around her" can stem from prejudice and personal opinions. They don't indicate exactly what the behavior is that warrants these labels. Is it because the employee sometimes calls in sick to care for her children? Does it mean she doesn't engage in sexual horseplay with coworkers, or that she once reported sexual harassment to company management?

Employers must keep criticism concrete and use specific examples of poor job performance, such as "Mary arrived late for work on ten separate days last month," or "Jane took two months to complete an assignment that took her coworkers only three weeks."

Your performance review should include a simple explanation of any problem, an explanation of how the problem hinders you from doing your job, and an explanation of how it impacts the company's productivity. It should also list specific improvements to be made and the time frame in which you will be expected to show improvement. Anything less concrete than that is too ambiguous to be considered objective.

Who Conducts Your Review?

Another practice that renders a performance review too subjective is having only one person complete the review. A one-person review is much easier for you to successfully challenge as discriminatory.

Some employers have more than one supervisor sign off on reviews. One lawyer even advised companies to do this "regardless of whether the other supervisors actually conducted the evaluation, because it gives the appearance of objectivity" and thus "strengthens an employer's defense if the employee ever pursues a discrimination claim."

If more than one supervisor has signed your performance review, make sure that all persons who signed the review took an active part in assessing you. If not, your employer may be trying to bolster the record against you. If this is so, you should either complain to the human resources department or make note of it on the performance evaluation itself.

Peer Reviews.

Some employers assemble a panel of peers to conduct performance evaluations, which presents other problems. Employers are advised that the biggest benefit of peer review is that it helps to keep problems out of court. Statistics show that judges and juries give a great amount of deference to reviews compiled by coworkers. At one employer seminar, a lecturing lawyer said, "Not only is it a better defense in court, but any employee with a poor review from her coworkers will have a very difficult time finding a lawyer to represent her in a discrimination lawsuit. By using peer panels, you cut these people off at the pass."

Sometimes peer review may indeed be a fair process, but if all your peers are men, you might want to note that fact in a response to the performance review.

Sometimes a company will allow you to choose between a supervisor or peer evaluation. You have to decide what's best for you. Some companies even allow employees to select the peers or supervisors who review them.

Also, members of your peer panel may become privy to information about you that you'd rather they didn't know. If any of the panel members spread private information about you—information they got through the review process—the company may be found liable for invasion of privacy and possibly even slander or defamation.

How to Respond to a Performance Review: Be Prepared

Chances are that your employer has thoroughly prepared for your performance review. Employees, however, often view their role in this process as that of a third-party observer. They merely walk into the meeting, sit down, and listen to what their boss has to say. To prevent getting sandbagged, I urge you to prepare for the review in the same manner your employer does.

Typically, an employer collects information about you from a variety of sources. These might include the original job description, letters from customers or clients, data and statistics on your performance (especially if you work in sales), written comments from other management personnel, and your personnel file. Some supervisors make a point of finding out typical obstacles or conditions that prevent an employee in your specific job from performing well.

Your boss may also have solicited feedback from others who've had an opportunity to work closely with you. Some supervisors take written notes on an employee's performance for a period of time leading up to the evaluation.

Most managers will also obtain your past performance evaluations to assess whether you have met the previous year's goals.

Collect this information and documentation prior to your meeting. You may be surprised to find that the material you collect is more extensive and detailed than the material your supervisor gathers. After all, you know more about yourself and your accomplishments than anyone. Your supervisor, on the other hand, may be charged with tracking the performance of many employees and be incapable of knowing everything you have accomplished since your last review.

Write a detailed list of all that you've achieved since your last performance review. Be specific, using phrases such as "Completed designing a public relations plan for XYZ Company, one of our biggest clients," or "Revamped the schedule for the third-floor nursing staff so as to better accommodate our hospital budget." Bring the list with you to the meeting. Perhaps you can even give a copy to your boss *before* he or she writes your evaluation.

Also, bring any letters or memos you've received from supervisors, coworkers, and clients that cast your work in a positive light.

Some employers even schedule "pre-appraisal conferences" between you and your evaluator. These meetings give both of you a chance to share information prior to the actual review. If this is the procedure at your company, take advantage of this time by sharing your accomplishments and job skills with your boss. It's a lot easier to head off a bad review than it is to change one that's already been written.

Recognizing "Progressive Discipline"

Many employers view performance reviews as an essential part of a "progressive discipline" system whereby an employee is put on notice when there is a problem, given incremental sanctions if the problem persists, and may eventually be fired. Since this system creates a documented history of an employee's poor performance, the employer is less likely to be successfully sued for discrimination. "An unbroken line of poor performance evaluations over a reasonable length of time can be an effective defense," reads a typical publication used in the training of human resources workers.

One problem with the system is that sometimes the "documented history" is nothing more than a hastily drawn up litany of minor complaints and contrived reasons for reprimanding the employee.

I was once told by a supervisor at CNN that he wanted to fire a certain videotape editor because a lower-level manager had complained that she had a "bad attitude." He told me he had begun documenting everything possible about her, including her slow editing and long breaks. He asked me whether I had encountered any problems with her. If so, he wanted to document them. He also told me he was verifying every fact on her original job application and résumé. If he found anything to be untrue, he said, he was planning to use it as a reason for firing her immediately. He seemed disappointed when he mentioned that her former college had verified her degree.

I realized he was prepared to use whatever criticism I might offer to support his already-made decision to fire her.

I told him that although she was somewhat slower than other editors, I didn't think the problem stemmed from an unwillingness to work. She was relatively new at the job and had less experience than the others. I also told him I'd seen the very person who'd complained about her talking to her in a very rude, demeaning manner at times. Perhaps it was just a communication issue, I suggested.

This supervisor was beginning a progressive discipline system that would justify on paper his firing of this person—and absolve the company of any legal liability for doing so. The problem is that other employees were committing the same infractions or exhibiting the same behavior but were not being written up or disciplined for it. Therefore, the criticism of this one employee was unfair and invalid.

Sometimes employers *accelerate* performance reviews for an employee they are trying to get rid of. For instance, if you're normally scheduled to receive reviews once a year, your employer may instead require you to receive them quarterly until either your performance improves or enough paperwork to fire you has been compiled. "You use your paper trail to good effect here," advises one employment lawyer, an advocate of the accelerated review schedule as a means of assembling additional evidence against the employee. "Once you have enough evidence, then escalate from warnings to suspension to termination."

Sometimes accelerated performance reviews are used for legitimate reasons. For instance, if you are reviewed annually, your employer may feel that the company cannot wait an entire year for you to improve. The thinking may be that you'll improve faster if you receive continual feedback for a while.

However, any sudden change in the way an employer documents concerns of this type can backfire on the employer. A court will look into whether the change was brought about by a valid need to get better performance out of the employee immediately, or whether it's just part of a smoke screen to cover up the fact that a decision was made arbitrarily or discriminatorily.

If you have had your performance reviews accelerated, try to find out whether other employees have ever had their reviews accelerated as well. Is this a regular procedure for employees who are not performing well? If not, is there something about your situation that demands this immediate acceleration? If not, then your employer is not being fair and consistent with you.

Requiring Your Signature

Some employers require workers to sign their performance reviews. They do this for several reasons. One is that they want to be able to document that you were informed of your poor job performance and were given time and notice to correct the problem, but didn't. If you ever seek a lawyer to represent you in a discrimination charge against your employer, your employer will probably send your lawyer a copy of your signed performance review, in which you acknowledge that you are aware of deficiencies in your work. This significantly weakens your discrimination claim, and your lawyer may even refuse to represent you from that point on.

If you receive an inaccurate performance review and you are not required to sign it, then don't. If your signature *is* required, then sign it under protest. See the section below on how to object to poor performance reviews.

If There Is a Real Issue

Sometimes even the best employees encounter difficult periods at work, when they are not performing up to par. Given the chance, most employees usually improve. The issue is how you and your employer handle these trying times. Your employer is required to give you a *reasonable opportunity* to correct whatever problem exists, and that includes any necessary training and assistance. If your company repeatedly criticizes you for a specific behavior on the job but never offers to train or retrain you to help you correct the problem, then the company may not discipline or fire you for it.

Moreover, your company must give this opportunity to *all* employees. Are others given more opportunity to fix their problems? Are they given broader time frames, or more lax parameters? Or are they given more training in response to their lack of skills?

If so, your company is not treating you fairly, regardless of your poor performance on the job.

On the other hand, if you truly deserve a bad review—if your work is substandard and your reviewer had no prejudicial motivation for giving you a poor review—then there's nothing you can or should do about it. Any claim of discrimination you make that you know to be false will be seen for what it is eventually—not to mention that it will needlessly injure others' reputations and, ultimately, your own.

Objecting to a Poor Performance Review

IF THERE IS A PLACE ON THE REVIEW FORM FOR YOUR INPUT

Some employers allow employees to write comments on the actual review form in response to the review. In fact, be alert for a statement on your performance review that says something like this: *If you have any objections, you agree to list them below; otherwise you agree with the evaluation.* Your failure to object may be considered passive consent on your part, which will have the same legal effect as if you had agreed with what's written in the review. You will also probably be prevented from ever challenging it.

If you believe your review is inaccurate and stems from prejudice, you must note it at this time. You needn't go into great detail, disputing every point. In fact, I advise just a simple statement explaining the situation, such as *I believe my supervisor's unhappiness with my work stems from the fact that I have evaded his sexual advances*, or *I believe my poor performance review is because of the fact that my supervisor prefers not to work with women.* If that is too confrontational for you, then simply write *I disagree with this evaluation.* Follow up your disapproval with a private visit to the person designated by your employer to take discrimination complaints.

Then, if the company tries to use the performance evaluation against you, you have created a contemporaneous record—one that preserves your side of the story.

IF THERE IS A FORMAL APPEAL PROCESS

Most employers don't have an appeal process that allows employees to object if they disagree with their performance evaluations. Employers are advised against it by employment defense lawyers who claim "it would open up a floodgate of complaints and provide little benefit to the employer."

Obviously, if your employer *does* have an appeal procedure, then you should use it if necessary. Carefully write out your complaint. If possible, do this at home so you can take your time and make sure you are clear and accurate.

If the appeal process consists of only a verbal meeting, I suggest that you still write your statement and distribute it to the person or persons present at the meeting. Then there can be no mischaracterization of your complaints.

IF THERE IS NO OFFICIAL AVENUE FOR YOUR OBJECTION

Some employers do not allow an employee to provide any input or response to their performance evaluation. If this is the case, I suggest that you complain anyway if you feel you have received a prejudicial review.

You can do this in several ways:

If there is a place for you to sign the review form, write the words *Signed under protest* just after your name.

If there is no place to sign, neatly write a sentence or two somewhere on the form stating that you disagree.

If that is not possible, write your own version of the facts, and ask that it be placed in your personnel file. Also state in writing that you were given no other opportunity to respond to the performance review. In your protest, write the name and job title of the supervisor who complained of your work or disciplined you, a detailed description of the behavior in question, and why you feel the criticism is invalid. List the names of any people who can bear witness to your side of the story.

Make sure you keep a copy.

Verbal Warnings

If you are called into a manager's office and given a warning, you should assume that the minute you walk out, the manager will document exactly what was said to you, how you responded, and what type of ultimatum you understood to have been given. This one-sided documentation will also include a list of any prior notification you received that improvement was needed, and perhaps even a statement that your performance had not improved since the prior notification.

The documentation will lay out specific goals you're expected to meet, along with deadlines for those goals. And it might say that you were warned that if you do not improve, you will be terminated. It will be signed and dated by the manager who gave you the reprimand.

Then, should you ever complain in court that you were fired for discriminatory reasons, those private notes, written without your knowledge or input, will be admissible in court against you.

Sometimes an employer will recap the meeting in memo form and then ask the employee to sign a statement, which might read something like this: *Please review this memo and confirm by signing below that it accurately summarizes our discussions on [date].* Or it might be worded: *My signature below indicates that the above memo is an accurate description of the meeting between me and my supervisor on [date] regarding my job performance and that I have been advised that I must improve the areas outlined above or I could be terminated.*

If the memo doesn't accurately define what was discussed, then don't sign it. If it does, be aware that you are probably being set up for termination.

It's crucial that you keep your own records in this matter. Note the name and job title of the supervisor who reprimanded you and describe the problem he was complaining about, including the date. Write down what you said in response and list your own explanation. List exactly what the supervisor wants you to improve, including the date by which the improvements are expected and what, if anything, the company will do to help you improve. Also list the names of any people who might corroborate your story. If possible, place these notes in your personnel file. At the very least, keep them in your file at home.

If Your Employer Doesn't Conduct Performance Reviews

Some companies have no formal review process at all. Typically, these employers randomly place things in your personnel file, often without your knowing it. Unfortunately, they usually do this only if there is a problem with your performance. When everything is going great, why bother?

Therefore, it's crucial that you regularly check your personnel file to see what might have been added without your knowledge.

Accessing Your Personnel File

One of the most important pieces of evidence in a discrimination claim is your personnel file. This is the "official" record of what events transpired during your tenure as an employee. Despite the vital importance of this record, many employees never bother to review it . . . until it's too late.

Typically a personnel file will contain your job description; employment application; résumé; job offer letter; past performance evaluations; documentation of salary increases, promotions, or transfers; documentation of any training you've received; resignation or termination letter; exit interview records; and settlement agreements, if any.

It's important to know the type and extent of the documentation your employer is keeping in your file so that you won't have any surprises if you file a discrimination lawsuit. Also, if you don't correct errors in the documentation or make objections in a timely manner, you may lose that right completely.

Laws regarding your right to access your personnel file vary greatly from state to state. In fact, they are so dissimilar and complex that it's impossible to effectively summarize them.

Although most states do guarantee a right of access, the laws differ with respect to how often and under what circumstances. Some laws are vague, saying only that employees should be granted "reasonable" access. Other laws specifically define how and when employees may review their files. Some limit access to once or twice a year.

A few states provide detailed breakdowns of the information an employer must include in—or exclude from—a personnel file. (For example, to protect the privacy of employees, some states specifically prohibit the inclusion of medical or financial records. Other states have no file privacy rules, and rely on constitutional privacy rights to deal with the issue.)

In many states you're permitted to photocopy your file, whereas other states allow you only to take notes or simply view the file.

Several states prohibit you from accessing any part of the file that infringes upon another person's privacy. This might include letters of reference or candid referrals that supervisors or coworkers have given that they expected to be kept confidential.

In addition, some laws allow or require employers to be present when you review your file.

Even though state law may not *require* your employer to grant access to your file, there's nothing to stop an employer from allowing you to do so. Check to see what your company policy is in this regard. And again, your employer must be consistent, so if other employees are regularly allowed to view their files, you should have the same right.

If you are a union member, your union contract probably guarantees you the right to view your file. In addition, the union itself is guaranteed access so that it can represent its members effectively.

If you are a federal government employee, you are guaranteed access under the Federal Privacy Act.

Most states grant a lesser right of access to *former* employees, so it's important that you regularly access your file while you're still employed. Some states allow former employees to access their files for only a specified period of time after their departure, usually ranging from a few months to a couple of years.

Regardless, should you ever file a lawsuit, you have the right to subpoena your personnel records. But if you wait until that happens, you may have an unpleasant surprise. Your employer may have conveniently added things to your file after you lodged your discrimination complaint.

Moreover, the items inside your file may help you decide whether you even *want* to file a lawsuit. They will assist your attorney in evaluating your case.

FINDING AN ERROR IN YOUR FILE

If you find an error in your file, you should attempt to correct it.

Some states do not guarantee you this right, but instead leave it up to the employer to make the rule.

If your employer allows it, then do so.

If your employer forbids changes, then *add to the record* by inserting your own explanation of the event in question.

Or send a letter to the human resources person or a supervisor that outlines your version of the facts and states that you're not being allowed to correct errors or misconceptions in your file. There's a good chance that your letter will be placed in your personnel file. Even if it isn't, at least you've gone on record as objecting to the inaccuracy of the documentation being kept on you. If your employer claims that your firing was based on parts of your record you know to be inaccurate, your side of the story will be more believable if you have objected from the beginning. Make sure you keep a copy of your letter.

BUILDING YOUR FILE

You should also make sure that your positive, productive accomplishments find their way into your personnel file. This is called "building your file to support yourself." Include memos from supervisors and coworkers commenting on your good work, letters of appreciation written by customers or other third parties, notices of raises and promotions, notices of any additional responsibilities you are given, and any other paperwork that reflects on your ability to do your job. If you receive any of these things without an accompanying written note, keep a log yourself. Include the date and any action taken, such as, "On March 15, at 2:00 P.M., my supervisor, Mr. Jones, called me into his office and told me I was doing such a great job that he was giving me a raise effective April 1."

13.

Lodging a Complaint with Your Employer

And they listened with the greatest of interest to everything he had to say. And then they ate him. —Mark Twain, describing a Christian missionary's visit to a South Pacific island inhabited by cannibals[1]

Most women dread lodging a discrimination complaint. And no wonder. They believe that no matter what they say, or how convincingly they say it, in the end they will be eaten.

For me, deciding how and when to complain was the most difficult dilemma I encountered. Looking back, there were several turning points when I could have complained but didn't.

I chose not to complain when I first heard that CNN's executive vice president, Ed Turner, upon hearing of my pregnancy, commented, "Another good reporter down the drain!" I'd hoped his remark was only a matter of miscommunication—that perhaps he mistakenly believed that I intended not to continue working after my baby was born. I thought I could clear up the matter myself by sending him a note explaining my intention to return to work.

I again chose not to complain three months later when I received his "mommydom" memo in reply. I thought I could fix the problem by demonstrating a serious-about-work attitude.

Two and a half years later, after my second child was born, I didn't complain when my bureau chief insisted on cutting back my hours, explaining that he and Ed Turner thought I wouldn't mind since I'd just had my baby. Only, at that time it was because I was *prevented* from complaining. My bureau chief had instructed me that I was *never* to directly contact CNN Center in Atlanta with comments—complaints or otherwise. Instead, he insisted that everything go through him. At about that time, I began keeping a log of our conversations. That log was subpoenaed by CNN, and during my deposition I was asked to read it aloud. Here is part of the transcript:

> Date: March 15
>
> I say, "Maybe I should call Ed [Turner] and ask for my job back." Dave says, "Absolutely not. Just be patient. I think Jim [my replacement] will go away." I say, "What do you mean, you hope he'll go away? . . . Do you mean Jim has the option to stay and keep half my job if he wants?" Dave says, "Don't worry about it. Trust me. There's nothing you can do right now. . . . Jim has no children and probably wants to keep himself busy."
>
> I say, "You know, Dave, I have a real problem with Atlanta. I think there is a stigma there. Next time [CNN president] Tom Johnson is in town or Ed Turner, I would like to know so I can meet with them and tell them that I think CNN gets preconceived notions about . . . women with children—that they are perceived somehow as second string." . . .
>
> Dave says Ed and Tom are not planning any trip out here soon, but will let me know if they are.
>
> I suggest I fly to Atlanta and meet with him.
>
> "Oh, don't do that!" he says.

So I didn't.

At the time, I knew very little about employment discrimination law, a highly specialized field in which few lawyers are trained. Had I been familiar with it, I'd have known that I should have complained the first time I heard about Ed's "down the drain" remark. It might have prevented the entire incident from escalating.

I also should have complained immediately after receiving the "mommydom" memo. Since I didn't, CNN's lawyers later claimed the memo was sent in jest, between two "friends," and that I'd never considered it inappropriate. CNN insisted it was not indicative of Ed Turner's attitude toward women, or at all related to his firing me following the birth of my second child.

I would also have known that CNN was derelict in not having a complaint system in place. Although CNN had instituted an Atlanta-based human resources department to take complaints of this nature, the network had never bothered to inform me about it.

I would have known that any complaint system is required to have a *bypass* provision, which in my case would have allowed me to complain to a person other than my own supervisor. Instead, I was put in the bizarre position of having to ask my boss for permission to complain about him and his boss to his higher-ups!

But I *didn't know* any of these things.

And I wondered. Since I, a lawyer, didn't know them, what must the average woman know about employment discrimination law?

The more I learned, the more I realized: not much.

For most women, encountering discrimination is simply a lose-lose situation. If they don't complain, they continue to encounter discrimination. If they do, they may face retaliation. Sometimes their complaint jeopardizes working relationships between themselves and their supervisors or coworkers—or their job altogether.

The complaint process not only distracts women from their

jobs, it creates anxiety and suspicion. Whom can they trust? How do they know whether the people they complain to will truly attempt to fix the problem? And even if those people do try, what if their efforts only make things worse? Perhaps their employers will respond by finding a fake reason to fire them. Or maybe the person they complain about will sabotage them in a way that leaves no trail of accountability.

Your employer is entering the complaint process armed with knowledge and experience. Why do women, myself included, continually enter it blind?

When lodging a complaint, you should know what will be asked and expected of you, and what you must do to protect yourself fully.

Only if you know ahead of time what your employer's obligations are will you be able to judge whether your employer is doing an adequate job responding to and investigating your complaint. Only then will you know why your employer is asking certain questions of you. You'll also be less likely to say something that can be taken out of context and used against you. What you say and how you say it will affect how your complaint is regarded and ultimately resolved.

You will also understand that once you lodge a complaint, you've begun to lay a paper trail. Paper trails often scare employers into doing the right thing. You might be surprised to learn that most employers don't readily side with the supervisor. Instead, they view the entire situation as if they are wading through a quagmire of legal responsibilities and pitfalls.

Most important, familiarity with the complaint process will lessen your anxiety and stress.

To Complain or Not to Complain

To complain or not to complain . . . why should women even be faced with contemplating which path will damage their career the least?

Many women tell me they'd rather not complain, because it makes them vulnerable. They fear they'll be viewed as "trouble-makers," or that their employers will respond by quietly searching for excuses to undermine their careers.

The truth is that you are more vulnerable if you *don't* complain, because you will likely continue to encounter discrimination and may eventually be demoted or fired because of it. If you then claim discrimination, no one is apt to believe you since you never brought it up before. Your complaint will be viewed as false—based on either revenge or sour grapes.

Moreover, it may even excuse your employer from liability. Remember that, according to the decision rendered in *Faragher v. City of Boca Raton* (discussed in chapter 10), an employer can use as a defense that there was an effective complaint system in place and that you failed to take advantage of it.[2] Imagine this exchange in court: "Well, Your Honor, we do have this grievance procedure in place. The fact that she failed to use it is beyond us, but we really *do* care about our employees. Our policy plainly shows that when it comes to discrimination, we have a no-tolerance history." Sounds great, doesn't it? Why give them this opportunity?

WHEN THE GRIEVANCE PROCEDURE IS BOGUS

Only if you can show a good reason why you *didn't* complain will it not be held against you.

More than four hundred women at the Mitsubishi automobile plant in Normal, Illinois, were subjected to sexual harassment, yet few, if any, complained, until the Equal Employment Opportunity Commission investigated and sued the automaker. The *Chicago Tribune* reported the stories of some of the women working there:

There were times that she would take her complaints to a supervisor. The process for reporting such incidents discouraged it, she says. First, the aggrieved party was very publicly called off the factory floor. Everyone within eyeshot knew she was turning in her coworker. Then the accused coworkers would be called off the floor. Complainers would become known as "narcs" and incur harassment such as lewd notes taped on their backs or sabotage of their workstations, she says.

It wasn't worth it, she says. Even when she did formally complain, frequently nothing changed.[3]

If you know or have reason to suspect that your complaint system is phony or incompetently run, then don't use it. But make sure your belief is based on solid reasons and not an unfounded fear on your part.

If possible, complain instead to a supervisor whom you trust. Inform this person, in writing, why you have chosen to reject the established procedure.

Understanding Your Employer's Perspective

To prepare for your employer's reaction to your complaint, you need to keep in mind some basic realities. This is knowledge your employer takes for granted, and often assumes you do as well. Yet some employees are not at all familiar with the concepts.

ONE: YOUR EMPLOYER IS NOT YOUR FRIEND

Your employer does not have your best interests at heart.

You have a financial arrangement, not a friendship. You give your employer time and expertise, and your employer pays you money.

This is not a cynical viewpoint; it's a realistic and professional one. Until you view the employment relationship for what it is—

strictly a business alliance—you will never fully understand an employer's response, like this one from Beth N., a human resources manager responsible for taking discrimination complaints at a midsize company:

> *I never understand why women come to me crying their eyes out and telling me things that can only hurt them in the long run. But it's not my job to counsel them on how to lodge a proper complaint. Sure I try to make things right for all the parties, but that's because it's a necessary requirement to avoid getting sued.*
>
> *As human resources manager, my job is not to comfort and baby a woman who comes to me. My job is to assess risk for the company (to see if one of our managers has done something wrong and if we would be held at fault), then to minimize the company's liability in the whole mess, and finally to fix the problem.*

From an employer's perspective, you are in the workplace *to make money* for the company. Therefore, everything, including your complaint, must be viewed from that perspective. How much will it cost your employer to fix it? How much will it cost if you sue? How much will it cost if your employer has to replace your supervisor?

All of this doesn't necessarily mean that your employer is a singular-minded Scrooge. Your employer knows that sound business judgment is achieved only through a financial analysis of any potential liability, including a possible discrimination lawsuit.

TWO: YOUR EMPLOYER IS NOT MORALLY DRIVEN TO MAKE CHANGES

My experience has shown me that the great majority of employers really have no motivation to make the workplace a more equitable environment. They are certainly not propelled by any sense of moral responsibility.

If you were to speak to your company's board of directors about the moral imperative to implement change to accommodate a more diverse workforce, I doubt the board's response would be immediate or decisive.

If you mentioned, however, that a more diverse workforce could bring in more sales, and hence more profit, their ears would perk up.

More important, if you mentioned that if they don't start hiring more women they might get sued for a lot of money, I guarantee that each and every board member would pull his or her chair up close to the table and ask, "What can we do to fix this problem?"

People often ask why I thought suing for money would help fix what happened to me at CNN. My answer is that after I'd tried several methods of communication with Turner Broadcasting, I realized the only language the company would truly understand was *corporatespeak*—aka money. After all, they are in the business of making money. Losing money creates a problem and triggers an alert status.

Don't expect moral enlightenment, or you will be disappointed. Management usually doesn't see the light. But they do feel the heat. As one corporate manager put it, "It's good business to be fair."

THREE: A LESSON IN BUSINESS ADMINISTRATION AND HUMAN RESOURCES

So who are these people assigned to hear your complaint, and what are their responsibilities?

It depends on whether your employer is a mid- to large-size company or a small business.

In mid- to large-size companies, discrimination complaints are usually handled by a human resources (HR) department. HR personnel oversee hiring, recruiting, wage and salary administration, employee benefits, performance appraisals, and exit interviews.

They conduct investigations for thefts, drug use, employee competence, performance, attitude, misconduct, and safety. They also advise management when the company is legally at risk or when employee morale is low. They conduct training, track expenses, interpret workplace policies, and keep abreast of changes in the job market.

Not all HR people employ the tactics I've described in this chapter. Many are sincere, hardworking individuals who are truly concerned about hiring and treating employees in the fairest manner possible. The leading national organization for HR people, the Society for Human Resources Management (SHRM), to its credit, offers a significant amount of literature and advice on how best to do that. But it also offers seminars that teach how to use some of the methods described in this chapter. The extent to which an HR person uses them depends on the aggressiveness of the individual and the preferences of the employer.

Many small companies, however, have no human resources professional at all. It's not cost-effective for a small-business owner to hire a full-time or even a part-time person to handle personnel issues. Consequently, you are likely to encounter a mishmash of situations.

Most small-business owners designate a particular employee for the task of taking discrimination complaints. Sometimes a worker will step forward in a leadership capacity and unofficially assume the responsibility of doing so. Often an office manager will take on the job, since he or she is already handling much of the paperwork. Sometimes a business owner's spouse will do it.

Other small-business owners expect employees to complain directly to their boss or to the business owner. Difficulties arise when the boss or owner is the person doing the discriminating.

In these cases, the law assumes that you will instead complain directly to a federal or state agency, such as the EEOC or the state equivalent. That's why employers are required to post notices of employee rights or face stiff fines. These notices typically outline your rights and list which government agencies to contact should you experience a problem.

In most small-business situations, the complaint procedure is informal and unofficial in nature. Even if there is a person designated to handle complaints, he or she may not have received training. In fact, they may know as little as you do about the process. Consider, for example, the following words, spoken by Matt D., a small-business owner:

> *Getting legal counsel and all that stuff is expensive, and frankly, we don't even know where to look sometimes. Every day or every hour that we spend away from our craft doing paperwork is taking time away from our generating income, so a lot of times you'd rather just roll the dice and hope that you hire the right people. You hope that if you treat them fairly, they won't file some frivolous lawsuit if the job doesn't work out.*

All in all, don't expect a small-business owner to have the same degree of sophistication with respect to workplace discrimination that a mid- to large-size company has. In fact, a small-business setting is one of the few circumstances where employees are likely to be on the same footing as employers.

Some small-business owners retain independent consultants who review and audit the company's books, ascertain whether the company is complying with the law as an employer, and offer advice and strategies on how the company might better protect itself. These consultants also provide hot lines for employers that offer advice on how to respond to specific situations.

FOUR: IT'S A TIGHTROPE

As I've already mentioned, many human resources professionals attend seminars to learn how to respond to discrimination complaints. These seminars are usually taught by employment defense lawyers, and on more than one occasion I've heard different lawyers repeat the same line: "The best defense is a good offense."

The first time I heard it, I was astounded. I thought, The idiots think they're playing football!

I was shocked that they would approach a serious issue such as discrimination as if it were a game. In fact, at one seminar, the speaker ended his opening presentation shouting the words, "You're in a war! And we're going to give you the tools and weapons to fight that war!" The audience responded with resounding applause.

Eventually I realized that these lawyers are not *personally* involved; they don't feel the pain and frustration of having been discriminated against. Their sole directive is to offer advice on tactical positioning and maneuvering, all aimed at avoiding liability for the employer.

It's their job to insist HR professionals be aware of legal risks and of the fact that any documents or tapes generated by an investigation are potential evidence in a lawsuit.

Once an employee officially complains, a series of events is triggered. Employers often compare it to walking on eggs. If they don't adequately investigate a woman's complaint, the woman can sue for negligent investigation. If they don't take proper corrective action, the woman can sue for hostile environment/sexual harassment. If they inadequately discipline the offender, other women who are subsequently discriminated against by him may sue, claiming the company knew about his propensity to discriminate and did not protect them. At the same time, employers who are overzealous in disciplining an offender can be sued by the offender. As one employment lawyer, Anna S., put it:

> *Women don't understand that when they bring a problem to an employer's attention, their employer's not going to be thrilled and say, "We're so glad you made us aware of this! This is terrible. This is unjust! Let us fix this for you!"*

> *Instead the employer views it as the beginning of what might be a long and costly problem. Even if you didn't cause it, you are the one throwing it in their lap. The employer is thinking, "Thank you for telling me, but now I have to walk a tightrope because the claim has a ripple effect."*

An employer who falls off the tightrope stands to lose a lot of money, not to mention face criminal penalties.

That is your employer's biggest concern.

As a result, sometimes when an employer says, "Let me help you," what the employer *really* means is "Let me fix the situation." There's a difference. As a result, the resolution of your discrimination problem may not be the very best solution for you. Rather, it probably will be the best solution *for all involved.*

Preventative Steps Your Employer Is Required to Take

An employer can significantly defuse this liability crisis by having an "effective" antidiscrimination policy in place. But what is considered effective under the law?

A policy must be clearly written and widely disseminated to all employees, including managers.

In addition, managers should receive appropriate training so they can comply with the policy, and the training must be *meaningful.* One woman told me that the "sensitivity" training the management in her company was receiving amounted to the men being told, "Okay now, guys, don't grope the girls' breasts."

That won't do.

Jemela M., a psychologist who used to conduct sensitivity training for large organizations, recalls that whereas some employers took her training seriously, other groups, usually those in male-dominated professions, viewed it as a farce:

Some wouldn't participate; they would stonewall me . . . fold their arms and stare blankly ahead. They did not give the impression that they came away with anything from the training because they did not want to come away with anything from the training. On the whole, the information was unwelcome and not well received. I've done a lot of training, and it was always extremely well received except for certain groups. These groups were marked in their level of anger and hostility toward the training, and my assessment came from the fact that they were formerly male bastions.

One of the first things you should ask your HR person is whether the person you're complaining about has received any training. You may or may not be given an answer. (Usually an employer will not disclose this information unless you sue them and force them to.) If they do answer it, and the answer is no training, I suggest you make a note and place it in your file at home. If the answer is yes, ask how much training and when.

For a complaint procedure to be considered meaningful, it should have a bypass procedure. This means an employee can go to an alternate person to complain if the designated person is biased or is the person doing the discriminating.

An employer is required to respond with a thorough and discreet investigation. If discrimination is found, the employer must take immediate corrective action.

From your employer's perspective, the complaint procedure is a smart, cost-effective business tool.

Lodging Your Complaint

Says Anna S., the employment lawyer we met earlier:

An employee is a babe in the woods, and unfortunately the stakes can be very high and people do get hurt. In the day-to-day trench warfare, there are just more resources on the employer's side. They want to do the right thing, but that's subject to economics.

Economics dictate that an employer spend time and money preparing to take your complaint in a manner that complies with the law and utilizes every strategy legally possible . . . and then some.

In view of the degree to which most employers prepare for complaints, you should do at least the same, if not more.

SIMPLE MECHANICS

Typically, an investigation is conducted by an HR person, but it can also be done by a manager, private investigator, outside consultant, or lawyer.

Lodging a complaint may not be as confrontational as you might expect. You needn't go stomping into the office, demanding to be heard. It can be a very civilized, low-key process.

Many human resources people tell me they respond to a complaint depending on the demeanor of the woman who filed it. Says Patricia N., a human resources director:

If she comes in with both guns drawn and threatening a lawsuit, I'm likely to simply document everything possible against this woman. My advice is if you really want to solve the problem, then come in with the attitude of solving it, regardless of how angry you feel at the guy who did this to you.

Some employers have forms they ask you to fill out; others allow HR people to take down the information in an oral interview. Regardless of what method your employer uses, it's always a better idea for you to write out your complaint, rather than rely on your memory during an oral interview.

HR people believe that no conversation is ever as important as the first interview. They are taught that this is when they get the most accurate story. One lawyer referred to it as finding "pay dirt." They believe that most complainers later change their stories and come up with better rationales, excuses, lies, or whatever. As a result, they are instructed to do an in-depth, documented interview the first time you complain. Then, as they continue to talk with you over days or weeks, they look for inconsistencies in your story.

Unfortunately, the first interview is also when you will be least likely to be organized and methodical in your presentation. You will probably be upset about the discrimination or harassment and you might be frightened of the complaint process itself. That's why it's crucial you organize and write out your thoughts *before* complaining.

If your employer uses a form, ask for a blank copy and take it home where you can take your time filling it out. If your employer prefers to take the information verbally, comply with that request, but start the interview off by handing in your written statement of the facts.

In no event should you allow your interviewer's notes to be the sole written record of your complaint. Those notes may be inaccurately or carelessly written. You may have said one thing, and he or she may have heard another. These notes are almost always subpoenaed as evidence in discrimination lawsuits. Imagine how you will feel having inaccurate, sloppy, or just plain untrue facts admitted into evidence as the official record of your complaint.

Sometimes an HR person will ask you to read and sign their version of what you said. You should agree to do this only if you are prepared to be extremely aggressive in correcting any and all mischaracterizations.

And watch out! Sometimes they will send you a memo reiterating everything you said. It will include a statement that if you don't reply, you agree it is an accurate and thorough recounting of the facts.

THE FOUR BIGGEST MISTAKES WOMEN MAKE

1. Taking It Personally.

Margaret L., a human resources professional, recommends that women strive for a certain professional detachment:

> *Women need to fight their battles on an impersonal level. When they do otherwise, it's one of the biggest mistakes they make.*

Fighting a discrimination battle on an impersonal level is easy—unless *you're* the one whose been discriminated against. I don't think most HR professionals realize just how difficult it is for a woman to come forward about a discrimination issue. HR professionals take complaints every day, so the entire process seems routine to them. Not being personally involved, it's easy to emotionally disentangle themselves. As a result, when a woman enters the HR office emotionally upset or in tears, they're apt to view her behavior as hysterical.

Try to prepare yourself so that when you lodge your complaint, your thoughts are in order and you don't sound as if you're ranting and raving.

Compile a list beforehand of details and concerns you want to bring up. If you cry, just take a deep breath and ask if you can come back later when you are feeling less upset. Then go home and write everything out slowly and deliberately. Most important, don't raise your voice and begin screaming at the person taking your complaint. It sounds ridiculous, I know, but many women have told me they've done so and regretted it later.

I'm not saying that you should hide the fact that the discrimination upset you. If it has, then you *should* bring it up, but try not to direct your emotion at the HR person.

2. Trying to Dictate the Punishment Your Offender Should Receive.

Rosemary M., a human resources director for a large corporation, offers these words of caution:

> *Sometimes a woman who's complained of discrimination tries to tell me what punishment to give. They come in my office demanding, "I want someone written up!" or "I want this guy fired!" But I'm not there as their advocate. The company will decide who gets written up or punished. Not her.*

Some HR people have a nasty, resentful attitude when it comes to soliciting your input on punishing the person who discriminated against you.

From your perspective, it's an opportunity for this person to be brought to justice. Since you were the one wronged, you feel you should have a say in the outcome.

From their standpoint, they were specifically hired to make these kinds of decisions, and they regard your input as a usurping of their realm of authority. Any recommendation you make is seen as biased—that of a hysterical victim wanting to extract a pound of flesh. (I find that ironic, considering that they, too, are "biased" in that they are hired and paid by an employer who directs them to analyze and evaluate facts, then make decisions deliberately calculated to insulate and protect the employer.)

This clash of expectations often leads to hostility and resentment. If you want to avoid it, refrain from mentioning that you want to see this guy paraded naked through the streets wearing a nose ring attached to the rear of a donkey. (Or at least try not to bring it up the first time you walk into the office to complain.) As one employment defense lawyer, Mary N., put it:

HR professionals realize that an employer is obliged only to take corrective action, enough so the problem won't happen again. It's not their mandate to make this guy turn over the family jewels.

Instead, express your input as a *solution,* not in terms of punishment. Stay away from statements like "I want this guy fired!" or "I want him demoted!" Rather, let the person know what you need to do your job—for instance, "I cannot take orders from him. I would like to be transferred" or "I will not feel that this problem has been solved unless one of two things happens. Either I get the promotion that I know I was entitled to, or you give me a valid reason in writing why I didn't." This type of statement focuses on how to make things right rather than on how to punish the wrongdoer.

3. Exaggerating.

Some women embellish or exaggerate when lodging complaints. Perhaps they believe that the HR person will not take action on their behalf unless the offense being reported is particularly egregious. Or maybe they feel the HR person isn't reacting strongly enough when listening to the complaint. (Later in this chapter you'll learn how some interviewers are actually taught to allow a few seconds of uncomfortable silence during the complaint process.)

If an HR person realizes you've overstated the facts in any way, he or she is likely to mistrust everything else you have to say. If you flat out lie about even the smallest issue, it would not be unreasonable for this person to assume you've lied about other things as well.

Don't jeopardize your complaint. Keep it truthful and accurate. Characterize things in a trustworthy fashion. Throughout my lawsuit, I was infinitely glad that I had never once been dishonest in my testimony. It would have been impossible to keep track of any complex set of lies.

If you tell the truth, you needn't worry about keeping your story straight.

4. Not Knowing the Company Rules.

HR people usually know all the company rules and regulations, because it's their job to do so. Sometimes they become so immersed in their job, they forget that most people don't study these rules, and they may get annoyed at you for not knowing them.

Make sure you freshen up on basic workplace rules and policies prior to lodging your complaint. Know the company procedure for lodging a complaint.

Employer Strategies and Tactical Ploys

BEFORE TAKING YOUR COMPLAINT

Prior to taking your complaint, an employer will usually research all applicable laws and company obligations. Then, in listening to your story, the employer will be able to identify exactly how, when, and where the company broke the law. (Don't expect the HR person to share this information with you.) He or she will also take into account all state laws that might apply. Some HR professionals even have flow charts or matrixes that list all applicable laws and obligations so they can apply your situation to them. Says Lori B., a human resources professional:

> *One woman came into my office complaining that her boss had sexually harassed her. I had checked my flow chart just before her interview. There's a list on it of things I should consider and ask. One of the questions was "Has she ever fraternized outside of work with her boss?" If you chose "no" as an answer, it said go to the next question. But if you chose "yes," it had a little arrow that pointed to a box in red that said, "This is a violation of a company rule that prohibits fraternization outside of work." So when she said she had dated him twice before, I knew we had her. We didn't have to find sexual harassment to take action.*

They had both violated company policy, and we could discipline or fire them both for it.

The HR department will also learn as much as possible about you prior to the interview. He or she will review your personnel file to learn of your employment history with the company; inquire whether you are presently subject to any disciplinary action (which makes your complaint suspect); learn whether you might have recently been denied a promotion, salary increase, or other benefit (which may make the HR person suspect that your complaint is based on sour grapes); find out whether you have ever made similar accusations; and verify that you've received and signed a copy of the company's sexual harassment policy (so your employer can hold you responsible for following company procedures, and also to prove that your employer did an adequate job informing you about it.)

Finally, an employer usually has a list of questions drawn up in advance—all calculated to elicit a thorough account of what happened and any information that might absolve the employer of wrongdoing.

These questions have been carefully worded and are usually drawn up by an attorney.

THIRTY QUESTIONS YOU'RE LIKELY TO GET ASKED, AND HOW TO RESPOND

Journalists are taught to ask certain basic questions when covering a story. They are: How? When? Why? Where? What? Who? You should anticipate answering the same questions when filing your complaint. When you have the answers clearly in your head, you are ready to lodge your complaint.

1. *What is your name and job title?*
2. *What is the name and job title of the person you are reporting?* Many women ask me whether they must identify

the person who has discriminated against them. The answer is yes. Failure to do so prevents your employer from being able to adequately investigate your complaint. Your employer will therefore not be held accountable for doing so.

3. *Do you have any reason to believe that I can't be fair and objective in taking and investigating your complaint?* One of the first things your employer will do is establish for the record that the investigation is a fair one.

If you are unhappy with the results of the investigation, you may later challenge it in court. The investigation will be carefully scrutinized to determine whether it was adequate, fair, and impartial.

If you voice no objection to this question, then expect your answer to be used as evidence against you if you ever challenge the fairness of the investigation in court.

If you don't believe the investigation will be properly conducted, then now is the time to say so. Be prepared to be specific as to what part or parts of it you perceive as unfair, and also to make suggestions as to what you require before you can feel that it *is* fair. The conversation might go something like this:

HR PERSON: Do you have any reason to believe that I can't be fair and objective in taking your complaint?

EMPLOYEE: Yes. I see you lunching often with the person I am about to complain about.

HR PERSON: What would you like me to do about that?

EMPLOYEE: That depends. Is there anyone else in the HR office who can take my complaint?

HR PERSON: Yes, my assistant, Jane Doe, can take it. Would that make you feel more comfortable?

EMPLOYEE: I'm not sure. Jane Doe works under you, so doesn't she have to answer to you?

HR PERSON: Yes.

EMPLOYEE: Even if she takes my complaint, will you still be overseeing her and instructing her on what to do?

HR PERSON: She can take the complaint on her own, without my intervention.

EMPLOYEE: After she takes the complaint, who will make the ultimate decision as to what to do about it? You or her? Or will it be someone else?

Get the picture? Don't be afraid to speak out at this point. If you don't, a court can later assume that you had no objections. In fact, some employers ask employees to sign a statement indicating their belief that the employer can do a fair and impartial job of investigating the complaint.

If they want you to sign such a statement, don't.

My advice is *never* make any kind of statement, either written or oral, saying you believe the investigation will be a fair one. After all, how do you know what factors are in place?

I suggest responding with something like "Given the fact that my supervisor has treated me in this manner, and he is so well regarded by this company, I am unsure that *any* investigation this company does will be fair and impartial." Or "Since you work for this company that allows so much discrimination to run rampant, I am doubtful that *any* investigation under the auspices of this company will be fair and impartial."

If they refuse to conduct an investigation because of your unwillingness to make or sign the statement, then file a complaint at the EEOC or your state's human rights commission.

4. *What happened?* It's best to hand in your own *written* version of the facts to accompany your answer to this question.
5. *What prompted you to complain?* This is another way of

asking you to explain what happened. Refer the interviewer to your written account.

6. *Recount the conversation(s) that took place during this ordeal.* Any conversation(s) that took place should already be described in your written account.
7. *Did this person make any physical contact with you? If so, when and where? Describe each incident.* This question gives your employer an idea of just how serious an offense it might be. Physical contact adds to the seriousness of a sexual harassment complaint.
8. *When did the alleged incident occur?* Many women are surprised to learn that they lose their right to sue an employer if they don't do so within a specified period of time. They will also have lost their right to lodge their complaint with the EEOC or equivalent state agency. Your employer is attempting to determine how close or far away you are from those time limits.
9. *How many people were involved?* The more people, the more serious the harm—not to mention the more people who might consider suing the employer. If others experienced the same treatment, then perhaps the employer is responsible for a "pattern and practice" of discrimination.
10. *Was this an isolated incident or part of a continuing behavior?* This question also elicits information as to whether your ill treatment might have been part of a pattern and practice of discrimination.
11. *Are you aware of other employees who have had similar experiences?* If so, list them.
12. *Were there any witnesses? If so, who are they and what did they see or hear?* Witnesses lend credibility to your claim. If you don't have witnesses, it doesn't necessarily mean that your claim is not credible. But witnesses can play an important role in the long run.

13. *Have you previously been subjected to sexual harassment or discrimination from this person? If so, describe each incident.* Here your employer is trying to get a sense of how weighty your discrimination claim is. If it has occurred over a long period of time, the court will regard it as considerably more serious than if it were an isolated incident.
14. *How long have you known each other?* This question, like the five that follow, helps the employer determine whether you might have "consented" to the behavior you are reporting. Consent would excuse the employer from liability.
15. *Describe your working relationship.*
16. *Do you have a personal relationship? If so, describe it.*
17. *Have you ever socialized with this person outside of work?*
18. *Has this person ever engaged in similar behavior that you have not complained of? If so, why did you not complain?* If the answer to the first part of this question is "yes," be prepared to give a good reason for why you didn't complain. Otherwise, your employer can use this fact to imply either that you "consented" or that the behavior didn't really bother you.
19. *Did you ever tell this person that their behavior offended you, or ask this person to stop?* See question 18.
20. *Do you have any documentation that will support what you say, such as photos, letters, journals, notes, diaries, or calendars?* If you do have any documentation, you should provide it. Don't give your employer any originals. Make copies, and if your employer wants to verify their authenticity, feel free to show the originals.
21. *Are you aware of the company's policies on discriminatory behavior?* This question forces you to admit that the company has done a good job informing you of its anti-discrimination policy. It also holds you responsible for

lodging your complaint in the manner prescribed under the policy. For instance, if you ever sue your employer for discrimination, you will be asked the following question: "Ms. Doe, you admitted you were aware of the company policy, so why did you not immediately report this so-called sexual harassment when it occurred?"

22. *What do you want us to do about your complaint?* Remember, think solution rather than punishment.
23. *Do you know of any reason this person might have for disliking you?* They are searching for motives, excuses, and defenses.
24. *Do you know of any reason this person might be sexually attracted to you?* They are fishing to see if you might reveal a personal relationship or encouragement on your part.
25. *Do you know of any reason why this person has behaved in this manner toward you?* More fishing.
26. *Identify all persons with whom you have discussed this.* The more people who know about a supervisor's discriminatory treatment of women, the more likely it is that those people, too, might sue. Then they can show that the company knew about the problem and did nothing about it. This can be very damaging, so an employer will want to make sure swift and appropriate action is taken.
27. *What effect has this had on your work?* This question stems from the sexual harassment criteria. Remember, if the discrimination's had no effect on your work, there is no harassment, because either you haven't had tangible job benefits taken away, or the ordeal is not "severe" or "pervasive" enough to prevent you from doing your job. Your employer will note this and use it as a defense if you ever sue for discrimination.

    If your work has been affected, say so.

If your work has not been affected, then tell the truth and acknowledge that it hasn't. The fact that it hasn't does not mean your employer will not attempt to remedy the situation. Tell your employer, "So far, my work has not been affected, but if you do not fix this problem, it probably will be, because I don't see the problem going away without your help." A smart employer will attempt to work with you to forestall an impending crisis.

Sometimes, if you complain *before* your work is affected, your employer has more breathing room to try to fix the situation.

28. *What effect, if any, has this had on your personal life, including your health?* This question goes to the damages you might recover in a lawsuit. Judges and juries give awards based upon how injured you are, both physically and emotionally. Your side will claim that all aspects of your life have been damaged. Your employer will claim otherwise and may use your answer against you.
29. *Is there anything else that we haven't talked about that you want to mention?* This question is posed so the employer can show that you had ample opportunity to bring up discrimination but didn't.
30. *Does this include everything?* Absolutely not! Don't ever acknowledge that your statement includes everything. You are not perfect. Chances are you've forgotten a detail here or there, or maybe even a major fact, that could seriously affect the validity of your complaint. It's best to answer, "I don't know whether that's everything. It's all that I remember right now."

WHILE TAKING YOUR COMPLAINT

Committing to a Time Frame.

"Most people trip themselves up on time frames," one employment lawyer states, "and it comes right off the page." Human resources professionals are advised to have you commit to a specific story or chronology of events as soon as possible.

Again, it's important that you have your facts straight *before* you complain. Even the most truthful story can sound fabricated if dates and times are mixed up.

Don't allow your interviewer to maneuver you into a time frame you're unsure of. Typically, a woman will say something like "I think it occurred the first week in February." The HR person will respond, "It'd be better if you could give me a more exact date." The woman then feels as if her complaint is deficient, so she estimates, "I'm pretty sure it was a Monday." The HR person responds, "So a Monday, the first week of February, would have been February 2. This occurred, then, on February 2?" "Yes, probably," answers the woman. The complaint is written up, "On Monday, February 2 . . ."

During the investigation, the HR person learns that the person you complained about was not even at work on Monday, February 2. Now you are in a position of having to change your story, which makes you lose credibility. Should you ever go to court over this matter, one of the first questions your employer's lawyer will ask is "Isn't it true you've changed your story since you first reported the incident?" or "If you weren't sure about that date, then what else aren't you sure about?"

Unless you are sure about a detail, don't commit to it. Keep your statement accurate. Accurate doesn't mean you must remember every minute scrap of information. A statement like "It occurred sometime during the first week of February" would be perfectly fine, or even "I can check my appointment book if you want to know the exact date." No jury is going to expect you to be a superwoman when it comes to remembering every single date. On the other hand, jurors will hold it against you if they think you are changing your story or fabricating events and time frames.

Stick to only what you know. No guessing allowed.

Conversational Tricks.
Human resources professionals are skilled in questioning employees in a manner that elicits the most detailed and revealing answers. They often use specific words and body language to induce you to feel at ease and speak freely.

HR professionals are instructed to save unfriendly, difficult, or embarrassing questions until they've established a rapport with you. If you know this ahead of time, you can mentally prepare for it. Just expect the interview to start out with fluff and end with a hammer on the head.

The HR interviewer sometimes compels an employee who is reluctant to speak by saying, "I'm getting only one side of the story here. John Doe says it happened differently. I need your side of things so I can get the information I need to take care of this properly."

Although this might be true, the comment is nevertheless meant to make you anxious. You think if you don't immediately spill everything you know, including details that are irrelevant and/or highly personal, the investigation will irreversibly take off in the other person's favor.

Another interview tactic HR people use is silence. "Take fifteen seconds and just look at them as if you're waiting for something," advises one lawyer. "They'll feel uncomfortable and resume talking, and then you'll hear things they never expected to tell you."

"Be a good listener," urges another lawyer. "Sometimes if you give her enough rope, she'll hang herself." This tactic is meant to smoke out women who lie or embellish.

Interviewers are also taught not to refer to the offending behavior as "harassment" or "discrimination." They will be extremely careful not to ask a question by saying something like "When did the harassment begin?" In that case, they themselves are labeling it harassment. It's an *admission* on their part.

Instead they'll ask, "When did this *behavior* begin?" If you feel like poking around, try responding with "Are you referring to the harassment behavior?" I guarantee they will not say yes. Instead they'll respond with "I'm referring to the behavior you are complaining about." They will never describe it as "illegal" or "discriminatory," because that would be giving up legal ground.

Failing to Cooperate.

Most employee manuals or handbooks have a statement saying that any employee who interferes or fails to cooperate with a company investigation may be disciplined and terminated. This means that if you lodge a complaint and are unwilling to fully disclose whatever relevant information your employer needs to further investigate it, you are violating company policy.

Sometimes women ask me whether they can be fired for failing to cooperate with an investigation that is biased and unfair. Probably not, but that doesn't mean your employer won't try.

You must have a valid reason for not believing in the integrity of the process, and be able to cite facts that indicate the system is biased or ineffective. You should send your investigator a note documenting the details. For instance:

> To: Human Resources
>
> I do not want to cooperate with this investigation because I fear retaliation. Jane Doe recently cooperated and was fired. Mary Brown complained about this same supervisor a year ago, and nothing was ever done. Instead, he continues to harass us, and Mary Brown's since been demoted.

If possible, inform someone else in a supervisory position at the company of your decision. If there is no supervisor you can trust, then inform a coworker. That way you'll have a record of your objections. It can be something as simple as an informal note like the following:

Dear Supervisor Jones,

Dorothy Smith in human resources wants me to answer questions about such and such, but I'm afraid. Jane Doe answered similar questions, and instead of fixing the problem, they fired her. Any suggestions?

Make a copy before you send it. Don't expect any solutions from the person you send it to. Your purpose is more to lay your own paper trail proving that you *did* have objections about the integrity of the investigation. Then, if you are ever fired for refusing to cooperate, you will have a written record as to your reasons why.

I also suggest you complain to the EEOC or your state's human rights commission about it. If possible, complain before or at the same time you refuse to cooperate with your employer.

Tape Recording.

Some interviewers will want to tape-record your complaint. I've heard HR professionals advise both ways on this issue. Most advise against it, because they believe a tape recorder is an "information blocker." It tends to make people clam up, whereas an interviewer wants you to feel at ease so you will speak openly.

If your interviewer is taping, he or she must tell you so, and the recorder should be in plain view. Sometimes an HR person will ask permission to record your conversation while the recorder is running so they have a recording of your consent.

Don't be afraid to say no. Recording the conversation will help only your employer. And with a recorder running, chances are you will be nervous and unable to recount your story fully.

The most accurate version of your story will be the one you yourself write in the privacy of your home without feeling pressured.

If the HR person records you and does not inform you, then he or she may have violated state law.

Attorney-Client Privilege.
If your employer decides to have an attorney take or investigate your complaint, be careful. One of the most evasive maneuvers employers use is the attorney-client privilege. Normally, this privilege protects an attorney-client relationship so that a client can speak freely with her lawyer without fearing the attorney will disclose the information to others. In that instance, it's a valuable resource that enhances our legal system.

In your case, however, it may be used to hide evidence. Here's how:

If you ever sue your employer for discrimination, you will probably be able to subpoena a human resources person's notes of the investigation. Those notes might prove that the company was derelict in investigating your complaint. They might also include other damaging information about your employer that could help you prove your case.

If your complaint has this potential, the HR person may turn the investigation over to a lawyer. The lawyer can then claim that his or her investigation is secret—subject to the attorney-client privilege—and you then lose your right to subpoena the investigation's findings. In effect, your chances of successfully proving your case have been sabotaged by this deceptive use of the privilege.

HR professionals are taught to use lawyers in instances where a complaint might evolve into a serious lawsuit or criminal claim, involves a large number of employees, could cost the company a lot of money, or might generate adverse publicity if it is made public.

As one employment defense lawyer put it:

> *We use the privilege all the time; even when someone just files a complaint. We give the HR people guidance on how to use it and when to call us in. They want to do a fair investigation, but if what they learn is hellish—well, they have to protect the employer and avoid liability.*

I truly don't believe any court would allow the privilege to stand in these instances. The problem is that it's usually impossible to prove the privilege was misused. A lawyer can come up with a dozen seemingly legitimate reasons for using it.

If a lawyer is used in your case, immediately ask the lawyer to tell you whom he or she is representing. The lawyer must then disclose that he or she is representing the company and not you.

Ask whether the investigation is or will be part of his or her "attorney work product" (and thus subject to the attorney-client privilege).

If the lawyer says "No," ask for that statement in writing.

If the attorney says "Yes" or "I don't know," I advise not to cooperate. Tell the lawyer that you don't believe the employer has your best interests at heart by conducting an investigation that can be kept secret. Tell the lawyer you expect your employer to conduct a fair and impartial investigation.

In either case, tell the attorney that in light of the fact that your employer has taken the adversarial step of using an attorney at this early stage, you feel you should have a lawyer present as well, and that you intend now to bring your complaint to the EEOC or to your state's human rights commission.

Sometimes, even though a lawyer attempts to use the attorney-client privilege, he or she is disallowed from using it. This occurs when an employer shares a supposedly "secret" investigation with people other than the attorney (human resources personnel, office workers, management, etc.). In that case, an employer has destroyed the privilege. Also, in order to invoke the privilege, the human resources person must bring in the lawyer at the onset of the investigation, not simply turn over an already prepared report. Finally, some companies have begun hiring lawyers to work in what is essentially a non-lawyer job—that of human resources worker. As such, they are responsible for investigating all complaints. In that instance, the lawyer is not acting in the capacity of an attorney, and therefore cannot use attorney-client privilege.

A Typical Investigation

After you lodge your complaint, your employer will begin an investigation to make a determination as to what happened. Usually this investigation starts within a day or two, depending on the severity of the complaint and whether anyone is in jeopardy of experiencing discrimination in the interim.

One employment defense lawyer put it succinctly, saying, "The investigation is time to document, document, document!"

Remember, the primary goal is to assess risk and minimize liability, not to assist you. In fact, one of the largest HR training organizations in the country lists ten goals for conducting investigations, and not one of them is to assist employees. Of the various lists put out by the numerous employer training organizations, most include the following:

- to evaluate and assess the legal risk to which the company will be exposed
- to implement strategies that minimize risk and liability
- to improve the factual basis of employer decision making
- to develop a thorough and complete record on which to base a legal opinion
- to prevent the likelihood of a government investigation (this includes an EEOC investigation)
- to curtail adverse publicity
- to avoid the costs of litigation and its disruptive effect on business operations

At this time, your employer will create a special file in which to put the information gathered. This information should not be placed in your personnel file. To do so would violate the law. Your personnel file is apt to be reviewed by others who are responsible for giving you raises and promotions, and the fact that you've lodged a discrimination complaint should not enter into any such decision.

This investigation file will be the beginning of what will likely be a swift but thorough investigation, and it will start . . . with you!

WHAT THEY WILL INVESTIGATE ABOUT YOU

Even though you are not the one who has been accused of doing something wrong, *you*, not the wrongdoer, will be the initial focus of the investigation.

Immediately after the interview in which you lodge your complaint, the HR person will make notes critiquing your demeanor, presentation, and attitude. He or she will also note whether you made any admissions, denials, or conflicting statements and whether you offered any evidence to support your story.

Your interviewer will research and document your relationship with your coworkers, your productivity in the company, and your prior jobs. He or she will also make notes about your personal life. For instance, if you've made any comments about having a "difficult" time at home, they will document it. Then, should you ever claim the discrimination caused you emotional pain and upset, your employer can point to your personal life as the cause, and thus avoid being held fully responsible for it.

WHAT THEY WILL INVESTIGATE ABOUT THE PERSON YOU ARE REPORTING

The next focus of the investigation will be on the person you've complained about. He is apt to be subjected to the same legal tactics your employer uses on you.

And why not? The accused is an employee, too. And he also

poses a threat of litigation—and monetary loss for the company—if the investigation is not done properly.

Your employer will begin by researching his credibility and reviewing the same type of documentation reviewed about you.

Most important is whether there have been complaints about him in the past. If so, his credibility is low. Your employer also realizes that if you file a lawsuit at this point, you can easily prove that your employer had notice of a problem but did not fix it.

Your employer will notify him that there has been a complaint lodged against him and request a private interview.

During the interview, the employer will ask him to recount what happened. They are taught not to immediately reveal to him all the details of what you said. For instance, they will not say, "Jane Doe tells me you called her into your office last Thursday, shut the door, and tried to kiss her." Rather, they'll ask, "Jane Doe tells me there was an incident last Thursday. Can you tell me about it?" It's an open question. It makes no specific accusations and it doesn't put him on the defensive.

In fact, one seminar specifically instructs HR people to "couch" their statements as suspicions rather than accusations in order to get more cooperation from him. An accusatory statement such as "Why did you try to kiss Jane Doe?" or "We have witnesses that saw you try to kiss Jane Doe!" usually only creates hostility and a refusal to cooperate.

Often, the accused will ask for "immunity" if he agrees to tell everything he knows. There is no such thing as immunity in this situation. HR people cannot guarantee it, and if they do, they have violated *your* rights!

Just like you, he can be disciplined or terminated for failure to cooperate with an investigation if he does not fully take part in the process.

WHERE THE INVESTIGATION GOES FROM HERE

The interviewer will then make a list of potential witnesses and any additional paperwork to be reviewed. This includes relevant memos, notes, time cards, expense reports, reimbursement records, logs, receipts, purchasing records, travel history records, sign-in sheets, video security tapes, managers' notes, samples of your work, personnel files of all parties involved, and any former complaints that might have been lodged by or against anyone involved.

The HR person will compare all this information to the stories both of you have told and fish for motivation on either of your parts. What motive might he have to treat you in this manner? Do you have a motive for lodging a false complaint? Have the two of you experienced any particular conflicts or problems with each other?

The investigator will also assess whether your claim has the potential to develop into a major lawsuit.

Finally, he or she will identify potential witnesses and begin listing questions to ask them.

WITNESSES

Connie B. is a human resources consultant. She says:

> *What I've found from interviewing people in my investigation is that stories can vary. It's not necessarily because people lie. It's because people see things differently. Everybody has their own truth.*

In most cases, witnesses are employees, either coworkers or supervisors. Their responses may surprise you. They will run the gamut—from those who are honest and forthright to those who tell outrageous lies. You will see your fellow employees as you have never seen them before.

I'll never forget the words I spoke to my attorneys immediately following a very disappointing deposition of one of my former coworkers. "Could you please take this out of my back?" I asked. Not understanding at first what I meant, they asked me to explain. "This knife," I said. "It doesn't feel very good."

You can save yourself a lot of disappointment and frustration by accepting *now* the fact that some of your witnesses will not come through for you.

In my own case, the witness had given a very explicit statement on two separate occasions, once to me and again to our investigator. She had ranted and raved about her discriminatory treatment from the network, and she had named names and related specific incidents in which she accused the company of sex-based prejudice. At one point, she even thanked me for having the "courage" to bring such a lawsuit.

Then we subpoenaed her, asking her to recount all she had said:

QUESTION: Did you at that time feel that there were males that were getting job assignments that you would have expected to have gotten but for some reason were being assigned to men instead of you?

ANSWER: No.

QUESTION: Did you ever make a statement to [CNN vice president] Bob Furnad to the effect of, "How many white males do I have to stand behind before I will get a particular job position or be able to cover a particular type of story?"

ANSWER: I don't remember. . . .

QUESTION: Did you ever have a feeling that story ideas that you had pitched—or came up with—a story that you wanted to do . . . for some reason those stories would be assigned to [a male reporter] to cover rather than yourself?

ANSWER: I don't remember specific stories.

We endured her denials for about fifteen minutes, until finally my lawyer just terminated the deposition.

I'm not saying all your witnesses will react this way. But you should be prepared for a variety of "truths." Some may be too scared to tell any truth at all. Others may feel they are being "loyal" if they lie for their boss. Some may color their testimony with minor mischaracterizations for whatever reason. Usually, however, witnesses tell it exactly as they see it. What will surprise you is that they probably didn't see it exactly as you did.

The only thing predictable about your witnesses is that they will be unpredictable.

Your investigator probably believes that witnesses provide the most objective input since, unlike you or the accused, they usually don't have a personal stake in the outcome. Therefore, if you know that a witness may have reason to mischaracterize events, tell your investigator. Explain the facts or situation that influences that witness's testimony. For instance, "Harry Smith witnessed John Doe grabbing my breasts, but Harry and John are best friends. They go out every Friday night."

Similarly, if one of your witnesses happens to be a close friend, expect the investigator to view that testimony as biased.

Normally, when a witness is interviewed an investigator will not tell him or her all the details of your accusation—for two reasons: A witness's testimony is more valuable if he or she hasn't heard an "official" version yet. Also, your employer is not allowed to discuss your complaint with others unless they have a *business need to know,* discussed later in this chapter.

It's better if witnesses are interviewed alone. Group dynamics and peer pressure sometimes suppress accurate responses. Try to learn under what conditions your witnesses were interviewed.

Some women ask whether they should first speak privately to their witnesses as a courtesy, to let them know that they can expect to be questioned. My answer is this: Only if you feel it's necessary.

Witnesses will be asked to recount *everything* you've said to them about the incident, including any warning you may have given them about being called as witnesses. If you try to put words in their mouths, it will come to light. Even if you don't try to put words in their mouths, the other side will imply that you did, or that you conspired to structure a story in your favor.

It's best to just ask witnesses to tell the truth and leave it at that. For instance: *You will probably be asked about the day you witnessed John Doe grabbing my breasts. Regarding your testimony, all I ask is that you tell the truth and tell it as clearly and accurately as you can.*

Sometimes an employer will not interview any or all of the witnesses whose names you provide. This might be for several reasons. Perhaps your interviewer feels the witness has nothing significant to say. Or maybe enough other witnesses have already corroborated an event.

If you feel that a particular witness should not be overlooked, point that out to the interviewer. If the witness it still not questioned, remind the interviewer again, but in writing this time, listing the name(s) of any witnesses not called. On your own copy of this list, write what you expected each to say and the reason given you, if any, as to why they weren't called. Then, should you ever object to the accuracy of the investigation, you will have a written record of the witnesses whose potential testimony was ignored.

CONFIDENTIALITY

Jane G., a human resources professional, cautions against expecting too much from the HR department:

> *No one should walk into an HR office and think things will come back to haunt them. On the other hand, if an employee asks for confidentiality, it won't necessarily be so. They cannot reasonably expect to come in and expect me to fix it without talking with anybody. Yet invariably the first thing women ask me when they come in to complain is, "Can you guarantee confidentiality?"*

Employers walk a fine line. If they are conducting an investigation, they must interview a number of people, including the accuser, the accused, and witnesses, including coworkers and supervisors. At the same time, they must refrain from spreading accusations and hearsay about all the parties involved, or they risk being sued for invasion of privacy, slander, libel, or intentional infliction of emotional distress.

Employers may disclose information about your complaint only to people who have a "business need to know." Everybody in upper management does not have a business need to know. Typically, it includes only those who conduct the investigation or make decisions to correct the problem.

Sometimes a coworker has a business need to know. For instance, an investigator may have to tell a witness some background about the case in order to ask questions about it. Even so, witnesses should be told only the information necessary for the investigator to conduct a thorough interview.

Although investigators will tell witnesses not to discuss the case with anyone, inevitably some do.

In view of all the people your employer must discuss this matter with, it's impossible to guarantee you complete confidentiality. However, employers must guarantee you that they'll tell only people who must know.

DO YOU HAVE A RIGHT TO BRING A LAWYER?

It's up to your employer whether you're allowed to have a lawyer present during the investigation interview. That doesn't mean you can't consult with one prior to filing your complaint. In fact, you can have a lawyer advise you every step of the way.

Most likely, your employer does.

Employment defense lawyers, however, advise employers *against* allowing employees to bring legal counsel. They believe it creates an adversarial situation early on and prevents their investigation from being a "meaningful" one.

Union employees, in both the private and public sector, are an exception. They have an absolute right to have a union representative or lawyer present whenever they lodge a complaint or go through a grievance procedure.[4]

Reaching Conclusions

It's important that your employer complete the investigation in a timely manner and that any correction be immediate and adequate. Timeliness is different with each case, depending on its severity and pervasiveness.

Make sure the entire complaint process has been handled in the manner prescribed by the company manual or handbook. Any inconsistency on your employer's part makes the entire investigation suspect.

Sometimes, prior to reaching a conclusion, your employer will take interim action. This might include temporarily transferring the person you complained about or changing his supervisory responsibilities. Or it might include suspending him until the investigation is completed. This is done to protect an employer from being sued by other women who might claim the employer knew about his propensity to discriminate against women and did nothing about it.

An employer will never use the word "suspend" in describing this interim action, but rather the term "administrative leave." "Suspend" implies he did something wrong. If he didn't, then he can sue the employer for intentional infliction of emotional distress, slander, libel, defamation, or even malicious prosecution.

I have heard more than one lawyer advise employers to lie about interim leave. "Make up a convincing cover story for a manager to stay home and work on a special project while you're completing the investigation," they urge. "That way there's no public embarrassment, hence no lawsuit from the accused." The purpose is to make the situation sound as innocuous as possible.

Sometimes at the close of the investigation a human resources person suggests a specific punishment or solution. If the management does not then follow the advice, and the complaint turns into a lawsuit, the HR person's notes can be subpoenaed and your employer will have a difficult time proving they took "adequate action" in correcting the problem.

When disciplining an offender, an employer will consider how long the employee has worked there; what his employment record is like; what your employment record is like; whether it's a first-time offense; whether the accused was aware of the policy; whether the discriminatory act was committed out of maliciousness or crass insensitivity; the seriousness of the conduct and the length of time it went on; whether you told him to stop his behavior; and how valuable and high ranking the offender is. An employer will also consider how likely *you* are to sue if the offender is not adequately disciplined. More important, an employer will review past incidents in the company so as to be consistent, and not arbitrary, in making discipline decisions in your case.

Unlike in a court of law, your employer does not have to establish "beyond a reasonable doubt" that the discrimination occurred. To comply with the law, an employer need only conduct a "good-faith investigation and reach a reasonable conclusion."[5]

Punishment can include any or all for the following: a warning that if it happens again the offender will be disciplined or terminated; time off without pay; sensitivity training; a change of title or job; a reassignment; a transfer; a demotion; or termination.

After the investigation, the HR person should meet with you to let you know it's finished. He or she should tell you what action is being implemented as a result of your complaint, and will probably expect you to keep some of the findings and actions confidential. To avoid getting sued by the person you complained about, your employer may not tell you exactly what action was taken.

If you were discriminated against in a salary issue, it would be reasonable for the employer to give you back pay from the time your discrimination began until now. Don't be afraid to ask for this if your employer doesn't offer it. Put your request in writing so if you are refused, you have proof that your employer was given an opportunity to correct the situation and didn't. The company is obliged to put you in the same position you would be in had you not encountered discrimination. That can mean back pay, or a promotion plus an increase in pay, or some other resolution depending on your situation.

If the discriminatory act is sexual harassment, the company must make the harassment stop *immediately.*

IF YOUR EMPLOYER "PROTECTS" THE PERSON YOU'VE COMPLAINED ABOUT

Sometimes it seems that an employer responds by "protecting" the very person you've complained about. In some cases, he isn't punished at all. You may be told that he has been "talked to," that it won't happen again, but that you must continue working under him. In fact, he might even get a raise or a promotion due him.

There are myriad reasons why one of these alternative scenarios might come about. In many cases, it's a matter of an employer choosing to take only the minimum action necessary to avoid liability. Some employers subscribe to an old adage: "Every dog gets one bite." They believe that fairness dictates that an employee's first misdeed should be corrected with only a warning. Then, if the behavior continues, the employee will be severely disciplined or fired.

Remember, the remedy need only be reasonably calculated to *end* the harassment and correct the injury. If a simple warning ends the harassment, then your employer is off the hook, and there is no incentive to do more.

If your employer chooses to demote or fire this person, don't expect such a move to be publicly announced. That would be admitting there's a discrimination problem. Then other women may step forward and sue, using the employer's own admission as proof. Instead, employers will quietly "transfer" someone from one position to another, usually to a position in which the offender doesn't affect the welfare of a lot of women employees.

Sometimes an investigation actually is inconclusive. An employer may be unable to determine which party is lying. In many cases, both parties truly view the incident in different ways. In this situation, provided the employer has thoroughly investigated the matter, there is no obligation to punish anyone. The employer may decide to do nothing at all. This is a risky move on an employer's part, because if the accused was guilty of the offense and he commits another subsequent one, the next individual he offends will have a very easy time proving her case. Her lawyers would be able to show that the company actually had notice of this man's propensity to discriminate but chose to do nothing about it. For that reason most employers will, at the very least, transfer the accused to another position.

An Appeal Process

If you feel that the final decision is not an adequate response, you should be able to appeal it to someone else in the company. If your company doesn't have an appeal process in place, the complaint procedure as a whole may not be adequate.

Some employers allow for an appeal to a higher management person. Others provide an employee review board. In any event, the appeal should offer you the right to bypass the person who committed the wrongful act.

You should be allowed to ask the appeal body to reconsider the outcome based on all the same facts, or on any new facts that have recently come to light. You should be able to address any comments made to you during the investigation that indicated a lack of thoroughness or impartiality on the investigator's part. You should also be able to challenge the investigation if it was not conducted in accordance with company policies and guidelines.

Retaliation

Your employer must guarantee that there will be no retaliation against you. If your employer doesn't bring this up, don't be afraid to ask about it. The answer must be an unqualified guarantee, or your employer is violating the law. The same law that prohibits discrimination also prohibits an employer from retaliating against anyone who complains of discrimination.[6]

This doesn't mean that your employer may not try to exact revenge on you. But if they are caught doing so, they can face steep fines and unusually large jury verdicts.

For an employer's action to constitute retaliation, it must consist of the following:

1. You must engage in some sort of "opposition activity," such as filing a complaint, or even threatening to file one.
2. Your employer must then take some adverse action against you to deter you from engaging in that activity—for example, discourage you from filing a complaint.[7]
3. There must be a cause-and-effect relationship between your activity and your employer's adverse action—that is, evidence that your employer's actions were in direct response to your activity. The evidence can be something tangible like a memo, or it can even be inferred from proximity in time—if you complain on a Monday and get fired on Friday, one can reasonably infer that one action caused the other.

If you are retaliated against, it's crucial that you complain again, laying your own paper trail. If you don't complain now, you will have no record that your employer's actions were discriminatory. Keep a log of every occurrence and place it in your file at home.

One of the most artful tactics I ever heard discussed at an

employer seminar suggested that an HR person, or someone else from the company, walk by the desk of the person who has lodged a complaint and ask, "How are you doing?" If the person says "Fine," then the HR person returns to his or her office and documents the response. Unbeknownst to the employee, she is now on record as having been directly asked about retaliation and responded that there was none.

Your Responsibilities: How to Behave

Here are some basic rules to follow to give your complaint the best possible chance of being solved quickly and correctly:

Try to be a model employee during this time. Don't be late. Do your job. Don't give your employer any grounds whatsoever to discipline you, even if this means doing more work than you regularly do. For instance, even if you and everybody else in your workplace typically come to work ten minutes late, make sure you're there on time from now on.

Don't be hostile. Under the circumstances, it's easy to see a conspiracy where there is none. You may feel as though the entire company is against you. Chances are it's not so, but even if it is, don't let it show. You'll just be giving your employer more ammunition to use against you. Keep your attitude and demeanor professional and focused on your work.

Don't chat it up with anybody who will listen. That will only create a swirl of gossip that cannot help you in any way. This doesn't mean you can't inform a coworker or two about the incident and the fact that you've complained. You *should* do that to help document what went on, unless your human resources department has instructed you otherwise. But don't stand by the watercooler trying to get others to agree with you about how terrible your boss or employer is.

If I could give you anything, it would be the ability *not* to have to ride the daily roller coaster that inevitably arises from filing a complaint. I realize this is easier said than done, but try hard not to let the ordeal affect your everyday life and work. One day you feel as if the investigation is going well. The next day, you hear a rumor that the guy you complained about is getting a promotion. Another day, you hear he's getting demoted. When you check with the human resources department, you learn he hasn't even been interviewed yet. Don't rise and fall with every tidbit of news and gossip you hear.

Lodge your complaint. Keep in touch with the person who took it. Don't believe or depend on anything you hear unless it comes directly from the person in charge. Wait until you hear "official" news before you allow yourself to react to it. It will save you precious energy and lower your stress level.

Trust me. I know.

14.

You're Fired

1832 Lost job
1832 Defeated for legislature
1833 Failed in private business
1834 Elected to legislature
1835 Sweetheart dies
1836 Nervous breakdown
1836 Defeated for house speaker
1843 Defeated for nomination to Congress
1846 Elected to Congress
1849 Lobbied to be appointed land commissioner and failed
1855 Defeated for Senate
1856 Defeated for nomination for vice-president
1859 Defeated for Senate again
1860 Elected President of the United States

—biography of Abraham Lincoln

I've started a club. So far it's just me and Abe. My club is for people who face failure, warranted or not, and continue striving for success. To join, you need a lot of self-esteem and a belief that you are good at what you do.

Getting fired can be a brutal experience. Some bosses are more graceful than others at informing you about it. In an effort to be kind, my own boss pointed out that I should feel *lucky* he was taking the time to tell me I was fired. He said a friend of his at CBS used to move people's desks to the corner of the newsroom, with no assignments, until they figured it out for themselves.

I didn't feel lucky, though.

I felt embarrassed, ashamed, angry, bewildered, resentful, confused, frightened, and belittled. Not to mention sick to my stomach.

Anything but lucky.

This chapter will hand-hold you through the firing process, including layoffs and situations where your employer forces you to quit. Both of those instances may be firings in disguise.

Even though getting fired may seem like the end of the world, it's not. You can, and will, go on to achieve many successes.

Join the club.

Be Prepared

How can a person ever be prepared for getting fired?

You can. Your employer is.

Although your firing may have seemed to come out of the blue, it was probably well thought out on the part of your employer. In fact, your file's probably already been peppered with a number of "legally defensible" reasons for the firing. "Every time you fire an employee, you should ask yourself how you will explain it to a jury," advises one management lawyer.

If you haven't been taking the preventative steps described in the previous chapters, then you're already at a disadvantage. Nevertheless, there are some things you can still do to protect your rights.

How Did They Fire You?

There's a right way and a wrong way to fire somebody. If you were yelled at, called names, or had disparaging remarks publicly made about the quality of your work, your employer may be liable for invasion of privacy, defamation, or negligent/intentional infliction of emotional distress. This may be so regardless of whether your employer had a right to fire you.

Sometimes when employers fire people, they force them to clean out their desk under the supervision of a security officer. In other instances, security officers physically escort them off the premises. Unless there is a legitimate reason for doing this (for example, the job position requires high security or a worker has been caught stealing or is prone to violence), an employer may be violating your rights. There is no legally defined procedure for firing someone. The general rule, however, is that the same termination procedure must be used with everyone, and it must not create the impression in others that the person being fired is untrustworthy.

BECAUSE YOU'VE BEEN OUT SICK TOO MUCH

When I was sixteen years old, I had a friend named Regina. She was fired from her job as a movie theater usher because she was "out sick too much." Actually, Regina *had* stayed home more than her allotted share of sick days, but only because her fellow ushers, all male, had teased and ridiculed her to the point where she was too upset to go to work. The ushers made endless jokes about Regina's large breasts. Among the many cruel things they did was to draw a full-figured caricature of her on the wall of the men's rest room with her home phone number written alongside it. When her boss saw the drawing, he physically dragged her inside the rest room to show her, then accused her of engaging in "funny business" with his male ushers.

Too embarrassed to tell her mother how she was being treated,

Regina began to feign illness to avoid having to go to work. And then she was fired.

An employer may not create or allow a stressful environment in which you cannot work, then fire you for calling in sick.

Regina should not have been fired. It would have been up to her, however, to prove that her employer had allowed a situation to develop that rendered her incapable of meeting his work-related demands.

Quite a task for a sixteen-year-old.

CONSTRUCTIVE DISCHARGE

These words are from Christine F., a producer:

> *Well, they didn't fire me, it's just that they took most all my responsibilities away and gave them to a guy who was half my age with practically no experience. Then, a few weeks later, they told me I was supposed to report to him. They offered to renew my contract, but it was absurd. I realized my boss had been demoting or transferring all the women in management positions, hoping they would quit. It was clear to me I was going nowhere. So I quit.*

If your working conditions become so intolerable because of discrimination that you're compelled to quit, legally your situation could be the same as if you've been fired. It's called "constructive discharge."

Here's how constructive discharge might occur in a sex discrimination situation. An employer may want to fire a woman for reasons that are discriminatory. That employer, however, may decide *not* to fire her for fear of getting sued, and instead transfers her to a different job or location—one much lesser in quality or status than her previous job. For all intents and purposes, she's been fired.

Three things must occur for a resignation to be considered a constructive discharge:

First, you must have resigned because of *intolerable working conditions.*

Second, the intolerable working conditions must have been caused by unlawful discrimination or unlawful acts by your employer.

Third, a reasonable person under the same circumstances would have felt compelled to resign.

Some courts add an additional requirement: that an employer must have the specific intent to make you quit, not just to treat you badly.

Employers absolutely hate the theory of constructive discharge. They refer to employee lawsuits that stem from constructive discharge as "quit and sue" lawsuits.

What Constitutes Intolerable Working Conditions?

There's no specific rule as to what specifically constitutes intolerable working conditions. Courts and juries make that decision on a case-by-case basis, but it usually entails more than just hurt feelings or humiliated egos.

Transferring you to a different job, like what was done in the example given earlier, may be regarded as constructive discharge if the transfer amounts to a substantial demotion.

Sometimes a woman is transferred to a position with no chance of advancement. Some employers would refer to her as a "zombie"—as far as her career future, she is the walking dead. That's constructive discharge.

An employer sometimes creates a "special job" for somebody they want to squeeze out—a phony job with few or no responsibilities. Phony jobs usually constitute constructive discharge.

A poor performance review alone is usually not enough to constitute constructive discharge, although it can be if an employer gives the poor review with motives other than offering sincere, accurate feedback.

A hostile environment in a sexual harassment situation can constitute grounds for constructive discharge, such as we saw with Regina's theater usher job. So can a variety of other things, such as assigning bizarre working hours or purposefully implementing burdensome rules. One supervisor, angry that a woman had been assigned to work on his road maintenance crew, began denying her access to a rest room, even when she was experiencing her menstrual cycle. Instead, she was ordered to "use the bushes like the men do." That constituted constructive discharge.

When You Should Quit.

It's important you don't quit the minute you encounter difficulties of this nature. Under the law concerning constructive discharge, you must give your employer notice that your working conditions have become intolerable, so your employer has a chance to fix the problem.

If your situation is construed by a court *not* to constitute constructive discharge, your employer will owe you very little, if any, damages. If, on the other hand, it *is* construed to be constructive discharge, your employer will owe not only for past wages but for any future wages as well. Unfortunately, you never know exactly how a judge or jury will regard your departure, so solving the problem by quitting creates somewhat of a risk of your part. Therefore, I suggest you quit only if your conditions are so intolerable that you feel you have no other choice, and *after* you've thoroughly documented your attempts to remedy the situation.

You will be better off in the long run if you solve the problem internally through whatever complaint procedure your company has put in place.

IF YOU'VE BEEN LAID OFF

Sometimes an employer disguises a discriminatory firing as a layoff. "Hire individuals; fire in groups" is a common management credo. It's an easy way for employers to get rid of "problem employees" without having to answer to charges of discrimination. For instance, if a woman has a recent history of complaining of discrimination and is then fired, there is a legal *presumption* that her firing was discriminatory. If a boss appears to have a legitimate business reason for dismissing the employee, however, such as a layoff, the burden falls back on the woman to prove the layoff is a pretext, which is more difficult.

If you've been laid off and you suspect it's disguised discrimination, find out how many other workers were laid off and what criteria were used to determine who would be laid off. Check to see whether there was a credible, systematic method used to determine who was laid off. Any arbitrary action in selecting candidates for dismissal or layoff by your employer may be viewed as discriminatory.

Ask your employer to tell you the reason behind the layoff. Be sure to take notes. Evidence of discrimination may be in the form of letters or memos, or possibly the testimony of others who overheard or took part in any conversations concerning the action in question. Statistics showing that your employer has exhibited a pattern and practice of treating women in a discriminatory manner, or laying them off at a rate disproportionate to that of men, could also be used as evidence.

In the case of Denise H., evidence came in the form of in-house profit-and-loss data. For six years she worked as an accountant for a major oil company and had an excellent track record. Then she was assigned to work under a man who had a reputation for treating women poorly. She began to receive unsatisfactory performance reviews, and eventually was given a letter from her boss informing her that profits were down, development expenses were up, and environmental restrictions had recently cost the company more money than expected. As a result, the company was reducing its workforce. Her employer offered her a "buyout"—

several thousand dollars as an incentive to resign, in addition to a standard severance package. The company indicated that if she didn't accept the offer, she would probably be laid off in the coming year and thus be eligible only for the severance package.

The oil company overlooked the fact, however, that Denise's job required her to monitor company profits and losses. She knew that even though costs had gone up, profits had been significantly higher. In fact, it had been a banner year.

She chose not to take the incentive buyout, and prior to going on maternity leave, she lodged a discrimination complaint within the company, labeling the company's supposed cutback as a pretext for discrimination. When she returned, she was reassigned to a different supervisor and has since received excellent performance reviews. She was never laid off.

How to Respond When You're Notified You've Been Fired

If you're notified of your termination in writing, make sure you keep a copy of everything that's given to you.

If you're given only verbal notification, then log what was said to you and who was present. Sometimes employers arrange for a second person to "observe" when you're informed of your termination. That way if there is any dispute as to what exactly was said, it's two against one.

If you're terminated without notice, you're entitled to receive pay equivalent to the amount of notice time you *should* have received. For instance, if company policy is to give two weeks' termination notice, and you're given none, you should be given two weeks pay instead. This is in addition to any severance pay to which you might be entitled.

If you feel your termination is based on discrimination, or retaliation for objecting to discrimination, immediately lodge a complaint in writing before you leave the premises. Describe what you believe and why. It's crucial you do so, since that will preserve your side of the record. Keep a copy.

If possible, make a copy of your entire personnel file before leaving the premises. As you photocopy it, number each page sequentially. (Do this on the original, if that is allowed. If it is not, then number your copy.) That way your employer cannot later add or subtract things from your file. Keep your copy intact. Do not add to it or take things out.

If you're asked to turn in any company paraphernalia, do so, but first make a photocopy of each item, including ID cards, credentials, badges, and credit cards.

Collecting Company Information and Records

Consider these words from an employment defense lawyer describing the search for evidence in employment discrimination lawsuits:

> *When the sheriff hears there's been a shooting in town, he rushes to the scene and the first thing he does is look for the guy with the smoking gun. In discrimination lawsuits, there's rarely a smoking gun.*

Few employment discrimination cases actually have "smoking gun" memos—that is, written documents that openly express discriminatory motives or prejudicial attitudes.

Most cases are instead proved by circumstantial evidence—putting all the facts together and deducing that discrimination was most likely the motive behind an action.

In some situations, however, women are aware of smoking-gun memos or other company records that document discrimination. They take these records home or photocopy them to help prove their case.

Be careful!

For thirty years, Christine McKennon worked for the Nashville Banner Publishing Company; at age sixty-two, she was laid off. The company falsely claimed her layoff was due to a workforce reduction because of cost considerations. McKennon sued and proved that her termination stemmed from age discrimination. She admitted that during her last year of employment, when she suspected she was about to be laid off, she had taken company records home as "insurance" and "protection." The documents showed the company's strong financial condition.

Removal of these confidential documents, however, violated company policy and was grounds for termination in itself.

The U.S. Supreme Court ruled in her case that an employee's right to recover damages in discrimination lawsuits ceases at the time an employer learns that the employee committed an act that would have been grounds for termination.[1] It's called the *after-acquired evidence rule.* Under this rule, an employee who sues for discrimination can be compensated only for past wages and only up until the time her employer learned of her misdeed. She loses completely her right to recoup projected future wages and to be reinstated to her job. She also loses the right to be paid for any pain and suffering that occurs after the time her employer learned of her wrongful act.

If you are considering taking company records to help prove your case, first determine whether those documents are confidential. Documents are considered to be confidential if they contain what's known as "trade secrets."

Trade secrets are any information a company uses to make money by virtue of the fact that the general public doesn't have that same information. For instance, the formula for Coca-Cola would be a trade secret. A trade secret might also include information or data about customer preferences, pricing, marketing strategies, cost processes, plans, designs, source supply, methods, techniques, computer software, sales training, and testing techniques.[2]

Whether a document is a trade secret or not, it may still be regarded as confidential. For instance, financial worth isn't always a trade secret, but it may be confidential.

Whether a document is considered confidential depends on the manner in which your employer treats the handling of that document. For instance, have you been expressly informed that a particular document or documents are confidential? Have you signed a confidentiality agreement regarding handling of the documents?

Even if there is no express policy or agreement in place, what are the overall security controls being used? Do these security controls imply that the company regards the documents as private? For instance, are the documents usually locked up? Are you required to sign them out in order to access them? Are there signs posted stating they are confidential records? Do you need a security-level clearance to view them? Is a computer password needed to access them? Are they printed on paper that cannot be photocopied? Are non-employees allowed to view them?

All of these factors, and more, contribute to an overall judgment as to whether the documents are confidential.

Second, determine what your company policy is regarding the removal of confidential documents. Is a violation usually overlooked? Is the employee usually only minimally disciplined for it? Or is the employee fired in most cases?

If the employee is usually fired, you should *not* take the document(s). Doing so will give your employer legal grounds to fire you, and the after-acquired evidence rule will apply.

What if you know that a confidential document exists that will prove helpful to your case? Make a note of what that document is and where it's located. Give this information to your lawyer as quickly as possible so he or she can subpoena it.

You can ask anyone else in your workplace who has approval to access this information to take note of it as well. That way, if your employer causes it to "disappear" when the subpoena arrives, your employer will be in violation of the law.

Also, be careful when you collect and remove your personal

belongings from your work area that you don't take anything that belongs to the company. Otherwise, it can be considered theft, and once again the after-acquired evidence rule will apply.

An Appeal Process

Some employers offer an appeal process to terminated employees. If your employer does so, use it; if you don't, you may be prevented from claiming discrimination later.

Union employees are usually guaranteed an appeal process through their contract. Public employees have additional rights that prevent them from being terminated without first receiving a hearing and having the opportunity to appeal. Under the United States Constitution, the government cannot deprive any citizen (employees included) from their *property* (in this case, their job) without giving them *due process of law.* Due process means a fair hearing before getting fired.[3]

The government also may not deprive you of your *liberty.* If you're fired or disciplined in a way that adversely affects your reputation, it may infringe upon your liberty to seek a new job. Again, the government cannot take this right away without first giving you *due process of law*—that is, a fair hearing.[4]

Moreover, if you are a federal government union employee, the Federal Service Labor-Management Relations Statute also guarantees you a hearing with representation prior to being terminated.[5]

Loss of Benefits

WORKERS' COMPENSATION

If your job becomes so stressful because of discrimination that you are unable to work, you may be eligible to receive workers' compensation. Your employer may not fire you in retaliation for filing for workers' comp or because you receive any money for a workers' comp stress injury.

UNEMPLOYMENT

If you've been fired, constructively discharged, or laid off without good cause, you are probably eligible for unemployment. The unemployment form will ask you to state your reason for leaving your last job. If you believe it was due to discrimination, state that on the form. For instance, if you're fired for being late to work, but every man in your workplace is late every single day, then don't write "Fired for being late to work," but rather "My termination was due to the fact that my employer imposed a stricter standard of behavior for women than for men. My employer used my tardiness as a pretext to fire me. My employer daily tolerates tardiness from all my male coworkers, and has never disciplined a single one of them for it." If your boss has made any sex-based comments to you, include them as well. For instance, write "In addition, last week my boss told me he didn't think women belonged in the workplace."

Be sure that everything you write on the form is accurate and truthful. You will be signing a sworn statement to that effect.

One of the first places defense lawyers look when a woman files a discrimination complaint is to any government agencies, like the unemployment office, where she might have filed a sworn statement. They search for any contradictions you might have made.

In fact, some lawyers advise employers to oppose your right to receive unemployment compensation because the state will then hold an informal hearing. Employers will be present and log everything you say, realizing that at this early stage you don't usually have an attorney. If you later file a discrimination lawsuit, they will hunt for even the slightest contradiction in order to discredit your story. They can also subpoena the hearing officer to recount what you said.

HEALTH BENEFITS

Normally, federal law requires that your employer continue to provide you with medical insurance coverage for eighteen months after your employment ends. The law that guarantees you this right is the Consolidated Omnibus Budget Reconciliation Act of 1986, or COBRA.[6] During this period, *you,* and not your employer, must pay the premiums. You will, however, be entitled to the group insurance rate that your employer receives.

This law applies to employers of twenty or more people.

You lose your COBRA rights if you are fired for *gross insubordination.* Gross insubordination involves more than just not being good enough at what you do. It entails deliberately violating company policy, lying, cheating, or stealing.

In some instances, an employee is fired under the pretext of gross insubordination when in actuality the firing was discriminatory. If this is the case in your situation, it's crucial that you lodge a discrimination complaint both within the company and with the EEOC or comparable state agency. That way, there is a better chance that you will receive COBRA benefits. Even so, you may have to fight for them.

Beware the Exit Interview

When you leave a job, whether you quit or were fired, you're usually asked to participate in an "exit interview." Most employers tout this interview as an opportunity for you to offer "valuable insight" into how the company might be improved. After all this time working there, your employer finally is seeking your advice about the future of the company. You can actually gripe about every little nitpicky thing that's ever bothered you, and have somebody from the company sit and listen to you.

Unfortunately, an employer who truly wants advice from an employee doesn't wait until the employee is leaving to ask for it. In reality, your employer is only trying to avoid legal liability, and this is just another tool to assist employers in doing so—and an unethical tool at that. The interview itself isn't unethical, but rather the deceptiveness in how it's presented to you is. It's deceitfully pitched as a warm and fuzzy good-bye when in reality it's a scheme to deprive you of some of your rights and document your responses before you've had a chance to consult with a lawyer.

The main reasons for conducting exit interviews are the following:

First, an exit interview determines whether you have a problem that could evolve into an expensive lawsuit. If so, an employer wants the opportunity to salvage the situation before it gets to that stage. If you *do* complain of discrimination at this time, and your employer has not had a chance to investigate it before now, your employer should either temporarily rescind your termination (if you were fired), or ask you to withdraw your resignation (if you quit) until the investigation is complete. Otherwise, your employer has failed to adequately investigate discrimination complaints. Typically during this time, the employer sends you home with pay until your complaint has been investigated.

A second goal of an exit interview is to allow an employee to vent her frustrations. Employers believe that "being heard" defuses anger and frustration. I remember a joke that used to go around television news circles. "The most important thing in broadcasting is sincerity and credibility. Once you've learned to fake those, you've got it made." When the person conducting the interview sits there feigning concern, just remember that it's their job to do so. Can you really feel any satisfaction knowing that their purpose in listening so attentively is specifically to defuse you?

A third goal is to document your state of mind and well-being. If you ever file a discrimination lawsuit against your employer, you must show that the discrimination caused you damages, some sort of physical and/or emotional pain. If your employer can document that you were relaxed and untroubled the day you left the company, the employer can offer this information to prove that you really weren't affected at all.

A fourth goal in conducting an exit interview is to pin

down your story. Employers believe that if they record the facts immediately after your termination, the risk that you will fabricate additional incidents later is minimized. Unfortunately, in an exit interview you don't always remember all the incidents that are relevant. Moreover, you may be particularly distraught over being fired.

Many women are on guard during the exit interview, unsure of just how candid they should be. They are distrustful of how the information will be handled. As a result, they make a point *not* to bring up incidents involving discriminatory behavior. Others feel that since they're leaving, it's of no use. Still others fear that being candid might ruin their chances of getting a good reference.

You only hurt yourself if you're not honest at this point. Your employer may give you a bad reference regardless of whether you complain of discrimination during the exit interview. If so, you'll have difficulty proving the bad reference was based on discrimination, because you didn't speak of discrimination during the exit interview. It will sound like you're whining with an after-the-fact, fabricated excuse.

TWENTY QUESTIONS YOU'RE LIKELY TO BE ASKED—AND WHY

1. *Why are you leaving?* If your interviewer can document a reason for your leaving unrelated to discrimination, your employer can then rebut any discrimination claims you might have later on. Sometimes a woman gives multiple reasons for leaving, such as "My supervisor, Mr. Jones, told me a woman will never make it to an executive position in this company. Plus the hours are getting longer and I can't pick up my children from school on time."

   Your employer can point to your second reason as being partially responsible for your job loss. Therefore, your employer will be held only partially liable if you ever sue for discrimination.

Some women will offer vague or partially true statements, such as "I'm leaving because I want the opportunity to look for work elsewhere. I think I might be happier." What a women might fail to add is the underlying reason for her current feelings—that her working conditions have become intolerably discriminatory. The problem with giving partially true answers is that should you ever lodge a discrimination complaint, your employer will claim, "Her departure had nothing to do with discrimination. In fact, she never even mentioned discrimination during her exit interview. She just said she would be happier with a career change."

It's crucial that you clearly state your reason for leaving, and let the reason stand by itself. Any secondary reasons you give may later be twisted and used against you.

2. *Did you receive adequate training, and thus did you know fully your job responsibilities?* Sometimes employers do not fulfill their duty to provide an employee with everything she needs to do her job, including training. Employers want to go on record as having provided you with an adequate amount of training, so that if you failed at your job, it can't be construed as being their fault.

   Another aspect of this question is that if you don't know your job responsibilities, after your employer has given you training and a reasonable amount of time to learn them, the employer is justified in firing you.

3. *Are you satisfied with the work you performed here?* This question is designed to establish the fact that you were satisfied when you left and had no complaints. Any later complaint by you will be regarded with skepticism.

4. *Were you treated fairly?* If you don't bring up discrimination in response to this question, you have pretty much quashed your opportunity to complain of it at any future date.

5. *Are you satisfied with your pay and benefits?* If you say you are satisfied, you will be contradicting yourself later if you complain that you did not receive pay or a benefits package equal to that of your male counterparts.
6. *Were there adequate advancement and educational opportunities available?* Same as pay issues, discussed above, only this deals with promotions.
7. *What is the name and title of your supervisor?* Remember that the criterion for whether an employer is liable for sexual harassment may vary depending on the status of the person doing the discriminating—that is, there are different standards for a supervisor, a supervisor not your own, and a coworker. (See chapter 10, "Just Who Is Doing the Discriminating?") Therefore, it's important to list *all* the supervisors to whom you answered. That way you'll be making sure the company will be held responsible for the actions of all of them.
8. *Did you receive satisfactory supervision?* If you did not, the company may be liable for negligent supervision, especially if you were sexually harassed as a result of it.
9. *What is your opinion of your supervisor?* If your supervisor has been discriminating against you, now is the time to spell out exactly what he did to you.
10. *Did your supervisor treat you fairly?* If he didn't, say so. Otherwise, your answer here will be used against you.
11. *What was it like to work for the organization?* This question can address a number of issues, including whether your workplace can be construed as a hostile work environment.
12. *Were you satisfied with your working conditions?* More hostile environment fishing.
13. *Have you had any problems?* If you don't mention the discrimination here, then it will be tough convincing others that it even existed.

14. *Do you like your fellow workers?* Answering "Yes" to this question might provide a good defense for your employer if you later claim you were sexually harassed by a coworker.
15. *Was your decision to leave influenced by anything in particular?* If you say there was no particular reason, then you cannot later bring up your discrimination problem without contradicting yourself.
16. *If a suitable opportunity comes up in the future with our company, would you like to hear about it?* This question teases you into believing that you might actually get offered a better job (under a better supervisor). In actuality, should you ever complain of discrimination, your claim will be regarded as absurd, since obviously things were so great you wanted to come back and work.
17. *Do you know what the company's policies and procedures are?* In other words, did you do your job by reading and learning all applicable procedures?
18. *If so, did the company apply its policies consistently?* Remember, an employer is obligated to follow its own procedures or it risks being viewed as arbitrary, capricious, and discriminatory.
19. *Is there any area of the company or department that needs improvement?* If the company has discriminated against you, I suggest you mention it here.
20. *Is there anything else you want to add?* With this catchall question, an employer can show that you had ample opportunity to bring up discrimination, regardless of whether you were asked about it directly. Some employers go even further and ask you to sign a sworn statement that you've answered all these questions *thoroughly and completely.* Then, if you later add to the record, your story will be viewed as something you concocted to bolster your discrimination claim.

TACTICAL PLOYS SOME EMPLOYERS USE

Some employers schedule the exit interview in conjunction with giving you a final paycheck, in the hope that this will induce you to attend. But an employer cannot *require* you to submit to an exit interview as a condition of giving you what you are already owed. An employer *can* schedule an exit meeting in which to disburse your final paycheck and take care of other administrative matters, but cannot force you to answer the exit interview questions during this meeting.

Nor can your employer insist you take part in an exit interview as a condition of receiving whatever information you need regarding pension or health benefits due you, or any references you need to find another job.

Additionally, sometimes during an exit interview employers ask you to sign a statement acknowledging that you were treated fairly and were discharged for just cause. If this was not the case, then don't sign the statement.

SHOULD YOU GO TO THE EXIT INTERVIEW?

If you don't deal well with confrontation, and you know you'll likely fudge or water down your complaints in an attempt to "be nice" or not be "too confrontational," I suggest you skip the exit interview entirely. Why give your employer an opportunity to freely document, characterize, and mischaracterize everything you say?

Send a note to the person who requested the interview informing him or her that, given the discriminatory way you were treated by the company, you don't feel the exit interview would be conducted in good faith, and therefore you won't be participating.

If you find that too confrontational, or if it's too difficult to disentangle the exit interview appointment from other bookkeeping matters, then show up at the appointed time, inform the interviewer that you are not interested in taking part in the exit interview, offer to fill out whatever other paperwork is necessary, and ask for your final paycheck.

If he or she refuses to provide it, then immediately write out a note stating the date and time, the fact that you did show up for the appointment, and that your employer refused to give you your final paycheck and other necessary information as a consequence of your unwillingness to take part in the exit interview. Write that you did not want to take part in the exit interview because you believed the company has acted unfairly in the past and would attempt to use the information as documentation against your discrimination claim.

Make a copy and ask that the original be placed in your personnel file. Usually, depending on the state in which you live, an employer has a specific number of days in which to give you your paycheck. If your employer goes beyond that deadline, your note will help show not only that the employer broke the law, but may have done so for a reason that could be viewed as discriminatory.

Separation Agreements

Some employers offer money to departing employees in exchange for their promise not to sue. These agreements have various names, such as releases, separation agreements, severance agreements, and waivers.

It's legal for an employer to make you this offer, but you're not required to accept it. In addition, there are certain legal requirements with which your employer must comply in drawing up the release. The laws vary from state to state, so if your employer offers you a separation agreement, take the unsigned copy to a lawyer to review whether it complies with the law. Or you can hire the lawyer to negotiate it for you, which will be slightly more expensive but may net you more money since the lawyer may have more clout in negotiating.

Despite the varying laws, there are some provisions that apply to all releases.

WHEN EMPLOYERS OFFER SEPARATION AGREEMENTS

An employer who offers you a separation agreement is not necessarily admitting you were wronged. Employers view separation agreements as a means of buying insurance against "lawsuit roulette." They pay some money and then don't have to worry about getting sued by you.

Some employers regularly offer separation agreements to departing employees. Others never have, and probably never will. And some employers do so only occasionally.

A number of factors determine whether an employer makes such an offer, and if so, in what amount.

They consider your length of employment and whether the company violated any promises or policies in its treatment of you.

If you're being laid off, employers consider the reason behind the decision. For instance, if there's a restructuring that eliminates your position, it defuses your discrimination claim. If other workers were laid off at the same time, that further defuses your claim. In that case, your employer may feel more secure about letting you go without a separation agreement.

If you were fired, they also consider how well they documented their reason for firing you, and whatever other evidence or proof of discrimination is available. They ascertain whether your firing is consistent with the company's past practices in dealing with similar issues.

Employers also rate your credibility and demeanor. If your termination involves a dispute you had with a supervisor or coworker, your employer will assess the credibility of that person as well, including whether the person has a history of similar problems.

Your employer will take into account whether there was more than one person involved in the decision to fire you. It's much easier for employers to defend themselves if more than one person in the company agreed that you should be fired.

Whether you have a history of filing lawsuits will also be a factor, since that would indicate whether you might be inclined to do so again.

They will also check to see whether you have recently complained of discrimination. If so, an employer might be afraid that firing you will give the appearance of retaliation.

Finally, being in a "protected group" under the civil rights laws deserves mention here. A protected group includes women as well as racial and other minorities. Employers regard these groups as "high risk" when it comes to firing, and may be more inclined to offer separation agreements to members of these groups.

TYPICAL PROVISIONS

Generally, in a release you agree not to sue your employer. The law says you cannot "bargain away" your right to file a discrimination charge, because to do so would deprive you of your right to lodge a civil rights complaint. Separation agreements get around this dilemma by having you waive your right *to recover money* from any civil rights complaint, not your actual right to file it.

Separation agreements release employers from all these claims, regardless of whether they are known or unknown to you at the time. For instance, if you later learn that your male coworkers were making more money, the release prevents you from filing a pay discrimination lawsuit. The only exception to this is if your employer was fraudulent in disclosing information to you. For instance, if your employer knew about the pay disparity but gave you false information about it or denied having information to give you, the release would not be valid. You could then sue for fraud or fraudulent suppression of information.

Also, a release *cannot* waive your right to receive any wages due you. Nor can it waive your right to receive unemployment compensation, or compensation from an industrial injury, unless you have approval from your state agency that handles those claims.

Most releases also include a statement acknowledging that

you're an at-will employee, confirming that your employer has the right to fire you at any time.

The agreement must be simply written so that the average non-lawyer can easily understand it. It must also have a sentence informing you of its significance.

Employers also usually require a confidentiality provision whereby you promise not to disclose how much you received or, in some cases, the fact that you even signed the agreement. Employers are concerned that if word gets out, every employee will ask for one.

OLDER WORKERS

If you are forty or over, you may also be protected by the Age Discrimination in Employment Act, commonly called ADEA.[7] A release under ADEA must have certain specific provisions to ensure that your waiver is a "knowing and voluntary" one.[8] It must:

1. Be written in language that's understandable to non-lawyers.
2. Specifically refer to the fact that you are waiving your rights under ADEA. In other words, it cannot say only that you waive "all claims whatsoever."
3. Cover only claims that arose *before* you sign the release.
4. Pay you some money or benefit in exchange for waiving your rights under ADEA. This money or benefit must be over and above that to which you are already entitled.
5. State that you should consult with an attorney before signing it.
6. Require that you be given at least twenty-one days to review the document prior to signing it. If the release is to be signed in connection with a group layoff or exit incentive program, an employer must give you forty-five days to review the document prior to signing it.

7. Give you seven days *after* signing to change your mind and revoke it.
8. If your departure is in conjunction with a group layoff or exit incentive program, you have a right to know the ages and job titles of all other workers involved. This gives you an opportunity to determine whether the program was age discriminatory, as was the case with Dolores Oubre.

A forty-one-year-old maintenance scheduler at a Louisiana nuclear power plant, Oubre received more than $6,000 in exchange for signing a release that she would not sue the company. She later discovered, however, that her incentive layoff stemmed from age discrimination. The Supreme Court allowed her to sue the power plant for age discrimination despite having signed the release, because it had not been drawn up according to ADEA standards. In addition, the Supreme Court ruled that she *did not have to return the severance pay, but could still sue.*[9]

Severance packages may be designed to offer a series of payments or one lump sum. It's a matter of personal preference. Some employers prefer a series of payments because it gives them more control if, after taking some money, you then decide to sue.

What They Tell Others About You

When a person is fired, people in the workplace tend to gossip about the circumstances surrounding the event. Your employer, however, is not free to discuss or disclose your personal work situation with others. To do so may cause your employer to be liable for invasion of privacy, defamation, intentional infliction of emotional distress, and several other causes of action described later in this chapter.

JOB REFERENCES

Your employer is also limited in discussing your work when giving references. For instance, an employer cannot discuss your prior leaves of absence or medical information without authorization from you. Nor can an employer disclose that you filed a discrimination claim or give you a bad reference in retaliation for having done so.

DEFAMATION

If your employer makes an untrue statement about you that harms your reputation, then the employer may be guilty of defamation.

There are four untruths that are considered so foul that you need not prove actual damage to your reputation. Instead, the law *presumes* you've been damaged. They are:

- that you are guilty of having committed a criminal offense;
- that you are infected with what the courts consider to be a "loathsome" communicable disease. This includes diseases that have a history of having a social stigma attached to them, such as leprosy, venereal disease, and AIDS.
- that you are "unchaste." This includes telling others that you are sexually promiscuous, or referring to you by derogatory names, such as "slut" or "whore."
- that you have a lack of ability or integrity in doing your job. Merely stating that you've been fired is usually not defamatory, but it can be if it insinuates misconduct or lack of professional competence on your part.

The above four instances are called *per se defamation.*

If what your employer says about you falls outside of these four categories, it can still constitute defamation. In that case, your employer must have said or written these remarks with malice—that is, in a vicious way intended to harm you or sabotage your efforts at getting a new job.

Even if your employer does make these untrue remarks, he or she may *not* be liable for defamation if the remarks are considered to be *privileged.* Privileged remarks include statements made in the context of giving you a job recommendation. This is called a *qualified business privilege.* This very narrow exception is recognized in most states, but not all. Your employer must have good faith in believing that what's being said is truthful and serves a legitimate business need, such as a job reference. An employer cannot tell any more than is necessary, and the statement must be made on the proper occasion—that is, when *asked* for by a prospective employer. Most important, it must be told only to those people who have a *business need to know.*

To some extent, an employer will not be held liable for defamation if you have consented or authorized your employer to speak about you. On your original job application, you probably signed a statement authorizing your employer to give and receive any references on your behalf, and agreeing not to hold your employer liable for anything said. Some employers require this in order to prevent you from later suing if they give you a bad reference. You might want to think about narrowing the clause by inserting your own statement following theirs—something like this: *This approval authorized only for those who have a business need to know.* Or perhaps you might want to write, *I would prefer it if you check with me first before giving out any references.* Then initial it.

Many courts have held that an employer's attempt to obtain this waiver from you is invalid and ineffective, because although you gave consent to your employer to give a reference, you did *not* consent to be defamed, in which case you may still sue for defamation.

Another instance when your employer is not liable for defamation is if your employer makes any statements about you in the context of a legal proceeding. The purpose of this exception is to encourage people to speak freely in a court of law without fear of getting sued for defamation.

I've often heard advisers tell employers to give references only if they had good things to say about someone, and to give no references if they don't. The problem there is that a brisk "No comment" suggests a problem, and that's just as bad as if an employer had said something derogatory. It can still constitute defamation.

Compelled Self-Publication.
In some states, defamation may occur even if you are the one saying derogatory things about yourself. In one case, four women were fired for "gross insubordination" when they did not fill out their expense reports in the manner prescribed by company policy. In actuality, the company had sent them out of town on business for the first time, and had failed to instruct them on how to fill out reports. The company then fired them for gross insubordination, presumably for mishandling company funds.

The women attempted to get new jobs, but each was forced to disclose she'd been fired for gross insubordination. In essence, each was forced to defame herself with statements that were untrue. The four women successfully sued their former employer for defamation. Only a minority of states recognize compelled self-publication as defamation.[10]

INVASION OF PRIVACY

Sometimes an employer's remarks about you, even though truthful, constitute an invasion of privacy. This occurs when there is a *public disclosure of private facts.*

To constitute an invasion of privacy, the information that your employer relates to others must be embarrassing or humiliating—to the point where it would be highly offensive to a reasonable person—and not of legitimate concern to others.

In one case, a supervisor informed employees that one of their coworkers had recently undergone a mastectomy. A court ruled that the employer was liable for invasion of privacy.[11] In another case, a supervisor sexually harassed an employee, forcing her to have sexual relations with him, then disclosed to others that she had done so. He, too, was held liable for invasion of privacy.[12]

INTENTIONAL INFLICTION OF EMOTIONAL DISTRESS

An employer who reveals things about you, truthful or otherwise, in order to purposefully and spitefully hurt you may be liable for intentional infliction of emotional distress. This occurs if:

- your employer either *intended* to cause you distress or caused it out of reckless disregard
- severe emotional distress then resulted
- your employer's actions constituted conduct so outrageous that it's regarded as atrocious, beyond the bounds of decency, and utterly intolerable in a civilized community.

MISREPRESENTATION (NEGLIGENT OR INTENTIONAL)

An employer who goes out of his way to misrepresent a fact about you may be liable for misrepresentation. For that to occur:

- the employer must know that the information would be needed for an important purpose, such as your getting a new job
- the potential *new* employer intends to act upon the information
- you are then harmed as a result of it—that is, not given a job or offered a lesser job
- the employer either *knew* the information was false or was *careless* in mistakenly giving out wrong information that was harmful to you

INTERFERENCE WITH PROSPECTIVE ECONOMIC ADVANTAGE

If a potential employer decides not to hire you based on a false statement or inappropriate facts disclosed by a past employer, the past employer may be liable for interference with prospective economic advantage. In that case (1) there must be an actual reasonable expectation that you would have gotten the job; (2) your current or former employer must know about your expectancy when making the statement; (3) your current or former employer must have intentionally interfered; and (4) this caused you not to get the job.

MORE ABOUT REFERENCES

To avoid the possibility of getting sued, many employers simply give a name, rank, and serial number type of reference. Unfortunately, employers seeking to hire are then prevented from getting adequate feedback.

Sometimes, even though you were fired, your boss will offer to mischaracterize your departure as a layoff, resignation, or retirement. Employers propose this to avoid being liable for giving you a bad reference. In essence, you are both joining in a conspiracy to lie. Even so, it's an extremely common and accepted practice in the business world. Whether you want to engage in a ruse like this is a choice you have to make for yourself.

Finally, if you suspect that your past employer is giving you a bad reference, there are companies that specialize in documenting reference checks. They will call your former employer, seek a reference, and then document and transcribe conversations.

PART FOUR

TAKING ACTION

15.

Civil Rights Laws

We are confronted primarily with a moral issue. It is as old as the Scriptures and it is as clear as the American Constitution. The heart of the question is whether all Americans are to be afforded equal rights and equal opportunities, whether we are going to treat our fellow Americans as we want to be treated.

—President John F. Kennedy, discussing his civil rights bill, June 11, 1963. The bill passed one year later, eight months after his assassination.

I'll let you in on a little secret, but you must promise not to tell the guys. Women weren't supposed to be included in the Civil Rights Act of 1964—you know, that law that prohibits employers from discriminating on account of race, color, religion, national origin, *or sex.* A southern congressman, Howard Smith, proposed to add the word "sex" just before the House was to vote on it. He hoped the notion of giving women equal rights would be so outrageous that Congress would vote the entire civil rights bill down. His attempts at sabotage failed, and the Civil Rights Act of 1964 passed as amended.[1] As it stands, no other law has come close to affording women equal rights in the workplace.

Thank you, Howard.

In this chapter I'll give you a simplified mini-lecture on some civil rights laws. Many lawyers would probably not bother to explain the details of these laws to their clients. They feel the material is too complex to be understood by the general public. I disagree. I think it's easily understood if presented properly. Besides, if you aren't given the opportunity to understand how our civil rights laws work to protect you, how will you recognize when your civil rights are being violated? You won't.

School is now in session.

Title VII

Title VII is that part of the Civil Rights Act of 1964 that prohibits discrimination in the workplace. Title VII reads:

> It shall be an unlawful employment practice for an employer—
>
> 1) to fail or refuse to hire or to discharge any individual, or otherwise to discriminate against any individual with respect to his compensation, terms, conditions, or privileges of employment, because of such individual's race, color, religion, sex, or national origin; or
>
> 2) to limit, segregate, or classify his employees or applicants for employment in any way which would deprive or tend to deprive any individual of employment opportunities or otherwise adversely affect his status as an employee, because of such individual's race, color, religion, sex, or national origin.[2]

Title VII applies to any and all terms, conditions, or privileges of employment.

Discrimination based on sex includes discrimination based on pregnancy.[3] It does not include discrimination based on sexual orientation.[4]

FIFTEEN PEOPLE OR MORE

Title VII applies to employers of fifteen or more people. The reason for this cutoff is that lawmakers wanted to protect the privacy of small mom-and-pop operations, and avoid putting them out of business as a result of the financial burden of complying with Title VII.

Assessing whether an employer has fifteen workers is complex at times. What if an employer has ten full-time and five part-time employees? Or what if an employer has fifteen people but eight work for a subsidiary? Or perhaps an employer has fifteen employees but fires one (you) for discriminatory reasons. Does your employer then qualify as having fifteen workers under Title VII?

Here's how the courts untangle these issues.

Fifteen employees means your employer has fifteen people on the payroll for twenty weeks out of the calendar year in which the discrimination occurred. The fifteen people need not all have been present in the workplace on the same day and during the same hours; they just must be officially on the payroll during that time in order to be counted. The twenty weeks do not have to be in a row; any twenty weeks during the year will qualify your employer.

Also, the twenty weeks need not include or overlap the time you actually worked there. As an example, if you are discriminated against and fired in January and your boss has only ten employees, he is not liable under Title VII. If, however, he hires five more employees in May, he now qualifies as having fifteen employees. After he's had these fifteen employees for twenty weeks, he's liable under Title VII for the discrimination he committed against you in January.

A part-time worker counts the same as a full-time employee, so an employer could have fifteen part-time workers and still be held accountable under Title VII.

If an employer splits a company into small subsidiaries, each of which has fewer than fifteen employees, then Title VII may or may not apply. You must ask, "Does the parent company have the right to control your work environment?" or "Does the parent company provide funding for the subsidiary?" If the answer is yes to either of these questions, the companies can be counted as one when tallying up the number of employees.

Some state antidiscrimination laws have thresholds lower than fifteen employees. For a state-by-state breakdown of the minimum number of employees required in order for an employer to be liable under each state's antidiscrimination laws, see Table I.

DISPARATE TREATMENT AND DISPARATE IMPACT

Under Title VII, your employer's actions can be considered discriminatory under two rubrics, disparate treatment and disparate impact.

Disparate treatment occurs when your employer institutes a rule, policy, or decision that treats you, or women in general, differently than your male counterparts. An example of a disparate treatment decision is paying a woman less than a man, or promoting her at a slower rate than men. An example of a disparate treatment rule would be "Women are not allowed to be police officers."

Disparate impact occurs when an employer institutes a rule, policy, or decision that adversely impacts either you or women in general. An example would be a rule such as "All police officers shall be a minimum of 5'10" tall and weigh at least 175 pounds." Even though this rule doesn't specifically *exclude* women, its *impact* eliminates most of them from this employment opportunity.

DISPARATE TREATMENT

To prove a disparate treatment case, you must be able to show that your employer *purposefully* treated you differently than men. You can do this with direct evidence, such as a written memo or a spoken statement by your employer that expresses a discriminatory reason for taking adverse action against you.

But having such direct evidence is rare. Instead, many women rely on circumstantial evidence. In this instance, you can show that you had substantially the same qualifications as your male counterparts but were treated less favorably.

Your employer must then come up with a valid reason for why the adverse action was taken against you. Typically, an employer might argue that you've violated company rules or policies; have lesser qualifications than your male counterparts; can't get along with coworkers or supervisors; had poor test scores; or another seemingly rational explanation.

Once your employer comes up with a "reason" for the adverse action, you must then prove this reason is a pretext—an invented excuse that masks discrimination. To do this, you can show that (1) men were treated better than women; (2) your treatment departed from standard policies and procedures; (3) your treatment departed from your employer's past treatment of you; (4) your employer's general policy and practice with respect to minority employment in general is discriminatory; or (5) statistics show a disparity in your workplace on hiring, pay, promotions, or other work-related issues.

Here are some examples of how my lawyers tried to prove these things:

We offered the "mommydom memo" as direct evidence.

For circumstantial evidence, we subpoenaed the salaries of all CNN reporters in an attempt to show a statistical disparity based on gender. We also subpoenaed an in-house "diversity study" that CNN had conducted on itself. I cannot discuss the contents of the study or the salaries, however, because our trial judge issued a "protective order" at CNN's request. When a protective order is issued, the court uses the information, but it is not to be released to the general public.

We attempted to show my employer's overall policy of discrimination and ill treatment of women by the testimony of various employees:

Example #1: The Disappearing Women.

ATTORNEY FOR PANICCIA: How long after you got there did you form the opinion that the L.A. bureau was discriminatory against women?

WITNESS #1: You know, I'm not sure I can give you a time frame. I just remember as time went on, one by one, women started disappearing from the [assignment] desk, except in the early-morning hours or except as desk assistants or as free-lancers, they wouldn't get hired on. The guys would get hired on, the women would be kept as free-lancers. . . .

Example #2: The Assertive Woman.

ATTORNEY FOR PANICCIA: [T]ell me in general what you talked to [CNN Human Resources] about. . . .

WITNESS #2: I spoke with her about the gender bias that exists in the bureau as far as promotional practices, that I felt that at least one person that I knew was let go and it was a gender-based decision.

ATTORNEY FOR PANICCIA: Who was that person?

WITNESS #2: [A CNN assignment desk editor.]

ATTORNEY FOR PANICCIA: What else?

WITNESS #2: I think the general feeling in the bureau of, again, as it being a very hostile environment and feeling of not really promoting creativity. It was one where you really can't have a personality; you have to be very, very staid and very quiet. And that a woman who is aggressive—to my knowledge, all the women that I've seen who are aggressive are not looked at favorably and in fact, may be driven out.

Example #3: What's a Girl to Do?

ATTORNEY FOR PANICCIA: Based on the knowledge that you do have of what people earn there, does there seem to be a bias against women when comparing the pay that women receive for doing the same job as men at CNN?

ATTORNEY FOR CNN: Objection. No foundation. Calls for speculation and conclusion. And it's irrelevant.

WITNESS #3: I think so. But it's probably true in any place you work these days. Yes, I believe so, that there's discrepancies in the way women are paid versus the way men are paid. And, of course, the management will probably have ways of justifying that. And, you know, what are you going to do?

BFOQ as a Defense.

In disparate treatment cases, employers are *allowed* to discriminate based on sex if they can prove that being of a certain sex is necessary to do the job. The exception is called *bona fide occupational qualification*, or BFOQ.

For an employer to successfully use BFOQ as a defense for discriminatory practices, the employer must establish that:

1. Gender is so essential to job performance that a member of the opposite sex could not perform the work. In this case, an employer must have a reasonable factual basis to believe that all or substantially all women would be unable to perform safely and efficiently the duties of the job involved. This factual basis cannot be a preconceived notion based on stereotyped conclusions about women's weaker physiques or incapacities.
2. The particular task they cannot perform is *essential* to doing the job. Specifically, is this task so reasonably necessary to the operation of the business that the essence of the business would be undermined if employees of the "wrong" sex were hired? For instance, if you are a restaurant food server and at the end of the night you're required to carry four cases of wine to restock the kitchen but are unable to lift them, then is carrying those four boxes essential to performing the overall duties of food serving? Probably not.

Problems often arise when an employer's definition of the essence of the business differs from the employee's definition.

In the 1970s, Southwest Airlines catered mostly to male business travelers and hired only sexy female flight attendants, who dressed in hot pants and high boots. Southwest, based out of Love Field in Dallas, Texas, instituted the company slogans "Somebody Up There Loves You" and "We're Spreading Love All Over Texas."

The airline refused to hire male flight attendants, claiming their presence onboard would cause the airline to lose passengers. Southwest contended that the essence of its business was sex appeal.

The court disagreed, saying that female sex appeal was not a bona fide occupational qualification of being a flight attendant.[5]

Let's apply the first prong of the test: Did Southwest reasonably believe that female sex appeal was so essential to performing the job that a member of the opposite sex couldn't do it? The court, not without a sense of humor, answered, "Love, while important, is not everything in the relationship."[6] Although sex appeal was one aspect of performing the job, it was not the main aspect. It was only tangential to the main duties, which included passenger safety, ticketing and assisting passengers, checking baggage, and similar tasks. The court ruled that if a job requires multiple abilities, some sex-linked (female sex appeal) and some sex-neutral (passenger safety), the sex-linked aspects must predominate in order to justify a BFOQ. In this case, the sex-linked aspects did not predominate, and therefore men should be allowed to be flight attendants.

Let's apply the second prong: Is female sex appeal such an essential part of the job that the essence of the business would be undermined if men were allowed to be flight attendants? The court said no. There was no proof that Southwest would lose business if males were hired.

There have been rare instances where courts have allowed female sexuality as a BFOQ. Usually these exceptions include jobs like topless dancer or prostitute (legal in Nevada). A job as a Playboy Club cocktail waitress was decided to be a BFOQ exception based on the notion that the essence of the job was to "titillate and entice" the male clientele.[7]

More recently Hooters Restaurant, known for its scantily clad cocktail servers, was sued for refusing to hire men. Hooters claimed that female sexuality was a BFOQ and that the restaurant's business purpose was "providing vicarious sexual recreation." Hooters ignored an EEOC ruling requiring the restaurant to hire men, and instead launched an ad campaign that showed a burly man in a blond wig and Hooters uniform with the words "Come on Washington. Get a grip."[8] Eventually, however, Hooters settled out of court, agreeing to hire men and pay a total of $2 million to those men who had previously applied and been turned down.

As for Southwest Airlines, the company abandoned its love policy and recast itself as a low-cost, no-frills airline. It has since become a highly successful enterprise.

Customer Preference as a BFOQ.

Even if Southwest Airlines had shown that customers preferred female flight attendants, that still would probably not have been enough to warrant a BFOQ exception.

If customer preference were allowed to be an excuse not to hire someone, then a restaurant owner could refuse to hire certain races or minority groups by claiming the clientele didn't want them there. Viewed in that light, it's easy to see why customer preference could end up being nothing more than a reflection of customer bigotry. Therefore, it should not be a valid excuse.

An American business, Wynn Oil Company, refused to hire women to deal with its South American clients. Wynn insisted that cultural prejudices would prevent South Americans from doing business with female oil company executives. The court ordered Wynn to hire women anyway, noting that "stereotypic impressions of male and female roles" was not enough to invoke the BFOQ exception, nor justify discriminatory conduct.[9]

A rare instance where customer preference *can* justify a BFOQ exception is when a safety issue arises. A female corrections officer was disallowed from working in the high-security area of an all-male prison because the court felt a female's presence would disrupt the peace and therefore undermine the essence of the business—which was to keep the facility peaceful and secure.*

Authenticity as a BFOQ.

Another instance where customer preference might be used to justify a BFOQ exception is for *authenticity's* sake. An owner of a French restaurant, for instance, might want to employ only a French chef. Similar reasoning might apply to a casting director who wants a male or female for the part (although even that situation has been successfully challenged at times).

Privacy as a BFOQ.

If a customer's preferences are based on privacy interests, they may be weighty enough to justify a BFOQ exception. This typically occurs with custodians (where the worker must clean public rest rooms); nurses (who must tend to intimate functions of a person's body); health club trainers (who touch the private areas of one's body); and any other job that requires the worker to be present while the client disrobes, sleeps, or performs bodily functions. As one court stated, "The purpose of the Civil Rights Act is to eliminate sex discrimination in employment, not to make over the accepted mores and personal sensitivities of the American people."[10]

The bottom line is that a customer's privacy must be balanced against an employee's right to work. The more invasive the intru-

*Dothard v. Rawlinson, 97 S. Ct. 2720 (1977).

sion into a person's private sexuality, the more likely an employer can use BFOQ as an excuse to hire only one sex.

DISPARATE IMPACT

Under the disparate impact theory, you must be able to show that a job requirement or policy impacts disproportionately on women, and that this requirement or policy is not related to job performance.

It's not necessary that an employer *intends* to discriminate against women, only that the *impact* of the rule or decision does so.

An unnecessary height and weight requirement, such as that in the police officer example discussed earlier, disproportionately impacts women. It would be up to you to show that this restriction has little or no relationship to the job of keeping the peace.[11]

Business Necessity as a Defense.

In order to use business necessity as a defense for a disparate impact claim, an employer must show that the particular skill, test, or attribute required has a *manifest relationship* to a legitimate business purpose.

In response, you can recommend other valid methods or procedures the employer can use that will serve the employer's interests in selecting someone who can do the job. For instance, you could recommend that an employer use strength and agility tests in place of height and weight requirements. If the court finds that the less-discriminatory methods you've suggested are just as good at winnowing out the unsuitable police officers, you've won your case.

OTHER TITLE VII DEFENSES

There are four other defenses an employer can use against either a disparate treatment or disparate impact claim. They are the same four discussed under the Equal Pay Act section of this book: merit, production, seniority, and "any other factor other than sex."

For a more detailed explanation of these defenses, see chapter 5, "Receiving Less Pay and Fewer Benefits."

REMEDIES AND DAMAGES

What remedies are available to you if your employer violates Title VII? You are allowed to ask for any of the following, but the final decision is up to a judge or jury. You can request that you be hired for the job or position you were denied or be given any seniority you've lost as a result of discrimination.

You can request a court order that your employer end a particular discriminatory policy or practice.

You can ask for back pay, which would probably include any lost earnings from the time the discrimination occurred. It would not, however, go back more than two years before the time you filed a complaint with the EEOC. Your back pay may include wages, bonuses, customary overtime, health benefits, vacation or sick pay, retirement contributions, and any other compensation you typically would have received. Remember, though, that under the after-acquired evidence rule (discussed in chapter 14, "You're Fired") your back pay may be severely limited if your employer learns you've committed a violation of company policy.

Also, if you find another job in the interim, your back pay will be offset by whatever you receive from your new job. In some courts, back pay is also offset by any unemployment compensation you might have received.

You have a duty to "mitigate" damages. This means you have a responsibility to seek another job with reasonable diligence, and accept any offer of comparable employment. You're also obliged to accept your own employer's offer of unconditional reinstatement. Otherwise, back pay cannot be awarded at all.

You can also request "front pay," which is lost earnings from the day the court decides your case until the day you receive a new job in a comparable position. Usually, front pay is an estimated amount.

Compensatory damages can also be awarded. This means you can be reimbursed for what you paid out, for your inconvenience, and also to make up for any suffering you endured.[12]

Finally, in most cases you can receive punitive damages. These damages are awarded when a court recognizes that your employer committed discrimination with malice or reckless indifference to your rights. The court (judge or jury) then decides to punish your employer by allowing extremely large punitive damage amounts. In doing so, the court is also sending a message to discourage other employers from discriminating.[13]

Punitive damages are allowed in cases of *intentional* discrimination—that is, disparate treatment cases—but not in disparate *impact* cases.

Under the Civil Rights Act of 1991, the amount of punitive and compensatory relief for intentional discrimination is restricted to the following amounts:

If your employer has 15 to 100 employees—$50,000
If your employer has 101 to 200 employees—$100,000
If your employer has 201 to 500 employees—$200,000
If your employer has 501 employees or more—$300,000

Punitive damages are not allowed if your employer is the federal government. Nor are they allowed in intentional cases that involve *mixed motives*, which is discussed in the next section.

MIXED MOTIVES

Sometimes an employer will fire or demote a woman for several reasons—only one of which is discriminatory. This kind of case is called *mixed motive.* If yours is a mixed-motive case, you are severely limited as to the amount of money you can receive in damages under Title VII.

If your employer can prove by a *preponderance of the evidence* that the adverse decision against you would have been made even without the discriminatory motivation, then you cannot receive any compensatory or punitive damages. In fact, all you're entitled to is an order from the court instructing your employer to stop the discriminatory behavior. You cannot ask to be hired, rehired, or promoted.[14]

It's easy to see why employers search so diligently for fake reasons to justify discriminatory firings. If they can convince a court they had at least one valid reason for terminating you, your damages are reduced to almost nothing.

Who's Excluded from Title VII and Why

Certain employers and organizations are exempt from Title VII for a variety of reasons:

RELIGIOUS ORGANIZATIONS

Religious organizations and churches do not always have to comply with Title VII because of the separation in this country of church and state. We don't want our government telling our churches what to do. (By "churches" we mean churches, temples, mosques, and other places of religious worship.)

What if a church insists on hiring only men for a job because church doctrine prohibits women from holding that position? It depends. If the job directly relates to an aspect of the faith, then Title VII will not force the religious institution to hire a woman. If, however, the job has nothing to do with the faith, such as that of a janitor on church grounds, then Title VII *does* apply.

A Catholic university was allowed to reserve a portion of its teaching staff jobs to Jesuit priests (all male) in the belief that their teachings would enhance the faith. But the university was *not* allowed to discriminate when it came to more secular jobs, such as school administrators and clerical workers.

A Christian school offered health insurance benefits only to its male employees, claiming that, according to the Bible, only men should be head of the household. A court rejected that argument, saying that the school could avoid having to comply with Title VII only with respect to persons hired to carry out the religious activities of the school.[15]

PRIVATE CLUBS

Private membership clubs are another exception under Title VII. The First Amendment guarantees us the freedom to associate without the government intruding upon us. Title VII is seen as government intrusion—telling us whom we must associate with or hire inside our private clubs.

The question is, just what constitutes a private club? The EEOC looks at several factors, including whether the organization:

- is a club in the ordinary sense of the word—that is, a gathering of persons for social and recreational purposes or for the promotion of some common objective (such as literature, science, or political activity)
- has specific requirements for membership, such as references, formal applications, or club rules
- limits its facilities and services strictly to members or to guests of members
- is controlled and owned by the membership
- is operated for profit
- uses public advertisement to solicit members or to promote use of its facilities by the general public

(Note that these criteria are slightly different from those discussed in chapter 9, "You're Not in the Club," which determine whether an organization is a private club for the purpose of falling under a state's public accommodations law.)

CONGRESS AND THE PRESIDENT

Until 1991, Congress did not fall under Title VII. Remember that there are three branches of government—the executive, legislative, and judiciary—all of which are supposed to remain independent of each other under our Constitution. This separation of powers is designed to ensure that no one branch gains too much control and thus has an opportunity to abuse its power toward the people. The system maintains a balance of power.

Title VII didn't apply to Congress because Congress, the *legislative* branch of the government, would have had to answer to the EEOC, the *executive* branch of the government. This would infringe on the separation of powers.

In 1995, however, the Congressional Accountability Act made Congress accountable under Title VII, with one exception. Congressional complaints are filed not through the EEOC but through the Office of Compliance—which is part of the legislative branch of government.[16]

Similarly, the Presidential and Executive Office Accountability Act, signed into law in 1996, holds the executive branch of the government (i.e., the president and presidential administration) accountable under Title VII.

Under the Presidential and Executive Office Accountability Act, discrimination complaints are lodged at and investigated by a newly formed office called Inspector General of the Executive Office.

JUDICIAL BRANCH OF THE FEDERAL GOVERNMENT

If you are a civil service federal courts employee, you are covered under Title VII. If, however, you are *non*–civil service, Title VII does *not* apply because of the separation-of-powers concern. Unlike Congress and the President, federal judges have had no law passed that holds them accountable under Title VII. Instead, any discrimination claim must be filed on the sole legal grounds that the discrimination violates the basic provisions of the United States Constitution. These claims are filed through an internal complaint procedure set up by and for the federal courts.

FEDERAL GOVERNMENT

Federal employees have also been granted Title VII protection, and they report violations to either the EEOC or the Merit Systems Protection Board (MSPB).

U.S. MILITARY

Members of the United States military are not covered under Title VII. Civilian employees working for the military are.

OTHER MISCELLANEOUS EXCEPTIONS

Indian tribes are not accountable under Title VII.

Foreign countries employing U.S. citizens must comply with Title VII unless doing so would violate the law of that country.

Other Types of Discrimination Lawsuits

Typically, a discrimination lawsuit charges an employer with violating not only Title VII but other laws as well, such as wrongful termination, intentional infliction of emotional distress, breach of contract, and breach of public policy. Therefore, even if Title VII offers limited damages, these other claims often allow for large punitive-damage awards.

Most must be filed in court within one year from the date the violation occurred, but this requirement varies from state to state.

Recovering Your Attorney's Fees

In all types of discrimination claims, you are entitled to receive attorney fees and court costs if you win. Although technically an employer can ask for the same if you lose, most courts will not grant them to an employer unless the employee's lawsuit is extremely unreasonable or frivolous.

Local Laws

Most states have their own laws that mirror Title VII. Usually you have a choice between using federal or state law. (See chapter 18, "If All Else Fails . . . See You in Court," for the advantages and disadvantages of both.) State laws are too numerous and varied to discuss in detail.

Occasionally municipalities or other local governments pass their own laws as well. San Francisco has a citywide ordinance that prohibits discrimination based on sexual orientation. Even though sexual orientation discrimination is not covered under Title VII, anyone within city limits is bound by that city's antidiscrimination law.

Schools and Title IX

Schools are subject not only to Title VII but to Title IX, which states:

> No person in the United States shall, on the basis of sex, be excluded from participation in, be denied the benefits of, or be subjected to discrimination under any education program or activity receiving Federal financial assistance.[17]

In 1997, Title IX nearly flunked out of school.

The National Coalition for Women and Girls in Education issued an official "report card" on Title IX, evaluating twenty-five years of progress since it was first passed.

The highest grade Title IX received was a B– in Access for Women to Higher Education. Most of the grades in subjects like

Career Education, Learning Environment, Math, and Science were C or C–. The very worst grade was in Sexual Harassment, which received a D+. The report noted that 81 percent of eighth- through eleventh-graders had experienced sexual harassment at school.[18] Title IX was passed initially to assist students. (Since students aren't employees, they had no protection under Title VII.) Our courts, however, have interpreted Title IX as giving protection to educational employees as well.

If you work for a school that receives federal funding, you can sue under both Title VII and Title IX.

A sex discrimination claim under Title IX is analyzed the same as those under Title VII, but the remedies differ. Under Title IX, there is a question as to whether your employer can be ordered to pay you damages. Although some courts have allowed it, others have ruled that only students, and not employees, can receive money damages under Title IX.

The sole remedy for employees under Title IX is a revocation of federal funding from the learning institution. Although this can be a powerful deterrent to discrimination, it may not adequately compensate you as an individual for any pain and suffering you might have endured. For that reason, many educational employees choose to proceed under both Title VII and Title IX.

Title IX complaints are filed not at the EEOC but at the Office of Civil Rights under the United States Department of Education.

16.

Complaining to the EEOC

CNN, recently merged with Time Warner, "acted like a typical large corporation," Paniccia said Wednesday. "They circled their wagons and began shooting at me."
—*USA Today,* January 4, 1996

I'll let you in on a very embarrassing personal thought. When I first filed my discrimination complaint, I actually thought that when Ted Turner and Jane Fonda heard about it, they would immediately say, "Oh, how terrible! CNN did that to her? This shouldn't be allowed to go on. Let's fix this thing right now."

Initially, my lawyer had written a fourteen-page letter informing CNN of my discrimination complaint. In response, we received a short, curt letter from an attorney in the corporate office of Turner Broadcasting. It stated that she had conducted an investigation and that my "sex and medical condition [pregnancy] had nothing to do with my departure." It also declared that CNN was "prepared to defend itself if necessary." CNN, however, would be willing to talk with me, presumably to offer what employers refer to as a "nuisance payoff." CNN probably was considering offering a nominal amount of money just to get me, a nuisance, out of its hair.

What a miserable solution, I thought. What satisfaction could I get taking a small payoff that would then allow the company to continue to treat women poorly and never acknowledge a problem, let alone try to fix it? Word of how I'd been treated just hadn't gone high enough, I figured. I needed to make enough noise so that Ted and Jane would hear about it. They'd make things right. I just knew it.

So if anybody has a bridge they want to sell, I guess I'm the person you're looking for.

It's foolish to expect an employer to acknowledge *anything* once you've filed a complaint. As one employment defense lawyer later told me, "At that point, just doing the right thing isn't always an alternative for an employer. Once you've filed a charge or hired a lawyer, for employers it just becomes a matter of defending themselves."

Sometimes the truth behind your allegations never reaches the top. Either the upper management is too busy to deal with problems of this nature, or midlevel executives are frightened of the repercussions from something that happened on their watch. As a result, they may not relay the full extent and truth of your allegations.

Although some companies have the civility and good intentions to work with you throughout their in-house complaint procedure, even those companies will now begin treating you like the enemy once you've filed a complaint. In their eyes, you've made serious charges that they cannot afford to take lightly. You may have jeopardized the company's financial stability, and possibly even tarnished its public image.

If they haven't already done so, many employers contact

lawyers at this point who advise them step-by-step on how to respond to your EEOC complaint. The lawyers will enter the process playing hardball.

What to Expect

Although Title VII protects you from retaliation for complaining of discrimination, it cannot prevent your employer from denying or discounting your allegations, or from offering false explanations to discredit your story.

Although you may have never heard a single complaint about your work, you should now be prepared to hear a wide variety of condemnations and criticisms.

Jasmine L. worked for five years as a records and file clerk for a large insurance company, never once receiving negative reviews. When a male coworker with less experience was promoted over her, she asked for the same promotion. Her boss agreed she was an excellent employee and told her she would be promoted to a new position that would be created the following month. Six months later, she still hadn't been promoted. Jasmine complained again and this time was told company cutbacks had prevented the new position from being made available. She then asked to be promoted to the same job as her male coworker, but the company refused. She filed a complaint with the EEOC.

> *I was shocked. They told the EEOC that this guy was a better employee! They said I was slow—that I didn't get files up to the offices fast enough and that sometimes files would be missing or hard to find. It was all bull. They never told me stuff like this before. They always said, "Oh, Jasmine, you're doing a great job. Oh, Jasmine, thanks for all your help. Oh, Jasmine, we can't organize this stuff without you." But what they told the EEOC . . . they were just covering their butts.*

You might ask yourself, as a friend of mine did, "Can I just walk away from it at this stage?" She was fearful of encountering this degree of aggression from her employer.

Only you can decide whether you are strong enough and motivated enough to take your fight to the next level. But if you decide to let it go, you must be resolved to tolerate the discrimination.

You could possibly wait it out until your boss retires, gets transferred, or is laid off. Or you could quit and find a new job. If you work for a large company, you might be able to apply for a transfer to a different department. Under the law, your new supervisor should not be informed of your complaint.

If you decide to go through with filing a complaint, however, don't be discouraged or frightened. The EEOC can be the great equalizer. It can allow a single person to fight a multibillion-dollar corporation . . . and win. Unfortunately, it can also be the great bureaucratic paper mess.

This chapter will give you a cursory overview on how to file your EEOC claim.

One piece of advice: If your supervisor believes you're a good employee, this is your last chance to get a letter of recommendation—*before* you file your charge. I managed to obtain two letters from CNN before they were notified of my complaint. Not only was I able to use them for prospective employers, but during my lawsuit, in the midst of CNN's attacks on my credibility and my work, the same letters were admitted into evidence.

Should You Have a Lawyer?

I usually advise consulting a lawyer *before* filing with the EEOC.

One crucial reason is that you'll be making a statement under oath that will be key evidence should you file a lawsuit.

CNN asked the court in my case not to allow evidence of other women's experiences. The network objected on grounds that I had never mentioned in my original EEOC complaint that other employees had experienced discrimination. Therefore I should not later be allowed to bring in evidence about other women.

In fact, my EEOC affidavit included the following statement: *I am aware of about six other females who have filed sex discrimination complaints, but they are afraid of losing their jobs, and I will attempt to secure the names for the investigator who receives my charge.*

My lawyers pointed this out to the judge, and CNN was ordered to turn over the evidence. Had I not included the statement about the other women, I doubt we would have had grounds to obtain the evidence.

There are many strategies, like this one, that defense lawyers will use to defeat your claim. An attorney will help you phrase your EEOC complaint so that you avoid inadvertently giving up your rights.

Another important reason for getting legal advice at this early stage is that you have two choices as to where to lodge your complaint—either the federal EEOC or your state's human rights agency—thus designating which court you will end up in should you file a lawsuit. This is a critical legal decision, and one that could ultimately mean the success or failure of your case. Some state agencies grant employees more rights than does the federal EEOC. Other state agencies overwhelmingly favor employers. You need to make a tactical decision at this early stage, depending on the state in which you live and the facts of your case. An attorney can help you do that.

Even if you don't retain an attorney to represent you officially at this stage, you should at least consult with one to have him or her review any paperwork before you file it. You will probably have to pay an hourly fee for the lawyer's time. If the lawyer is familiar with employment law, it should take no more than two hours.

I realize paying for an attorney may be financially difficult, especially if you've just been fired. On the day I was fired, I came home to find eight workers on top of my house, installing a new roof. (I had scheduled them two weeks before, but had managed to forget about them during the confusion surrounding my termination.) For the next three days, I sat inside crying while their incessant pounding overhead served as a continual reminder of how much money I would owe when they finished the job.

Not to mention that it just made my head ache.

I know it's tough to justify spending money if you've just been fired. But paying a lawyer makes sense. (It beats paying a roofer.)

Federal Versus State

Since each state differs when it comes to discrimination laws and procedures, it would be impossible to describe each state's organizational setup. The overall procedures in the various states are similar enough to the EEOC's that this summary of federal procedures should give you a basic understanding of the process.

You should call your state human rights commission to determine specific deadlines and investigation procedures. For a state-by-state list of human rights commission offices, see Table III.

What Is the EEOC and Why File?

The Equal Employment Opportunity Commission (EEOC) is the federal agency Congress established to take discrimination complaints under Title VII, the Equal Pay Act, the Age Discrimination in Employment Act, and the Americans with Disabilities Act.

There are two reasons why you would want to file an EEOC charge.

First, the EEOC may solve your discrimination problem without your having to hire a lawyer (other than for the hour or two advising you on how to file your complaint). If your resources are low, the EEOC may be a good alternative.

Second, it's the "gateway" to filing a discrimination lawsuit. You cannot file a Title VII lawsuit unless you first lodge an EEOC complaint. The EEOC gives you permission to file a lawsuit by issuing you a *right-to-sue letter.*

Is There a Deadline?

The deadline to file with the EEOC depends on whether your state has its own antidiscrimination agency.

If your state has none, then you may file directly with the EEOC and must do so within 180 days from when the discriminatory act occurred.[1]

If you were discriminated against by not being hired, then the 180 days begins the day someone else fills the position. If you were refused promotion, the 180 days begins the day your employer notifies you that someone else will fill the position. If you were fired, it begins the day you were terminated or the day you were notified of the termination, whichever is sooner.

If your state has its own antidiscrimination agency, you must file with that state agency *before* you file with the EEOC. You can then choose to stay with your state agency or the EEOC.

If you choose the EEOC, you may refile your charge with the EEOC sixty days after you've filed with the state. You might be able to file sooner than sixty days if your state agrees to terminate its proceedings before the sixty days are up. You then have thirty days after the state terminates its proceedings to file with the EEOC.[2]

If you intend for the EEOC, and not your state agency, to ultimately investigate your claim, you can file your state claim directly with the EEOC. In that case, the EEOC will forward your complaint to the state, but the state will not act on it. At the end of the sixty-day waiting period, your complaint will automatically be considered filed at the EEOC.

If you miss these deadlines, you will probably be prevented from pursuing your discrimination claims.

THE LAST ACT OF DISCRIMINATION

Don't make the mistake of miscalculating when the last act of discrimination took place. A college professor was denied tenure and then dismissed one year later because he had failed to make tenure. Did the actual discrimination occur when he was denied the tenure, or on his last day of work? The U.S. Supreme Court ruled it was the day he was denied tenure and that he had 180 days from that date to file a complaint. Therefore, he had missed the deadline.[3]

Employment defense lawyers love these gray areas, because it gives them legal grounds to have your case dismissed. As one defense lawyer said, "The law is vague when it comes to determining exactly what constituted the last act of discrimination. And it's a big fat question on those EEOC complaints as to just when the last act of discrimination occurred. If you mess up, you may be handing your case on a platter to some defense lawyer."

Sometimes a woman undergoes a *series* of discriminatory actions by her employer. She may try to avoid filing an EEOC complaint, thinking she can work it out herself. Eventually, things may get so bad that she has no other choice but to file. She must then prove that the last act of discrimination occurred within the last 180 days. If she can also prove that her employer engaged in a *continuing violation* of the law, then all past acts can be linked together as one continuing violation. As such, they are all admissible, even those acts that occurred before 180 days. It's not necessary that all the acts be committed by the same person in the company.

Locating the EEOC or State Agency

You can file an EEOC complaint in person, by mail, or by telephone. To find the nearest EEOC office, look in the white pages of the telephone book under "U.S. Government," or check out the EEOC Website at www.eeoc.gov/.

The Website and phone number will also give you brief descriptions of how and where to file.

If you are filing with your state, look in the phone book under state government listings. If you don't know the exact title of your state human rights commission, call your state's main telephone number, or see Table III. Some states also have Websites.

Actual Filing Process

INTAKE QUESTIONNAIRE AND INTERVIEW

The first form you'll be asked to fill out is an intake questionnaire. It asks you to list your employer's name and address, your hire date, job title, salary, the name of the person(s) who committed the discriminatory act, the date the most recent act of discrimination took place, and a basic description of what happened.

It's important you name *all* supervisors involved. If you omit a name, you may later be prevented from suing that person.

After you complete the questionnaire, an intake specialist will conduct an interview with you to determine whether your claim is valid. This is done in person or over the telephone. Everything you say is on the record, and it may end up in your EEOC files and eventually be subpoenaed by your employer.

If you have an attorney representing you, the EEOC will ask you to fill out a statement officially informing the EEOC of this. The EEOC will continue to contact you directly, but will probably send copies of all relevant documents to your lawyer.

If you've consulted with an attorney to have your complaint looked at before you file it, but have not signed an agreement for that attorney to represent you, then you have not officially retained an attorney. Although you should feel free to mention that you've consulted with one, you should not fill out the form stating that you have retained legal counsel.

CHARGE OF DISCRIMINATION

At the end of the interview, the intake specialist will draft a formal *charge.* The charge is a one-page document that briefly states who discriminated, on what basis (i.e., on account of sex, age, etc.), and how and when the discrimination occurred. You must sign the charge under penalty of perjury.

A typical charge might state:

> I. From [date] until [date], I was subjected to harassment in the form of disparaging remarks about my gender, my pregnancy, and the fact that I had children, by John Doe, President of XYZ Corporation. On [date] I was discharged from my position of systems analyst. I was employed by XYZ Corporation since [date].
>
> II. Human Resources Director Fred Smith of XYZ Corporation told me I was being replaced because my supervisor was upset that I had become pregnant with my second child.
>
> III. I believe I have been discriminated against because of my gender, female (including pregnancy), in violation of Title VII of the Civil Rights Act of 1964.

In filing this charge, you walk a tightrope. The charge defines the parameters within which any lawsuit you file will be limited (as was the case with me when CNN sought to limit information about other women's experiences). It must be broad enough to permit a wide array of evidence to be allowed into your case, but narrow enough to constitute a specific act of discrimination.

Employment defense lawyers brag about their success in drastically limiting an employee's lawsuit based on the narrowness of the original EEOC charge. As one lawyer said, "Eighty percent of employee cases are thrown out because we know what they've missed. The advantage goes to those who know their way."

AFFIDAVIT

You will also be asked to formulate and sign an "affidavit"—a sworn statement describing what happened. Usually this takes place during your intake interview, but it can also be done during the investigation that follows, over the telephone, or by mail.

For me, drafting the affidavit was a lengthy, torturous ordeal. For two hours, I related my story to an EEOC intake specialist, who typed it up *in her words.* She then printed out the statement and asked me to read and sign it.

Some of her interpretations of what I'd said were slightly off, although not totally inaccurate. For instance, I'd mentioned that my bureau chief had telephoned me and said he wanted to talk about my job. So I went to see him at the bureau, and he fired me. The intake specialist, however, wrote that my bureau chief "called to talk to me about my job and then told me I was fired." Her version was confusing, since it implied that he had fired me during the phone conversation. There were several passages, like this one, that could easily be misinterpreted.

I told her I was concerned that the statement wasn't precise enough—that CNN might later claim that I was somehow "changing" my story when I attempted to clarify it. She insisted it was accurate enough and was visibly annoyed when I asked her to change the phrasing of this and several other passages. One more correctional change, I thought, and she's going to throw me right out of here. It was Friday at 5:00 P.M.

John and Christine weren't my lawyers at the time. My first lawyer had merely asked his administrative assistant to tell me to "go file a complaint" because my 180-day deadline was approaching. When I asked the assistant which agency this lawyer wanted me to file with—the federal EEOC or the California Department of Fair Employment and Housing—she was unsure. Several days later, she was still unable to get an answer from him, so she suggested that *I* choose. As a result, I was pretty much on my own throughout the entire filing process.

My investigator finally convinced me to sign the statement as written, assuring me it didn't really matter because CNN would not be given a copy of my affidavit, only the one-page charge. The affidavit, she said, would be used only to assist the EEOC in investigating my case.

But she was only partially right.

Over the weekend, I noticed a statement on the affidavit that read: *I have been given assurances . . . that this Affidavit will be considered confidential by the United States Government and will not be disclosed as long as the case remains open unless it becomes necessary for the Government to produce the Affidavit in a formal proceeding. Upon the closing of this case, the Affidavit may be subject to disclosure in accordance with Agency policy.*

I knew enough law to realize that the upshot of this statement was (1) if I filed a lawsuit, CNN would have a right to my affidavit; and (2) after my case was closed, my affidavit could still be disclosed to who-knows-who under some vague "agency policy."

For the rest of the weekend, I was deeply upset that I'd allowed myself to be dissuaded from making my statement as accurate as I'd wanted.

Monday morning, I tried to reach my lawyer, but he was unavailable to talk with me.

So I returned alone to the EEOC, determined to correct the inaccuracies. I told the investigator that although it was an administrative headache for her, for me it was my life. I explained that long after I left there—when she had forgotten all about my case—I'd still be left poring over my statement. More important, I'd have lawyers from CNN trying to make me eat each and every word, and trying to have my case dismissed based on how I phrased every sentence.

I believe she thought I was an hysterical nut.

But she made the corrections.

And sure enough, CNN's lawyers eventually attempted to twist and pick apart every phrase and word written there.

YOUR EMPLOYER IS NOTIFIED AND RESPONDS

Within ten days of your filing the complaint, the EEOC will send, by mail, a copy of the charge to your employer.

An employer will usually immediately conduct an internal investigation.

If you complained to your employer prior to lodging your EEOC complaint, your employer probably has already conducted an investigation, in which case the original investigation will now be reviewed and updated.

At this stage, the investigation is almost always done by a lawyer, so whatever information is uncovered can be protected by the attorney-client privilege.

Your employer is allowed to interview your supervisors and coworkers, and obtain sworn statements from them. However, your employer *cannot* use retaliatory tactics or harassing measures to obtain these witness statements, because to do so would violate Title VII.

If you are still employed there, your employer can also interview you, but must not do so in a retaliatory manner.

Your employer will decide whether to (1) keep fighting you; (2) settle the case with you by having you withdraw your EEOC complaint; or (3) settle the case with the EEOC. Even if your employer settles the case with the EEOC, you still have a right to sue the employer.

Your employer may also file a "position statement" with the EEOC. Although not required to do so, most employers will, on the advice of their lawyers. They want the EEOC investigator to fully glean their version of the facts. They also want to inject your file with legal points that will influence the EEOC attorney who will eventually review the file. In addition, they want *your* lawyer to get a good look at the strengths of their case. It's a reasonable strategy on their part, and one that can be very effective.

On the other hand, position statements have sometimes been used against employers. This happens when an employee files a lawsuit and the employer then attempts to deviate from the facts and legal conclusions stated in the original position statement.

The EEOC Investigation

Whether or not your complaint is actually investigated by the EEOC depends on how busy that particular EEOC office is and the magnitude and scope of your case. All complaints are "investigated," but as one EEOC attorney told me, "the degree and penetration of each investigation varies from case to case."

If you want your case ardently investigated, it's important that you communicate this to your intake specialist. In determining to what degree a case will be investigated, the EEOC is likely to consider your request, your credibility, the strengths and weaknesses of your case, the scope and magnitude of your case—that is, whether other women are affected—and whether anyone is currently suffering as a result of discrimination still occurring.

In many cases, the person who takes your initial charge is also assigned to investigate your case. In conducting the inquiry, the investigator will seek to answer the question, Is there reasonable cause to believe that the charge is true?

The EEOC may interview and receive testimony from your coworkers and supervisors. Your employer is not allowed to have a representative present when the EEOC interviews a witness, unless that witness is a management-level employee.

The EEOC may send written questionnaires to your employer; inspect company records; subpoena documents; request that an employer compile data that might show disparities in salary, hiring, termination, or other treatment of women; or hold a "fact-finding hearing." A fact-finding hearing is an informal conference with both parties. In it the EEOC will attempt to define the issues, determine which elements are undisputed, resolve those issues that can be resolved, and ascertain whether there is a basis for negotiated settlement of the charges.[4]

RESULTS OF INVESTIGATION

At the end of the investigation, the EEOC will make one of several determinations:

It can find that there exists *reasonable cause* to believe your allegations are true.

Or it can find there is *not reasonable cause* and your case will be dismissed *without particularized findings.* This isn't ruling against you, it's just that the EEOC was unable at the time to find proof of discrimination. Whether or not this can be used against you at trial varies from court to court. You should consult with an attorney at this stage to determine whether it's wise to proceed, and whether your case has merit regardless of the EEOC's findings.

The EEOC can also find that your case should be dismissed because of technical considerations: you missed the deadline to file, your complaint is not of the type which the EEOC has the authority to investigate, your employer did not have the requisite fifteen employees in order to be held accountable under Title VII, or any other reason that would render the EEOC unable to enforce the law. This is called an *administrative dismissal.*

If your complaint is dismissed for any reason, the EEOC will hold a conference with you to go over the results and give you information about your right to file a lawsuit in federal court. Even though the EEOC is dismissing your case, you still have a right to file a lawsuit against your employer. A court is a higher body than the EEOC.

If the EEOC finds there *is* cause to believe your employer committed the discriminatory act, then your file goes up the EEOC chain of command, where it is reviewed by an attorney.

The EEOC will try to help you and your employer reach a settlement.

In some rare instances, the EEOC itself will file a lawsuit against your employer. This might occur if the EEOC believes a case may set new precedent, a case has garnered a significant amount of public reaction, or your employer is acting in a particularly egregious manner. This lawsuit can either be filed on behalf of an individual or on behalf of a group, as was the case against Mitsubishi Motor Manufacturing of America.

The EEOC filed its largest class action suit ever against the Japanese automaker. Initially, thirty women came forward (called the "Dirty Thirty" by some of their male coworkers) complaining of sexual harassment. When EEOC investigators looked into the matter, they found that 400 of the 940 women at Mitsubishi had been subjected to sexual harassment. The experiences of some of the women were reported by the *Chicago Tribune*:

> [One woman reported that] while building a car chassis at the Mitsubishi plant, over the numbing din of the assembly line, she once asked for permission to go to the bathroom by making the letter *P* with her fingers.
>
> In the tone of voice you might use to ask someone to pass the ketchup, one of her coworkers sidled up and asked [her], "Do you have to pee or did you want to suck my peter?" . . .
>
> [A second woman's] miseries included the coworker, "who would come up and hump your leg. He would say, 'Can you feel me getting hard?'" as he rubbed up against her while she was unable to shove him away—her hands were filled with tools, working on the car above her head. . . .
>
> This same offensive coworker put a sign on another woman's back that read, "Sperm Bank. Deposit here."[5]

Mitsubishi's initial response to the investigation was probably partially responsible for the EEOC's tough stance against the company:

Fifty-eight buses, paid for by Mitsubishi, brought nearly 3,000 workers to Chicago. Receiving their regular shift pay (and a box lunch), they streamed onto West Madison Street wearing their maroon and gray uniforms, massed in front of the skyscraper housing the EEOC's offices and sang out protests against the harassment charges.

"Two-four-six-eight, we're here to set the record straight," they hollered, holding aloft hand-lettered signs that read, "I am not a harasser."

Mitsubishi's strategy backfired when it was discovered that the company helped stage the rally and some workers had been coerced into making the telegenic public display of support for their wronged employer.[6]

Since the EEOC chooses to litigate so few cases, it's not considered a poor reflection on your case if the EEOC does not file a lawsuit.

Finally, if your employer refuses to cooperate with the EEOC's investigation or destroys or hides evidence, the EEOC can draw an "adverse inference" against your employer. It's a presumption that the company did wrong and is covering its tracks. An adverse inference may be taken into consideration by a judge or jury should you file a lawsuit.

RIGHT-TO-SUE LETTER

Six months after you file your complaint, the EEOC must give you a right-to-sue letter, regardless of whether the EEOC has completed its investigation.

You can ask the EEOC to consider giving you a right-to-sue letter sooner. If the EEOC is inundated with complaints, they may agree to release the letter sooner.

Another way of obtaining an EEOC right-to-sue letter more quickly is to file your complaint with the state agency first and then ask the state to dismiss the claim after sixty days. You then have a right to file in federal court. You must make sure the state does not dismiss your claim on the grounds that it has no merit. The dismissal should state that it's for the sole purpose of allowing you to sue in federal court. Otherwise, the fact that it was dismissed can be used as evidence against you.

After the EEOC issues you a right-to-sue letter, you have ninety days in which to file your complaint.

There are numerous ways to maneuver around the deadlines and time limits on the various filing requirements. They are so complex that it is yet one more reason why you should at least consult with an attorney at this stage.

Exceptions

FEDERAL EMPLOYEES

If you are a federal employee, you must first lodge your complaint with the agency or department where you work. The law requires there be an equal employment opportunity (EEO) counselor onsite.

You must file your complaint within forty-five days of when the discrimination took place. The EEO counselor then has thirty days to provide you with counseling. During that time, the counselor will give you a "proposed" ruling in your case, along with written notice that you have fifteen days to lodge a formal complaint if you still want to proceed.

Once you lodge a formal complaint, the EEO counselor either accepts or rejects it.

If it's accepted, the counselor must conduct an investigation within 180 days. You are allowed to review the investigation results and, if unsatisfied, request that the EEO counselor conduct an informal hearing to reconsider.

If the complaint is rejected, you can then file a complaint with the EEOC and receive a formal hearing before an EEOC administrative judge. If, however, your dispute involves discrimination issues and other grievances, then before receiving an EEOC hearing you must file with the Merit Services Protection Board (MSPB). You then have thirty days to appeal that decision to the EEOC or to a federal court. If you choose the EEOC and the EEOC rejects your appeal, you then have ninety days to file a lawsuit in federal court.

CONGRESS

Congressional employees do not file with the EEOC. Under the Congressional Accountability Act of 1995, Congressional employees must first file informal complaints with the Office of Compliance within 180 days of the discriminatory act. The office then provides counseling over the next thirty days, after which you are required to enter into mediation.

If, after mediation, you are still unsatisfied, you may lodge a formal complaint with the Office of Compliance or file a lawsuit in federal court.

EDUCATIONAL EMPLOYEES AND TITLE IX

Title IX allows you to go directly to court without first lodging a complaint with a federal agency. You are not required to go through counseling or mediation.

UNIONS

Labor union employees need to read their union contracts, which usually outline all rights and procedures for objecting to discrimination. The contract may require you to first file a grievance through a union arbitration process. At the end of that process, you can proceed to the EEOC just as any other nonunion employee would, and eventually sue in federal court.

17.

Understanding the Lawyers

If we are to keep our democracy, there must be one commandment: Thou shalt not ration justice.

—Judge Learned Hand, address before the Legal Aid Society of New York, February 16, 1951

Imagine my surprise when CNN's lawyer informed me that I had scheduled a mediation with CNN. Or at least my lawyer had scheduled it. (I was still using my first lawyer and hadn't yet hired John and Christine to represent me.) He had casually mentioned to me several weeks before that CNN had offered to mediate my case, and I had replied with an emphatic "No."

But my lawyer was either remiss in getting back to CNN or just plainly ignored what I'd said. As a result, I was now listening to CNN's attorney tell a state hearing office that I had agreed to mediate my case. This particular hearing was for the purpose of settling a wage discrepancy that was part of my overall claim against CNN.

The hearing officer asked me, "Is this true? Do you have a

lawyer for this problem?" "I do have a lawyer representing me on the overall discrimination claim," I said, "but he didn't want to pursue this minor pay issue because he said it wasn't worth his time."

"We can easily include that in the mediation," the CNN lawyer interjected, "and postpone this hearing until next month in hopes that everything will get worked out before then." The hearing officer looked at me questioningly. "It's okay with me to postpone the hearing," I replied, eager to have some time to find out what exactly was going on.

Inside, I was furious that my lawyer had scheduled a mediation without my consent.

The hearing officer must have sensed something was wrong, and she asked to speak with me privately. After the lawyer left, the hearing officer asked me what was up. I told her I'd never seen or heard of CNN's lawyer until now and that I knew nothing about any scheduled mediation. I didn't want to bring it up in front of the attorney because I didn't want CNN to know how scattered my relationship with my own lawyer was.

She asked me to tell her about my discrimination claim, then told me how sorry she was that the entire ordeal was unfolding for me in this manner. She spent the next ten minutes advising me on how she thought I should proceed with my claim.

As I was packing up to leave, she said, "I hate lawyers. Don't you?" I suddenly realized I'd neglected to mention that *I* was a lawyer. I rarely bring it up, because I tend to think of myself as a journalist with a law degree.

I thought about it for a minute and then truthfully replied, "Some of them—yes, I do. I really do."

But not all of them. If you find the *right* lawyer, your life will be infinitely easier.

Finding the right lawyer doesn't necessarily mean the one who works for the biggest law firm, although it can. It doesn't mean the lawyer who gets the most press or went to the most noteworthy law school, although it can. Nor does it mean the one who offers you the best deal, although that, too, can be a factor.

The right lawyer depends on your individual case.

Attorneys run the gamut in terms of their knowledge, preparation level, and commitment to cases and individuals. Some are just plain incompetent, whereas others are as good as gold.

They also run the gamut in terms of the kinds of experience they have. Some are adept at pushing paper and writing letters but are terrible in front of juries. Some are great talkers but couldn't write a motion to save their lives. And some have fantastic negotiating skills but can't seem to find time to return a phone call. A few have it all.

Most important, lawyers on both sides of your case have very different mentalities and goals. It's crucial that you grasp the mind-set of both your attorney and your employer's attorney. Only then will you fully comprehend their motivations and interest (or lack thereof) in your case. Only then can you pick the right lawyer for you.

Understanding Your Employer's Attorney

Large employers sometimes have their own lawyers who work full-time for the company, called in-house counsel.

An in-house counsel may or may not be motivated to settle your case, depending on the input and directives he or she receives from the company.

In some cases the in-house counsel is not an expert in employment law, but rather deals only with negotiating contracts or conducting other business affairs for the employer. If that is the case, the in-house attorney will immediately assign your case to an outside law firm, or handle it only until it becomes too complex or time-consuming.

Most smaller employers don't have in-house lawyers and will always immediately hire an outside firm to handle your case.

In fact, the great majority of employee discrimination lawsuits are handled by outside law firms. Your employer will most likely use a mid- to large-size law firm. These firms usually represent *corporate* or *business* clients, as opposed to individuals. Most have offices in various cities around the country; some have offices worldwide. Their lawyers defend against employee lawsuits and are commonly called *employment defense attorneys* or members of the *defense bar.*

Most of the best students from the best law schools are solicited by these large, high-paying firms.

On rare occasions, these firms will represent a worker rather than an employer. For instance, if one of their important business clients were to call and say his niece just got fired and needs a lawyer to represent her, they might consider obliging him. They also might oblige him for his divorce, his bankruptcy, the escrow on the sale of his private residence, and any other reasonable request he might make. But if a person off the street were to walk in and ask for assistance, they would probably refuse the case. To do otherwise presents an "issue conflict"—that is, the lawyers might be placed in the awkward position of having to argue publicly on the "wrong" side of the law, not to mention that they might irritate some of their employer clients.

Within the hierarchies of these large firms, senior partners are on top. They act as "rainmakers," wooing large corporate clients into retaining the firm to handle all the company's legal problems. Once a senior partner secures an account, he or she usually assigns it to a junior partner. Partners share company profits, and senior partners receive a larger percentage than junior partners. Associates, less experienced, are beneath junior partners and work on a salary basis (no profit-sharing), hoping to make partner someday. They do a lot of nose-to-the-grindstone legal work.

Now that you understand this hierarchy, you might be able to discern how your employer regards your case. If senior partners are directly involved, your employer is taking this situation very seriously, which might mean you have a strong case or that your employer is stubborn and willing to defend at any cost. If, however, you're dealing with a low-level associate, your employer may believe your case has no merit. Or perhaps your employer is not a very important client. In many instances, a low-level associate will take directions from a partner until a critical juncture in the case, when the partner will step in—for depositions, hearings, et cetera. In that instance, the low-level associate is probably not making any of the tactical decisions.

In my own case, CNN hired one of the largest employment defense firms in the country, which then assigned its most senior partners, as well as junior partners, associates, paralegals, and numerous other support staff. CNN also used its in-house attorneys to oversee and track the litigation. In view of this situation, it was easy for me to discount CNN's constant public claims that my case "had no merit."

Understanding Your Attorney

You will use a *plaintiffs' lawyer.*

Plaintiffs' lawyers typically file lawsuits on behalf of individuals or groups against businesses and corporations. Plaintiffs' firms are usually smaller and don't have branch offices, as defense firms do.

One of the biggest differences between your lawyer and your employer's lawyer is how they charge for their time.

Generally, plaintiffs' lawyers work on a contingency basis—that is, they take a share of the profits if they win the case, and otherwise don't get paid. That's why individuals like yourself can afford to fight large businesses and corporations. Defense law firms charge their corporate clients on an hourly basis to defend against your lawsuit.

There are some startling repercussions in this regard.

First, defense attorneys have no incentive to decline a case, because regardless of the outcome, they will make money. That means they will usually be brought onboard regardless of the merits of your case.

Since they get paid by the hour, they actually have some incentive to keep it going. While most feel an obligation to do what's best for their clients, some rack up countless hours on a case that might otherwise have settled. Depending on how vigilant an employer is in scrutinizing a law firm's time and expenses, a firm might accrue an abundance of unnecessary hours. In fact, in some firms, if junior partners and associates don't accrue a certain amount of billable hours per month, they get shown the door. Sometimes a few very large employers become the milk cow for a firm's employment law department, or perhaps become an associate's ticket into partnership.[1]

Employers often use their in-house counsel to closely monitor the hours and expenses logged by an outside law firm. Many company managers, however, have no way of judging just how much time and money are really needed to fight a lawsuit.

There's no love lost between defense and plaintiffs' lawyers. Many defense lawyers believe plaintiffs' lawyers are responsible for a needless amount of litigation in our society. They refer to plaintiffs' attorneys with distaste and irreverence. At one employment defense conference I attended, the speaker referred to a plaintiffs' lawyer as "C. Leigh Zee" and to the lawyer's client as "Ms. Liza Lot."

Plaintiffs' lawyers, on the other hand, point out that defense lawyers usually represent big money, big companies, and big bullies. They believe defense lawyers can't afford to have a conscience—not if they want to keep those valuable corporate accounts. And if that means legally attacking a woman who's complained of sex discrimination, fine.

Plaintiffs' lawyers also note that many big defense firms team up with insurance companies to convince the public to pass laws that limit jury awards and plaintiffs' lawyer fees (although defense firms don't work *too* hard doing this, because they realize that if *all* the high-stakes litigation goes away, there won't be much business left for defense firms). Unfortunately, voters don't always realize that a stiff jury verdict and a well-compensated plaintiffs' lawyer are the only means available to the ordinary person to fight big business and succeed.

Frankly, I'll take a plaintiffs' lawyer any day. They equalize a legal system that would otherwise favor the side with the most money—and that's usually the employer. Once you've been stuck, as I have, on the small end of a big-business court battle, you realize the value of that.[2] On the other hand, there are honest, hardworking lawyers on both sides of the fence.

What Exactly Do You Need in a Lawyer?

If you haven't already retained an attorney, you must do so now if you intend to pursue your claim. Although the law does allow people to file lawsuits on their own behalf, don't. It's great in theory, but fatal in fact.

Bigger isn't necessarily better. Ideally you want a law firm big enough to handle the financial strain an employer's resources are apt to put on you and your lawyer. At the same time, you don't want an extremely large firm that doesn't regard your case as being very important, or that might send you exorbitant hourly billings.

You do want a lawyer who's adept at bulldozing through the defense's paperwork in order to push your case to court.

You also want an attorney with trial experience. Employment lawyers gain this training in many different ways.

Some work for firms that specialize in employment law. Sometimes smaller firms of this nature represent both employees and small employers.

Others work for firms that don't specialize in a particular area of law, but rather focus exclusively on going to trial, or litigating.

Still others come from civil rights backgrounds, and may have worked for women's organizations, the American Civil Liberties Union (ACLU), or a similar nonprofit group.

There are numerous other avenues a lawyer can take to gain experience in this area.

Some have general practices, in which case they have no experience in employment law. In a small town, a lawyer must wear many hats. If your employer's lawyer is not highly specialized in either employment law or trial practice, this type of lawyer may be okay for you. Otherwise, try to find a lawyer who has some specialty in employment law or trial work.

More important, if you intend to go all the way to trial, make sure the lawyer you choose can and will take your case that far. Some lawyers either have poor trial skills or they're just plain lazy. Defense lawyers know who these lawyers are, and can call their bluffs. As a result, their cases don't settle for much.

Some lawyers have reputations for conducting thorough investigations prior to ever filing a case, or for representing only clients who are extremely credible. Defense lawyers know that a phone call from *that* lawyer means serious business.

HOW DO YOU FIND THE NAME OF A GOOD LAWYER?

Referrals are always a plus. If you know someone who has a good lawyer, ask them whether their case involved an employment issue. It won't do you much good if your uncle Frank had a great lawyer when it came to probating Aunt Martha's will. I cringe when I hear a comment like "Gee, sounds like your uncle Frank had a great lawyer. Does this lawyer take employment cases too?" Yikes! Why would you want a probate lawyer taking your employment case?

You should also consider what criteria this person is using to judge the attorney. I sometimes hear the observation that an attorney is "so nice." That's fine, but what about the attorney's skills, commitment, and interest in the case? I like nice, but I prefer attorneys who can eat my opponents for lunch . . . and still be hungry.

You can sometimes find a good lawyer by reading the local newspaper. Occasionally, an employment discrimination case will make a media splash and the lawyer's name will be mentioned.

I found John and Christine by asking a very prominent *defense* attorney to name her law firm's most rigorous opponents. If you personally know any lawyers, try asking them whom *they* would use if they needed an employment lawyer.

Also, state and local bar associations often provide lawyer referral services at no charge to the public.

The EEOC keeps rosters of attorneys and will give you two or three names if you come in to file a charge. The only problem is that they usually don't offer them to you until *after* you've filed your complaint, and that may be too late. You could, however, contact your local EEOC office to see whether they might share some names with you before you file.

Table VI lists a number of private organizations that can either refer you to an attorney or provide one.

RESEARCHING AN ATTORNEY'S BACKGROUND

After you've come up with a couple of names of attorneys, call your state bar to see what information about the lawyer is available to the general public. In many states, you're entitled to know whether a lawyer is in good standing with the bar and whether he or she has ever been subjected to disciplinary action.

Meeting and Interviewing an Attorney

Your next step is to personally interview the attorney. Call his or her office and tell the receptionist you'd like to speak with the lawyer about filing an employment discrimination lawsuit.

The receptionist should be able to tell you what normal office procedure is in that regard. Some lawyers will send you a questionaire to fill out; others will allow you to immediately schedule an appointment, although you may have to wait several days or weeks. Some will see you at no charge, while others will require an introductory fee for the lawyer's time.

During the initial meeting, the attorney will ask you to describe the events surrounding your employment and/or termination.

You should bring your résumé, termination notice, employee handbook, employment contract (if you have one), personnel file (if you've been able to obtain it), past performance reviews, and any other documentation that might prove helpful.

During this time, you shouldn't be made to feel as though you're imposing. If the attorney is too busy to focus on you and your case at this early stage, it will only get worse as time goes on. Do you want to deal with the stress and headache of an inattentive lawyer in addition to whatever strain your employer puts on you?

I was impressed the first time I met and interviewed my lawyers, John and Christine. John spoke with me for two hours—at no charge. He held all his calls and listened attentively to what I had to say. When I met Christine, she invited me into her office and encouraged me to ask questions.

TEN QUESTIONS TO ASK WHEN INTERVIEWING A LAWYER

1. Do you have a background in employment law? If so, what is it?
2. Have you ever taken a case like this before? If so, how often or how many? Some attorneys try to puff up their experience in an effort to get your case, so ask for specific examples of cases this attorney has handled.
3. Have you ever gone up against the particular law firm that my employer is using? If so, when and what was the outcome?

4. How many lawyers work in your firm? Do they specialize in the same area of the law?
5. Does your firm have the resources to fight my employer's law firm? How large is your support staff? In some firms, the support staff consists of one administrative assistant. Other firms have an entire team of assistants, paralegals, file clerks, receptionists, and law clerks. The size of the support staff will give you some idea of the firepower this law firm has. It can be an important factor if your employer has unlimited resources and is using a law firm that's capable of papering you to death.
6. What is your approach to litigation? For instance, how aggressive are you in taking depositions and filing motions? Or do you prefer to respond passively to motions, et cetera from your opponents? (You want an attorney who is aggressive in this regard, and willing to spend time, effort, and money fighting your case.)
7. Do you take cases to trial? If so, what percentage of your cases go to trial? What percentage settle?
8. What happens if my employer makes me a settlement offer that I don't like? Will you leave the decision of whether we settle my case up to me?
9. What do you think of my case?
10. How are you at returning calls? Will you keep me updated on what's going on in my case? If so, how do you intend to do this?

TELL YOUR LAWYER *EVERYTHING*

When you meet your lawyer, don't sugarcoat the facts of your case. During the lawsuit, everything will eventually come to light. Why allow your lawyer to get blindsided by the defense? As one plaintiffs' lawyer told me:

> *Sometimes a client comes in and she's telling me about her story, which sounds like an amazingly strong case. But then, a couple of weeks or months down the road, I find out all kinds of things that she "forgot" to tell me. Usually I find all this out from the defense attorneys, who are all too happy to make me feel like a fool.*

If you don't disclose everything, how can you expect your lawyer to adequately evaluate your case? You might be surprised to learn that your case is still worthwhile. And since your lawyer knows the worst of it, he or she may be able to prevent any bad evidence from sandbagging it.

At the very least, you will have an objective legal evaluation of your circumstance. As one prominent plaintiffs' lawyer put it:

> *If a lawyer knows the good and the bad and tells you that you don't have a case, then you can save yourself a lot of heartache by taking the advice now, rather than going ahead and filing it and then losing.*

CAVEAT EMPTOR (BUYER BEWARE!)

Don't be swayed into signing with the first lawyer you meet, no matter how enticing it may seem. Try to interview two or three lawyers, not only to give you a good idea of what's out there but to get a good evaluation of your case. Some lawyers will take weak cases in hopes of extorting a few bucks from an employer who might be apt to pay just to avoid the nuisance of a lawsuit.

Also, beware of lawyers who try to make suggestions on how to build up your damages. Some lawyers will run you through a mill of their bought-and-paid-for doctors who document your stress. These lawyers also encourage you to remain unemployed, telling you that if you get another job, your case may be worth less money. This is a dishonest approach, not to mention one that is not in your best interests. A good lawyer will tell you to get on with your life and try to rise above the discrimination. A good lawyer doesn't approach the case by suggesting you debilitate yourself just to get a few more bucks. My lawyers *always* told me to concentrate on myself and my future, and to let them handle the lawsuit. This is how it should be.

What Your Lawsuit Is Likely to Cost Your Employer

Employers pay defense lawyers to go through company records, interview supervisors and coworkers, conduct legal research, and write memos on the strengths and weaknesses of your case.

Senior partners charge somewhere between $175 and $400 per hour. The higher amount is charged in larger urban areas where a lot of big business is transacted. The lower amount is typical in smaller towns and rural areas. Junior partners charge between $150 and $275 per hour. Associates bill from $90 to $125 per hour.

In a large city, the minimum cost of defending a discrimination complaint is about $25,000. At least $10,000 to $20,000 of that might be spent taking your deposition. Employers in smaller towns might pay half that amount.

The vast majority of cases last about one year, after which time an employer is usually ready to ask a court to dismiss your case on summary judgment grounds (see chapter 18, "If All Else Fails . . . See You in Court"). If a case goes to summary judgment, an employer will have spent between $50,000 and $75,000 in a large city, less in a rural area.

If the case goes to trial, in many cases an employer will spend between $30,000 and $100,000, and sometimes significantly more. CNN told the court that a case could easily cost "a quarter-million dollars" and was sometimes "into seven figures," but that's not usually the case.

An employer who loses will also have to pay whatever damages the judge or jury awards, which could range from zero to several million dollars. Only a small percentage of cases actually go to trial.[3]

INSURANCE MAY SUBSIDIZE THE COST

An employer with an insurance policy may not have to pay quite that much money. A growing number of companies are now carrying Employment Practices Liability (EPL) insurance to cover discrimination lawsuits. These employers will usually owe only the deductible, which may range anywhere from $5,000 to $25,000, depending on the policy. Employers typically pay anywhere from $5,000 to $100,000 per year in premiums. Some insurance companies, however, refuse to pay the high rates charged by some defense firms, in which case the defense firm may ask the employer to make up the difference. For more about EPL insurance, see chapter 18, "If All Else Fails . . . See You in Court."

What Your Lawsuit Is Likely to Cost You

The payment terms you agree upon with your lawyer will probably be based on a contingency arrangement. This type of agreement gives your lawyer a percentage of what you receive *only if you are successful.* Otherwise, you don't pay for the lawyer's time—only for expenses incurred. A typical percentage in a contingency agreement is in the 33–40 percent range.

In most contingency agreements, you agree to pay for expenses, filing fees, and court costs. These typically include paying for an investigator to work on your case; travel costs to another city to interview or depose witnesses; court reporters who transcribe any depositions taken; photocopying; subpoena costs; parking; postage and delivery fees; court filing fees; messenger services; telephone long-distance charges; and other related costs.

If you use any "expert witnesses," they can be quite costly, ranging from several hundred to several thousand dollars per day. They might include doctors, psychologists, engineers, scientists, construction experts, or experts in your particular line of work who can testify to your competence on the job.

The court will usually charge a filing fee and make you pay any other incidental court costs. In addition, there's usually a fee to serve your employer with notice of the lawsuit.

All this can add up to hundreds or even thousands of dollars, depending on the scope and magnitude of your case.

Not all law firms will require you to pay these expenses up front.

Read your retainer agreement to see whether you're expected to reimburse your attorney for these costs if you lose.

One question that often confuses clients is whether expenses are deducted before or after the money is divided up. For instance, say your lawyer is entitled to 33 percent and you are awarded \$100,000. If your expenses amount to \$25,000, does your lawyer take 33 percent of the \$100,000 or 33 percent *after* the expense are paid, which would be 33 percent of \$75,000? Make sure you discuss this clause with your lawyer and that you understand it.

The actual contract you sign is called a "retainer agreement." Sometimes a lawyer requires you to pay a "retainer" fee. This is a certain amount of money, usually ranging from \$1,000 to \$5,000, that your lawyer applies toward expenses or compensation for his or her time. This is a reasonable request. Sometimes it actually works in your favor if you pay a retainer, because lawyers who work on a pure contingency basis are sometimes reluctant to put in the hours required. They may try to do as little as possible in hopes of an early settlement and quick payoff. Depending on your personal goals, a quick payoff may or may not be acceptable.

One strategy defense lawyers use is to make a plaintiffs' lawyer feel as if they have a loser of a case. The plaintiffs' lawyer then becomes reluctant to "throw away" any more hours without hope of receiving compensation.

Some lawyers require retainer fees to separate the serious clients from the flakes. They believe that if you are willing to put some money forward, you are expressing a conviction that your case is worthwhile and are not just looking for a free ride.

CREATIVE SOLUTIONS FOR AN EMPTY POCKETBOOK

Don't be afraid to get creative with your lawyer. You want to pay a fair fee, but if your case is a good one, your lawyer may be willing to adjust the normal fee arrangement.

For instance, one woman I know wanted to hire a particular lawyer, but that lawyer required that he be paid on an hourly basis. She couldn't afford it, so she suggested a fee arrangement whereby she agreed to compensate him for the first twenty hours that he worked on her case. After that, he agreed to work on a contingency basis.

I don't know how willing your lawyer is to consider an alternative arrangement, but if you're in a fix, it's worth a try. It would not be unreasonable for your lawyer to refuse such an offer. But you'll never know unless you ask.

At the same time, it would be unwise to grind your lawyer's fee down to a point where it would be financially unfeasible for him or her to work on your case.

After talking with your lawyer, you'll get a sense of what kind of fee arrangement he or she needs to properly handle your case.

Why Your Employer's Lawyer Is Likely to Stall Your Case

In addition to securing more billable hours, defense law firms have other interests in delaying your case.

In most employment lawsuits, time works against the employee. If you're unfamiliar with the process, you may find it frustrating that months or even years go by before your case nears conclusion. The entire process may be demoralizing and even frightening. Defense lawyers, however, find this time frame normal.

In addition, most employees have usually suffered some sort of economic loss, such as losing a job or failing to get a pay raise. As a result, the employee may be experiencing financial difficulties, whereas the employer may have more resources to weather a lengthy case.

If you're still on the job, you may be anticipating a policy change that will end an uncomfortable situation. A delay only prolongs your distress.

Defense lawyers purposely try to make you feel as miserable as possible throughout the litigation. If they add to your anxiety by delaying your case, all the better. The more miserable you are, the more likely you are to accept a poor settlement offer.

Delay also makes it more difficult for you to prove your case. The law assumes there was no discrimination unless you, the plaintiff, prove it. This becomes more difficult with time, because witnesses forget or move out of the area. In addition, the company sometimes uses this period of delay to appease and defuse witnesses who are vocal and incensed about the discrimination.

Also, your own memory becomes less clear over time.

Finally, strategy-wise, defense lawyers focus their strengths not on the trial itself but in the paper wars leading up to trial. This means that the defense will put most of its efforts into various motions before trial, all of which translates into delay.

18.

If All Else Fails . . . See You in Court

Judge HUNT: The Court must insist—the prisoner has been tried according to the established forms of law.

Susan B. ANTHONY: Yes, your honor, but by forms of law all made by men, interpreted by men, administered by men, in favor of men, and against women; and hence, your honor's ordered verdict of guilty, against a United States citizen for the exercise of that citizen's right to vote simply because that citizen was a woman and not a man. . . . So now must women, to get their right to a voice in this Government, take it; and I have taken it, and mean to take it at every possible opportunity.

Judge HUNT: The Court orders the prisoner to sit down. It will not allow another word.

Susan B. ANTHONY: When I was brought before your honor for trial, I had hoped for a broad and liberal interpretation of the Constitution and its recent amendments—that should declare . . . equality of rights the national guarantee to all persons born or naturalized in the United States.

Judge HUNT: The Court must insist—(*Here the prisoner sat down.*)

Judge HUNT: The prisoner will stand up! . . . The sentence of the Court is that you pay a fine of one hundred dollars and the costs of prosecution.

Susan B. ANTHONY: May it please your honor, I shall never pay a dollar of your unjust penalty.

—transcript of the trial of Susan B. Anthony, convicted for voting, New York, 1873

Susan B. Anthony went to jail. Another thirty-four years would pass before the Nineteenth Amendment granted women the right to vote. She would not live to see it.

Throughout history, women have had to fight for rights that men have taken for granted.

Even today, when a woman files a lawsuit demanding equal treatment, she may be looked at as a whiner, a complainer, a troublemaker.

The day after I filed my own lawsuit, a friend of mine overheard two women in an airport rest room talking about me. "Why do these women sue?" one said. "Don't ask me," the other replied. "You'd think they could rely on their own capabilities and just do their work without whining and drawing attention to themselves."

Sometimes women are their own worst enemies. They reject "feminism" because they associate it with all that is divisive in our society. In their opinion, feminists are hostile, uncaring people who leave their children at home to plow out into the business world. "Feminists" disrupt and disrespect established patterns of business. They don't respect, or even like, men. It's their fault that the family as a cohesive unit has disintegrated, leaving behind a wake of juvenile delinquents who grow into dysfunctional adults.

Any of this sound familiar?

In response to the feminist movement comes a powerful backlash of tradition-bound women who believe the only solution is to go backward in time and assume conventional roles that historically have been defined as being within a women's sphere.

With conventional roles, however, come conventional limitations.

But what about the notion of going *forward*?

We can start by throwing away stereotypes of what "feminism" represents.

Consider this. Feminism is the ability *to choose.* In fact, choosing is the greatest gift the feminist movement has given us. We can choose without being ridiculed, questioned, or told our choice "doesn't fit" with society's expectations of us. Feminism is about respecting the choices of others—stay-at-home moms, career women, sexy divas, or whatever—without imposing stigmas or attitudes that degenerate or degrade. It's realizing that we have far more in common with each other than most of us care to believe, and acknowledging that we are all valuable contributors to our community. It is also refusing to use each other as stepping-stones in order to show others how much better we are in the particular path we have chosen.

So why do women sue? A better question might be, Why don't some women understand why other women sue?

In case you don't know, here's why.

Women sue because they don't have power. Women sue because they want to make things fair. They sue not because they are "victims" but because they refuse to be victims. Women sue because they are strong. They sue because in the business world, created and perpetuated by mostly men, money talks.

Women sue because it's their right to do so. Congress and the Supreme Court would not have created all these laws if they didn't intend for women to use them. Women sue because they want to be heard.

Women sue because they have daughters who will someday grow up. Women sue because they have sons who will someday grow up.

Women sue because they know what they are doing is right.

Employers and defense lawyers would have you believe that the great majority of women who file lawsuits are motivated by greed, wanting nothing more than to extort money. I don't doubt that women like that exist, but I beg to differ as to their numbers.

If you've ever spent an hour or a day at the EEOC, you'll find countless women whose sincerity and pain are quite real.

What *is* true is that an increasing number of discrimination lawsuits have been filed in recent years.[1] In fact, some people complain that the entire legal system has gone overboard with ridiculous litigation.

Litigation, yes. Ridiculous, no. The litigation stems from the fact that the workplace is simply not changing fast enough to provide women with fair opportunities. In addition, women are just beginning to understand their rights . . . and are fighting back.

Those women who do not understand how and why "a little discrimination" could completely dishevel a person's life have probably never faced such discrimination.

For instance, some homemakers (not all) may be partially buffered from discrimination simply because their lifestyle is more "acceptable" to most men. As a result, they encounter discrimination less often than a woman who chooses a nontraditional lifestyle or career. And they may find it difficult to relate to the devastation some women undergo as a result of discrimination.

Or sometimes an attractive woman finds that what little problems she encounters can be easily taken care of with a friendly smile. "So what's all the fuss about?" she may wonder. At some point, however, a friendly or flirtatious gesture may no longer be sufficient to open the doors she needs or solve whatever problems she's facing.

Still other women are extremely smart—smart enough to figure a clever way out of most predicaments . . . at least most of the time.

Eventually, though, if you keep demanding your share of the pie, you will also encounter your share of the world.

Then you'll fully understand why "some women" sue.

What You Want

Filing a lawsuit can accomplish many things. You must determine exactly what it is that you want to accomplish by filing yours. Is there something specific you want, such as getting your job back or getting a promotion you deserved? Is there any amount of money that will make you feel better about what's happened? Do you want new policies and procedures instituted by your employer or ex-employer?

If necessary, reread the section "Remedies and Damages" in chapter 15, "Civil Rights Laws," which lists all the possible remedies a court can grant, such as back pay, front pay, compensatory damages, and punitive damages. Consider whether any of those solutions might adequately compensate you.

Sometimes a woman just wants an apology or an acknowledgment that her employer wronged her. Some women want a letter of recommendation so they can find a new job and move on with their lives.

If your motivation is revenge or anger, a lawsuit will not cure your problem. It will probably make it worse. Similarly, if you're motivated by greed, no amount of money (or the expectation of it) will get you through this ordeal. You must have a strong moral belief that what you are doing is right and that what your employer did was wrong.

Take some time *before* you jump into this to examine your motives.

Keeping a Notebook

The lawsuit may dominate your thoughts at times. When it does, take advantage of it! If you haven't already begun doing so, keep a notebook with you at all times so you can write things down as they occur to you.

As a journalist, I had gotten into the habit of carrying around a "reporter's notebook"—a long, skinny, spiraled notepad, about the size of a business envelope. Reporters use them to collect information about whatever news stories they're covering. After my lawsuit started, I began using my notebook to keep track of the many thoughts and ideas that were constantly occurring to me. For instance, my notebook usually contained a list of evidence I thought my lawyers might want to subpoena; any questions that I wanted to remember to ask my lawyers; names of people I thought would make good witnesses; any facts that might help rebut the latest allegations CNN had made about me; a list of particular occurrences or events that I wanted my lawyer to question various witnesses about; and any other details that I thought might help my case.

This may seem like an inconsequential piece of advice, but I know from experience that you'll never be able to remember everything that occurs to you. Good ideas will pop into your mind one moment and be gone the next. This is especially so if you're under stress. In most instances, you won't even remember them long enough to write them down—unless you have your notebook on hand.

Demand Letter

Upon taking your case, the first thing most attorneys do is review all the documentation you've given them and send a "demand letter" to your employer. This letter lays out your case and asks your employer to rectify the situation by either implementing a change of decision or policy or by paying you some money.

Some attorneys will write lengthy, detailed synopses that describe every discriminatory episode you encountered on the job, every piece of evidence you intend to use, and every witness you plan to call. Others write a single paragraph informing your employer that you now have an attorney and are demanding your job back, or whatever else you might be asking for.

Some attorneys don't bother to send demand letters at all. They just sue.

You should discuss with your attorney which approach is best for you. The posturing done in this early stage may set the tone for the rest of the case.

Mediation

Mediation is an informal gathering of both parties and their attorneys. A neutral mediator tries to bring everybody together to settle the case.

Mediation differs from arbitration (discussed later in this chapter) in that the mediator does not have any power to make a decision in your case—only to encourage settlement.

I entered mediation for my own case, but I signed a confidentiality statement that I would not disclose what was discussed. Various laws also require confidentiality. This is to encourage candor on both sides during the mediation process. Nothing anyone says during mediation can be used against them in court.

What I *can* discuss, however, is what mediation is like, and what you should know if you are considering it.

At the onset of my mediation, I looked around and realized that I was the only person in the room with a personal stake in the outcome. Present were a mediator, two lawyers on my side, a CNN in-house lawyer, a lawyer from CNN's outside law firm, and a CNN vice president. None of the CNN employees responsible for the discrimination was present. To everybody there except me, it was just another business day.

It may be difficult for you to derive any real satisfaction from mediation unless you can confront those who committed the discrimination. Are they regretful of the incident, or do they feel self-righteously indignant about it? If you want your job back, can you endure working for this employer?

Moreover, a roomful of detached professionals probably will not understand, or even tolerate, the upset you are feeling.

On the other hand, it might be too upsetting for you to have to face those responsible for the discrimination, in which case you may prefer they *not* be there. (Employers are sometimes advised *not* to bring along the employee who committed the act, because it tends only to annoy and anger you, the aggrieved party, and thus lessen the chances of reaching a settlement.)

So you can tailor the process to best suit your needs, you should fully understand the implications of all of these factors *before* you consent to mediation. For instance, you might consider insisting that a spouse or friend be allowed to attend the mediation if you need moral support. As one mediation expert put it, "The mediation is a voluntary process, and it can be shaped any way the parties want it to be shaped. A woman should not be afraid to ask for what she needs."

YOUR CONSENT

Normally you are not forced into mediation. It's something both parties choose to do.

Sometimes, however, a judge will order you into mediation, or "strongly suggest" that you attend.

In some cases, you may have signed an agreement with your employer to mediate all disputes. Even if you didn't specifically sign an agreement, employers sometimes place these mediation clauses in employee handbooks, employee manuals, job offer letters, or employment contracts. If that is the case, you're probably bound by it.

Even if you are required to enter into mediation, no one, not even a judge, can force you to settle your case in mediation.

CHOOSING A MEDIATOR

Usually both sides take part in picking a mediator by using a process of elimination. In court-ordered mediations, the judge will sometimes choose the mediator.

Your mediator should have expertise in employment law. You may also want to consider requesting a female mediator, or a mediator who has specific experience in sex discrimination, especially harassment. In sexual harassment, a lot is left open for interpretation—for example, the reasonable woman standard. If your mediator doesn't acknowledge and understand this standard, he or she may inadvertently undervalue your case.

TYPICAL PROCEDURE

Usually your mediation begins with a joint session of both parties, each of whom makes a brief statement of their case. The parties are then placed in separate rooms, and the mediator holds private meetings with each side, bringing ideas and suggestions back and forth until a settlement is reached.

Some mediators will not separate the parties, but rather conduct the mediation in a face-to-face confrontational manner. In most mediations, witnesses are not called, although sometimes a witness might be interviewed if a mediator feels it's absolutely necessary.

When an agreement is reached, it's put into writing and signed by all parties. The parties also have the option of submitting the agreement to a court, which will then rubber-stamp it. This gives the agreement the weight of a regular court decision. In that case, however, the settlement becomes a matter of public record.

Some mediators will offer their expert opinions with regard to settlement value or strengths and weakness of each case. Others provide no advice at all.

In picking a mediator, you should make sure he or she is not too cozy with your employer's defense firm. At one symposium I attended, put on by a large defense firm, one of the invited speakers was a mediator whom the firm regularly used. Together, he and the firm lawyers told war stories about various mediations they'd done together. I couldn't help but wonder whether the women whose cases they'd mediated (or the lawyers who represented them) knew the extent to which these parties regularly interacted.

ADVANTAGES OF MEDIATION

One of the advantages for you in mediation is that it drastically shortens the process. Delays leading up to trial can drag on for years.

Mediation can also be confidential. If some of the events surrounding your discrimination are humiliating, you won't have to worry about having to disclose all the ugly details at a public trial.

DISADVANTAGES OF MEDIATION

Sometimes the very fact that a mediation is confidential is used by a mediator and the defense to pressure a woman into settling her case. They will continually remind her that if she doesn't settle, she will face an embarrassing trial.

A mediator may also tell her that in his or her evaluation her case is weak, and if she insists on going to trial, she may lose everything. The mediator will encourage her to take a "sure bet" of settlement, rather than risk losing it all. Sometimes the mediator's assessment in this regard is accurate, but not always.

I know one woman, Nancy I., an administrative assistant, who was pressured not only by the mediator and defense lawyers, but by her own lawyer as well. In fact, together they convinced her to sign a settlement agreement during the mediation, a move she later regretted.

The next day when I read the agreement, it just didn't say everything I thought they said it would. Plus they all told me that the amount of money the company was offering was pretty good. But now when I think about it, I don't think so. I think maybe my lawyer was just lazy. He just figured it was an easy way out—no work and free money.

I don't feel very good about the whole thing. But I signed it. There's nothing I can do.

It's a common strategy for defense lawyers to bring an actual settlement agreement to the mediation so they can hurriedly get your signature if you agree to settle.

I walked out of my mediation after nine hours. I had made myself a promise not to sign or accept anything negotiated in haste, or at the end of a long, torturous day.

If it's a viable offer, it will still be good in the morning. It's amazing what a clear head will do to help you see whether an offer is right for you.

Finally, it can be disadvantageous to mediate your claim too early in the process in cases where the employer has not been adequately briefed on all the evidence. Sometimes the upper management remains insulated in the beginning from knowing the true extent of the discrimination. As a result, they may tend to view your claim as not being of much merit, and be unwilling to offer you a fair settlement.

Arbitration

Nowhere will the deck be more stacked against you in getting a fair shake for your employment dispute than in arbitration.

Basically, arbitration is a privately funded courtroom where a third party acts as a judge and informally decides your case. In most cases, the arbitrator is a former judge, a lawyer with expertise in employment law, or a law professor.

At the beginning of the arbitration, both lawyers make opening statements. After that, each side presents their evidence, usually with the employee going first. The arbitrator has the option of limiting evidence in order to save time and money. He or she may also limit testimony, such as by restricting it to key witnesses. In many cases, however, an arbitrator will allow as much as, or more than, a judge.

Lawyers for both sides then make closing statements, and the arbitrator issues a ruling.

Arbitration may be binding or nonbinding. Nonbinding means that neither party has to accept the decision, and retains the right to pursue the matter in court. In binding arbitration, however, the decision is final and the arbitrator's decision will be filed with a court, which gives it the same weight as a court judgment.

Arbitration can take place either before or after a lawsuit's been filed. It may be voluntary or by court order.

It can also stem from an agreement your employer forces you to sign. And that's when most problems arise.

MANDATORY ARBITRATION

Some women are pushed down the arbitration path because employers require it—as a condition of your being offered the job, you agree that you will submit all disputes to "binding arbitration."

One defense lawyer summed it up like this: "Have them sign it when they take the job, stick it in their file, and they won't even think about it again until they have a problem . . . and then wham!"

"Wham" meaning employees are then sucked into a process that is inherently biased against them.

In 1995, the EEOC issued this statement about mandatory binding arbitration:

> An increasing number of employers are requiring as a condition of employment that applicants and employees give up their right to pursue employment discrimination claims in court and agree to resolve disputes through binding arbitration [even though] mandatory arbitrations systems include structural biases against discrimination plaintiffs.[2]

The fact that defense lawyers refer to arbitration as an "effective management tool" should indicate to you how favorable employers judge this process to be.

The EEOC doesn't discourage employees from arbitrating their cases, only from being forced to do so by employers without being given the opportunity to understand fully the implications and biases that come into play.

DISADVANTAGES OF ARBITRATION

Your Arbitrator Is Not Bound to Follow or Apply the Law.
Usual courtroom rules of evidence can be disregarded, including those that protect your procedural constitutional rights.

Most arbitrators, however, *do* follow the law, and are very knowledgeable about it. As one arbitrator put it, "We try to be fair, and insofar as the law reflects that, we'll follow it. We try to do what's right."

The problem is that if you stumble across an arbitrator who either blatantly ignores the law or makes a serious error in applying it, you have little chance to appeal the arbitrator's decision.

Difficult to Appeal.
The only grounds for appeal in an arbitration is if the decision bears no relation to the evidence, or if your arbitrator acted in an unethical or irrational manner. The exact standard varies, depending on whether you are following federal rules or a particular state's rule, but most of the standards are similar. These extremely limited grounds mean that appeals are rarely successful.

Your Employer Does This All the Time—You Don't.
Most likely, your employer has arbitrated other issues in the past and thus has a better understanding of the process. You, however, are what the EEOC refers to as a "one-shot player." The EEOC warns that the arbitration system favors employers who enjoy the advantage of being "repeat players." An employee is "less able to

make an informed selection of arbitrators than the employer, who can better keep track of an arbitrator's record."[3]

As one defense lawyer put it, "On the employment side, we specialize. This is all we do. So we know a lot more about what mediators and arbitrators are out there."

A good plaintiffs' lawyer will research an arbitrator's background before selecting one. As one arbitrator said, "An attorney can find out a lot more about an arbitrator than about a judge or jury. So you know what you're getting into, and you have some say about who is chosen. If the attorney does his or her homework, then you have that advantage."

One exception to the "one-shot player" disadvantage is labor unions. A union is most likely a "repeat player," and as such, is probably familiar with the arbitration process.

Some Arbitrators Aim to Please . . .
the One Who Hires Them Most.

Arbitrators are working individuals. They want and need repeat business. They are considered successful only if others request them as arbitrators.

Whose repeat business do you think they can get? Certainly not yours. Your hope is that this is the last time you'll ever need one.

An employer, however, may find dozens of uses for an arbitrator. And it can be quite a coup for an arbitrator to secure an employer as a regular client.

Even though the great majority of arbitrators are fair and honest, some cannot help but worry about stepping on the toes of potential or existing clients. It's not necessarily something they do purposefully, but they do it nonetheless, at least according the EEOC, which released the following warning: "Results cannot help but be influenced by the fact that the employer, and not the employee, is a potential source of future business for the arbitrator."[4]

In a study of employment cases, the EEOC found that "the more frequent a user of arbitration an employer is, the better the employer fares in arbitration."[5] (The study was conducted on only nonunion cases because the EEOC believes that unions have the same degree of clout that most employers do in their ability to offer repeat business.)

Other studies have shown similar results. One legal scholar concluded that arbitrations are "virtually assured employer-favored outcomes," given "the manner of selecting, controlling and compensating arbitrators, the privacy of the process and how it catalytically arouses an arbitrator's desire to be acceptable to one side."[6]

In fairness to arbitrators, however, most believe that even though the system itself creates a potential for bias, they take care to guard against it. They reject the notion that they succumb to bias in the interest of securing clients. As one experienced and well-respected arbitrator told me, "I take personal umbrage at the insinuation that we make judgment calls based on what business we might get in the future. I look at myself in the mirror every time I make a decision and ask, 'Have I made a call based on what's fair and reasonable?' "

Each arbitration is different, just as each arbitrator is different. It's crucial you pick one who's knowledgeable, experienced, and fair.

Less Money.

Arbitrators typically award smaller amounts of money than do juries. The overwhelming conclusion among defense lawyers with respect to arbitration awards is that "even a bad arbitrator is better than the best jury." They feel juries are "unpredictable wild cards," capable of awarding huge verdicts with little regard for the law.

You Lose Your Publicity Clout.

Employers also prefer arbitration because it keeps embarrassing or damaging facts private. Unlike a trial, which is a matter of public record, arbitration can give your employer an opportunity to quietly solve (or hide) a discrimination problem.

You, too, may prefer that the details of your situation be kept private, in which case arbitration may be an excellent choice.

However, the EEOC points out that you lose leverage when you abolish the threat of public exposure. "As has been illustrated time and again, the risks of negative publicity and blemished business reputation can be powerful influences on behavior."[7] If your primary goal is to influence your company's behavior toward other women, then a quiet arbitration may not be the best tool for you.

Mandatory Arbitration Privatizes Our Court System. The last disadvantage of arbitration is a social concern that may not directly affect you but does affect the overall enforcement of our discrimination laws. Mandatory binding arbitration *privatizes* enforcement of our laws. It takes disputes out of our public courts and puts them into a private justice system. This goes against every premise in our Constitution. According to the EEOC, "When employees are forced into private, employer-designed arbitration systems to resolve their discrimination claims, there is no public accountability for decisions that are made or for employers who violate the law."[8] Court rulings have the effect of setting precedent and making laws that will affect others. This opportunity is lost when a discrimination issue is settled behind closed doors.

ADVANTAGES

If the arbitration is nonbinding, it's almost always a good idea to use it, because it offers one more opportunity to solve your problem while still not interfering with your right to go to court. Binding arbitration, however, greatly limits your other legal options and usurps your right to file a lawsuit.

Arbitration, binding or not, costs less money. If you've been fired from your job and are having difficulty finding another one, money may be an important consideration. Unlike trials, which often require costly experts, exhibits, and court fees, a simple arbitration costs only a couple of thousand dollars for each side—a nominal amount compared to a trial. (On the other hand, if you have an extremely low income, a court will sometimes subsidize your court costs. This is called "in forma pauperis." The court will waive filing fees and pay for reimbursement of your witnesses, your costs for publication, preparation of evidence, printed or typewritten briefs, and investigatory expenses. In addition, the court may provide you with an attorney.[9])

Arbitration is also a much speedier process. It can cut months or even years off the court process.

If these features are attractive to you, then arbitration is something you may want to consider, but only after you have weighed all the factors involved in this option.

FORCING NEW EMPLOYEES TO ARBITRATE DISPUTES

The law is still unsettled as to whether employers can force employees to arbitrate discrimination claims. One reason arbitration agreements may not ultimately hold up in our courts is that Title VII guarantees us the right to pursue a discrimination claim in federal court. Arbitration prevents us from doing so and therefore abridges that right. Still, many courts have upheld such agreements, provided certain conditions are met.

Specifically, any agreement to arbitrate must be a "clear and unmistakable" waiver of your right to use the federal courts for your complaint.[10] It cannot be some generally worded clause, such as "all matters affecting wages, hours, and other terms and conditions of employment will be decided by arbitration."

Also, simply including a statement, even a clear and unmistakable one, in an employee manual, handbook, or job application may not be enough to be considered an agreement to arbitrate. In order to be effective, the agreement must be a stand-alone document that is signed by both parties which specifically states that the employer is offering you the job in exchange for your consent to arbitrate disputes.

FORCING EXISTING EMPLOYEES TO ARBITRATE DISPUTES

Employers have an even more difficult time trying to force existing employees to agree to arbitrate their disputes, since arbitration was not part of the original offer when the employee took the job.

An employer may ask an existing employee to agree to arbitrate all future disputes, but the offer must be made in exchange for something that the employee receives in return, such as a raise, a promotion, a stock option, or a similar benefit. Otherwise, the agreement will not constitute a valid, binding contract. Also, the raise, promotion, or whatever is given must be something you are otherwise entitled to receive. In addition, the contract must specifically mention that the employee is agreeing to arbitrate her rights under Title VII.

At one employer seminar I attended, a defense lawyer urged employers to "market arbitration in a positive light," even though there was not much positive about it. He told the employers attending, "It's obvious that it's somewhat cynical for you to say that it's really in the employee's interest, because we know what we're doing here. But market it as to why it's good for both sides. Emphasize the benefits to the employee."

An employer cannot force an existing employee to accept the arbitration offer by threatening to fire or discipline her if she doesn't. That would be considered *retaliation* under Title VII; that is, the employer would be retaliating against you for asserting your right to go to court under Title VII.

OTHER ASPECTS OF ARBITRATION

Overall, despite the EEOC's objections to the contrary, and despite the fact that the law is presently unclear as to whether employees can be forced to arbitrate their civil rights disputes, many employers continue to require they do so.

Also, it's important to note that with regard to issues other than civil rights, such as wrongful termination, breach of contract, and intentional infliction of emotional distress, the law is more clear. Agreements to arbitrate will be upheld, provided there has been a clear and unmistakable waiver.

Moreover, insurance companies are beginning to offer significant discounts to employers that force their employees to arbitrate disputes.

One interesting twist to the arbitration issue is that binding arbitration clauses have at times been used *against* employers. Sometimes an employer will fire a person, claiming that person is an at-will employee. (At-will employees have no right to their job and can be fired at any time at the will of the employer. See chapter 2, "You're Hired.") An arbitration clause contradicts the at-will status, since it implies that you *cannot* be fired at will, but rather have a right to object through arbitration.

Finally, a company's internal grievance procedure is *not* an arbitration, even if your employer insists that it is. In most internal grievance procedures, you have no right to an attorney and the final decision maker is somebody who works for the company. A true arbitrator should be an outside person who is fair and impartial.

Going to Court

Your lawyer will file a "complaint," which is then served on the party or parties being sued.

The length of time it takes from the time you file your lawsuit until you actually go to trial varies greatly, depending on where you live, with smaller rural areas being as short as a couple of months, and large urban areas taking as long as five years.

You have your choice of filing your complaint in either federal or state court. Some state courts offer more advantages to employees than federal courts, whereas other states offer fewer advantages.[11] Advantages include matters like longer deadlines; right-to-sue letters issued sooner; higher allowable compensatory and punitive damages; higher frequency of having high damages awarded; and laws that make it easier for an employee to prove her case.

Federal judges are appointed for life and often run a tight ship, meaning they are less apt to allow a trial to drag on or put up with theatrics from lawyers. The entire demeanor in federal courts is more formal than that seen in most state courts. Attorneys are required to argue their cases from behind a podium, whereas in many state courts they are allowed to move around the room.

Cameras are *never* permitted in federal courts, but they are allowed in many state courts.

More important, several task force studies on gender bias in federal courts have reported that a significant number of women (lawyers, employees, and litigants) have experienced discrimination in federal courts.[12] Some federal judges have expressed beliefs that employment matters are too trivial for federal courts, and have diverted their attention away from "larger, more significant civil cases."[13] One task force concluded that this belief had the potential to "easily translate into actual unfairness to a litigant."[14] For instance, some lawyers complained they were frequently "pushed through the courts without adequate time" to conduct their case.[15]

If, however, you live in one of the few states that tend to favor employers, you may prefer federal court. Your lawyer should know which is best for your case.

As a general rule, defense lawyers prefer federal court. They believe that most plaintiffs' lawyers are less familiar than defense lawyers with the rules of federal court. For instance, in federal court, your lawyer has ten days to request a jury trial, after which you lose that right completely. Defense lawyers also prefer federal courts because they believe they have a better chance of convincing a federal court to dismiss your case on summary judgment grounds (discussed later in this chapter).

My own lawsuit ended up in four different courts (five if you count the fact that we were assigned to one court twice).

We first filed in state court and were assigned to Judge Kathryn Doi Todd. But CNN successfully filed a motion to have our case removed to federal court. This was a tactical move on their part, since we would lose the advantage of California law, which tends to favor employees. It would also greatly diminish the potential for a large punitive-damage award. In addition, federal verdicts must be unanimous, but California state verdicts in noncriminal trials require only nine of twelve jurors to agree.

We were initially assigned to one federal judge, but then the federal court reassigned us to a second federal judge.

We wanted to remain in state court, however, where we had originally filed our case. The basis CNN had used in asking that our case be moved from state court to federal court was that we had sued under Title VII, a federal law. So we dismissed our case and refiled in state court—this time claiming that CNN violated only state law. We were assigned to another state judge, but CNN requested that our case be assigned back to the same state judge who had first received the case, Kathryn Doi Todd. That's where we ended up.

Some attorneys "forum-shop" by playing courtroom roulette until they get a particular judge with whom they're happy. This is not a good practice, and it is one that can anger a court, especially if a lawyer tries to maneuver out of a particular courtroom and is unsuccessful.

CLASS ACTION LAWSUITS

Sometimes lawyers bring class action lawsuits. These are lawsuits brought on behalf of a large group of people, in this case, all of whom have been damaged because of discrimination.

In a class action lawsuit, anybody who fits the "criteria" for the lawsuit is eligible to join. Typical criteria might include "Any woman who worked for XYZ Car Company from 1990 to the present and who applied for a promotion and was denied."

Courts allow class action lawsuits when (1) there are so many people that it would be burdensome, if not impossible, for each person to have their day in court; (2) everyone in the group has the same question of law or fact; (3) the claims or defenses being used by the people who are bringing the lawsuit on behalf of the class are typical of those in the rest of the class; and (4) representative parties will fairly and adequately represent the interests of the class.[16]

Usually class action lawsuits take many years to be resolved, and you are rarely required to be in court, only to be able to verify that you are eligible to join the class.

WITNESSES

In the end, we will remember not the words of our enemies but the silence of our friends.

—Martin Luther King, Jr.

Good luck. You'll need it. People aren't always willing to risk their careers to come forward about what they perceive as someone else's problem. They justify their silence by pointing to the mouths they are obligated to feed.

Although they may not go out of their way to testify, you can only hope they will tell the truth, if asked. Some may get angry at you for forcing them to do so.

If you've already complained, either directly to your employer or to the EEOC, you should have a good idea which of your witnesses are truthful and forthright.

Your attorney or your attorney's investigator will contact any coworkers or supervisors who are potential witnesses prior to trial and interview them. Your lawyer may or may not decide to depose them before trial—that is, ask them questions under oath.

Your employer or your employer's attorney will also contact your coworkers or supervisors. Your employer's attorney must disclose to these witnesses that he or she is conducting the investigation as a *representative of the company, and not as a neutral third party.* This is to make sure that the witnesses do not get the mistaken impression that the attorney is representing *their* interests. Sometimes an employer's interests conflict with a witness's. For instance, if a woman in your workplace is interviewed by the company attorney about your lawsuit, everything she says can be used against her later if she files her own lawsuit. This is true even though she did not have her own lawyer present at the time.

The employer's attorney may or may not obtain sworn statements from these witnesses. The attorney is more likely to do so if the witness is testifying in your favor. The attorney will try to elicit proof that the witness has no knowledgeable basis for drawing the conclusion that you were discriminated against. Also, once the attorney has a sworn statement from a witness, the witness can be more easily discredited at trial if there is even one scintilla of contradictory testimony.

The defense lawyer will probably treat these witnesses well if they still work for the company. If they have since left, however, the lawyer may be more aggressive.

In my own case, one woman who had left CNN testified on my behalf and was treated in a very aggressive manner when it came time for her deposition. She related an incident about how, in response to a news story idea she'd proposed, a lower-level supervisor had responded by emulating masturbation. CNN's attorney forced her to describe, redescribe, and then demonstrate the event:

CNN: Now, you described the gesture like masturbating. Could you tell me or try to describe the gesture that he did?

WITNESS'S LAWYER: No. Demonstrate for [the CNN lawyer] and let [the CNN lawyer] describe it.

WITNESS: You want me to demonstrate it?

CNN: That's right. So his hands were about chest level?

WITNESS: No, they were about—they were groin level.

CNN: His hands were at the level of his groin?

WITNESS: He was showing us how he would masturbate.

CNN: You could stand up if you want to, but I'd like you to do the gesture so I can understand what it is you're saying.

WITNESS'S LAWYER: Don't stand up, because everybody in this room knows what the gesture is, everybody knows what she's talking about.

WITNESS: He went like this in his groin area up and down.

WITNESS'S LAWYER: That's enough. That's enough. You know what the gesture is. If you want to describe it further for the record, go ahead. But everybody in this room knows what it is and I'm not going to allow—

CNN: I'm not going to guess what she thinks is a masturbatory gesture. He had his hand cupped; is that correct?

WITNESS: Yes.

CNN: And he moved his hand up and down; is that correct?

WITNESS: Yes.

CNN: And he did that two or three times; is that correct?

WITNESS: I didn't count.

CNN: Do you have any estimate?

WITNESS: Two or three times sounds fine.

WITNESS'S LAWYER: Do you know how many times he did it?

WITNESS: Probably turned my head in disgust.

CNN: So you don't know.

WITNESS: No.

CNN: How far away from him were you?

WITNESS: About as far away as we are, maybe closer. It was a very small office.

CNN: Four to six feet?

WITNESS: Approximately.

CNN: Did you say anything to him?

WITNESS'S LAWYER: After he made the gesture?
CNN: Yes.
WITNESS: I believe we just walked out of the office.

In the closing seconds of her deposition, the CNN lawyer asked whether she had complained of that incident and one other, which concerned another low-level supervisor making comments about how much he liked her butt. She was obviously humiliated that she had not objected to the incidents, and as the deposition ended, she looked as though she was about to cry. But then my own lawyer decided to ask one more question:

FURTHER EXAMINATION BY ATTORNEY FOR PANICCIA: Did you think a man that made masturbatory gestures to you concerning your ideas would be terribly receptive to complaints about another man commenting about your butt? I'll withdraw the question. I don't have any more.

DEPOSITIONS

Usually defense lawyers like to depose women complaining of discrimination as much and as soon as possible. They view it as a strategic coup if they're allowed to do so, because the sooner you commit to a story, the better chance that you will contradict yourself at a later date. And a lengthy, confrontational deposition will wear down even the most credible witness.

Your deposition is usually the first look the defense lawyers have at you. Until now they may have been at a disadvantage in assessing the strength of your case because the person responsible for the discrimination may have covered up his wrongdoing. If the business owner himself committed the discrimination, then he may be motivated to disclose everything to his lawyer, since he hired the lawyer and the lawyer works for him. In larger companies, however, the lawyer is brought onboard by the upper management and does not represent the individual accused of discrimination. That individual has no motivation to be candid with these lawyers, since he might be disciplined or fired if he tells the truth. Instead, he may try very hard to give them the impression that you are a flaky she-devil.

The defense also wants to see how you react under pressure. Do you reply with bitterness, so that a jury is likely to dislike and distrust you? Are you believable in your presentation? Do you have a thorough understanding of the facts? Are you able to recite them without sounding mixed up and confused?

More important, a lengthy deposition taken in a skillful manner can be used to convince a court to sharply limit your evidence or even dismiss your case.

One tactic defense lawyers use is asking "close-out questions." These are questions that cause you to swear you've stated all the relevant evidence, the effect of which is to prevent you from adding anything else to the record that you might subsequently remember. Your best response is something like this:

CNN: Have you now told me all the ways in which you believe you were discriminated by CNN or any of its employees?

PANICCIA: I have now told you everything that's occurring to me at this moment as I'm answering your question.

Or:

CNN: What documents other than the May 15 ["mommydom"] memo by Mr. Turner, if any, do you have to support your belief that you were replaced because you had a baby?

PANICCIA: Just give me a moment. I'm recounting some things so I can answer the question.

(Pause in the proceedings.)

PANICCIA: Were you asking for documents?

CNN: Yes.

PANICCIA: Documents. As I sit here now, none that I recall, but there may be some.

CNN: Is there anything that would refresh your recollection as to whether there are such documents?

PANICCIA: Probably a lot of things would refresh my recollection. Conversations, recounting conversations, talking to lawyers, or looking at my notes.

CNN: Do you believe there are any documents?

PANICCIA: Possibly. I'm not sure. I—I don't think I—at this moment, that's the best of my recollection—that there are no more. However, there may be.

It's important that you leave the door open in case you remember other incidents or documents that are relevant to your case. A deposition is not a spelling test. In other words, you are really not expected to be able to call up every minute detail at any given moment. So don't allow yourself to be forced into "closing out" the question.

Also don't allow your testimony to be mis-summarized by the defense. This is a tactic commonly used in order to lay down a good record to get your case dismissed. What happens is that you give an answer that's not quite what they wanted to hear, or isn't put as clearly and succinctly as they want it. They are thinking ahead and know how your testimony will read when used as evidence to support a dismissal based on summary judgment. They will summarize your answer with their own words and then ask you to confirm that what they said was a correct and accurate rendition of your testimony. In most cases, their statement will be much broader than your original answer. For instance:

CNN: Is it fair to say that if it had not been for you having a baby, you would not now be suing CNN?

PANICCIA: It's fair to say that if CNN hadn't fired me, then I wouldn't have sued. But considering the disparate treatment that has been given to women there, there is no saying that they might not have fired me for another reason for being a woman, in which case I might have sued as well.

CNN: So is the answer to the question no?

PANICCIA: The answer to the question is what I just told you. I don't think it can stand alone without the qualifying statement that I just made. Otherwise, I think it would mischaracterize what I just said.

Defense attorneys also sometimes use leading questions to establish that you had a friendly, cordial relationship with the man you are accusing of discrimination—that this man, in fact, did nice and helpful things for you. This will impress a jury and give the defense more leeway in attempting to prove that your claim is not credible. For instance:

CNN: Can you think of anything else along the lines that we have discussed that [your boss] did for you that you would consider to be nice?

ATTORNEY FOR PANICCIA: That's a meaningless term.

CNN: Are you instructing her not to answer?

ATTORNEY FOR PANICCIA: It's a meaningless term. It's an overbroad question. If he bought her lunch, if he opened the door for her, if he wiped up a spill, if he picked up something and handed it to her, if he brought her a Kleenex on one occasion, these might be nice things.

Or:

CNN: Did you request [your boss] to give you a letter of recommendation?

PANICCIA: Yes, I did.

CNN: Would you agree that it was nice of him to do so?

PANICCIA: I would have thought it was his professional obligation to.

Try to stay away from offering any characterizations that might be taken out of context and used against you.

Most of the defense's strategies will be readily distinguishable by your attorney, who will advise you on how to respond. It's not that your attorney will change what you have to say, because that's the truth and should not change. Rather, your attorney will advise you on how to phrase things so they cannot be improperly summarized, taken out of context, misconstrued, and used to defeat your claim.

INTERROGATORIES

"Interrogatories" are another way of eliciting answers and information from you. They are written questions that you are required to answer and sign. Usually, your attorney will go over your answers before giving them to the defense. If any of the questions are inappropriate or irrelevant, your attorney will object.

CNN inundated us with interrogatories. Here's part of what one set of questions was like, and what you can expect if you are served with interrogatories:

- Identify the name, title, and assignment of all persons who affected the pattern and practice of discrimination.
- Detail how that person was adversely affected.
- State all facts which support, confirm, or otherwise establish that the person's pay was based on sex, rather than a legitimate, nondiscriminatory reason.
- State all facts that support, confirm, or otherwise establish a pattern and practice of pay discrimination.
- Identify all persons you contend were adversely affected by the pattern and practice of discrimination in work schedules/work hours.
- For each person identified, state the work schedule/work

hours which the person was assigned to or denied as part of the pattern and practice of discrimination.

- If you contend that the acts encompass a pattern or practice of sexual harassment, identify all persons you contend were adversely affected by pattern and practice of sexual harassment, promotion, or constructive discharge.

The questions were endless—pages and pages of them. And even when we did answer them, CNN filed a motion to compel us to answer the questions more thoroughly, forcing us to go over and over every answer.

INVESTIGATORS

It's quite common for defense lawyers to use private investigators to uncover information about you.

During my lawsuit, I received many phone calls from people claiming they were conducting "surveys" (even though I had an unlisted phone number).

One woman wanted to know about my health care and health care claims.

I received a similar survey by mail that asked about customer service in the insurance industry. It wanted to know who my insurance agent and company was, the kind of coverage I had, what I paid for premiums, what type of claim(s) I might have recently filed, and the outcome of those claims.

Although I cannot say for sure that these surveys stemmed from the lawsuit, coincidentally they were all soliciting information that's highly important to defense lawyers. And they all ended when the lawsuit did.

One phone survey asked questions about cable television, such as "What do you think of when you hear the words 'Made-for-TV movie'?" It seemed innocuous enough, except that the next question was "What do you think of when you hear the words 'cable news'?"

My husband received a call from somebody wanting to know whether he was happy with his financial situation. (Perhaps they expected him to reply, “No, so I thought I’d put my wife up to suing CNN.”)

We never answered any of the questions. In most cases, we asked the caller to please list the questions we were expected to answer. We logged them, and then, when we had the complete list, we’d inform the caller that we had no intention of answering them—and hung up.

Through a variety of methods, investigators can learn where you live, what you owe on your home mortgage, what you pay for rent, whether you have credit cards—and if so, whether you pay them on time—what schools you attend or attended, how you are regarded by coworkers on your past and present jobs, whether your marriage is a happy one, and many other seemingly personal bits of information.

One defense lawyer told me that she typically uses information from a plaintiff’s first deposition to launch investigations into any area in which the woman’s testimony indicates that there might be damaging information about her.

SUBPOENAS FROM YOUR SIDE

At one employer seminar I attended, a person in the audience asked the seminar leader, “If you conduct an investigation of a discrimination complaint and learn that your company’s at fault, aren’t those documents subpoenable?” The seminar leader responded, “Yeah . . . if they’re around.”

I have no way of judging just how many employers hide or destroy evidence, but I do know that they make it very difficult for you to subpoena it. There are many ways, all within the law, to prevent you from obtaining the valuable evidence you may need. In my own case, CNN fought hard to protect evidence we wanted:

USA Today. CNN Lawsuit. May 8, 1995

A former CNN reporter who says she was fired in 1993 because she decided to have a second child has won a strategic victory in her ongoing lawsuit against the cable network. A California judge ruled Friday that Turner Broadcasting, CNN's owner, must give lawyers for Patti Paniccia key parts of a Turner-wide employee study on diversity. Superior Court Judge Kathryn Doi Todd ruled that Turner must disclose parts of the study that involve complaints on issues such as gender discrimination, work environment and marital status. Todd also said that Paniccia's lawyers could review salaries of all CNN and Headline News reporters and complaints of discrimination lodged against three key male CNN execs. It is unclear whether Turner will appeal the ruling. The company had no immediate comment.

In fact, CNN did petition a higher court to order Judge Todd to change her ruling. (Her ruling had allowed us to amend our complaint so as to broaden the scope of the evidence that would be allowed in.) But the California Court of Appeal refused to intervene. Nevertheless, it took us nearly six months to obtain the evidence.

Much of the defense lawyer literature I've read advises employees to object to just about everything on whatever grounds possible, including alleging that your request is not in the proper form, is not specific enough, is vague or ambiguous, is irrelevant, fails to explain why the evidence is needed, or is not reasonably calculated to lead to the discovery of admissible evidence.

Whether you're successful in retrieving the evidence you need depends on how much hardball your employer's lawyers are playing and how much money your employer is willing to spend on the defense firm's time to frustrate your efforts. It also depends on how hard your lawyer is willing to fight for you.

The items your lawyer will probably request include the qualifications and background of anybody who was treated more favorably than you; the company's official policy statement on discrimination; the company's procedure manual for reporting complaints; your personnel file; information on other complaints lodged against the person or persons you are complaining about; any studies the company may have conducted on discrimination; information concerning personnel practices, including statistical information regarding the number of females versus males who have been promoted, terminated, et cetera; and any information compiled by the employer on itself, such as the diversity study we fought so hard to possess.

In the case of an in-house study, some courts recognize a "self-critical analysis privilege." They don't want to discourage companies from conducting in-house analyses. If employees are continually able to use the analyses against employers, then employers may no longer perform such studies. Whether you are allowed to subpoena this kind of evidence depends on your court and how vital the information is to your case.

SUBPOENAS FROM THEIR SIDE

One afternoon I walked into my lawyers' office and was handed a file. "Here's what they've gotten so far," John said. "Gotten so far?" I asked. "What does that mean?"

It meant that CNN had sent out subpoenas and received back everything that was inside the file he was handing me. I opened it to find my employment records from past and present employers, and my medical records from every doctor, laboratory, and hospital I had visited in the last ten years, including my OB-GYN's personal notes about the deliveries of both of my children.

CNN had subpoenaed the files from my family doctor back to the day I had first walked into his office. I sat and read about the flu I'd caught after returning from my Central American honeymoon. I read about the respiratory illness I'd contracted when I was pregnant. And I read about the time I cut my leg surfing. In other words, you should expect that every one of your medical files will be reviewed by your employer's lawyers.

In most cases, the defense is within the law in seeking information about your personal medical conditions. Here's a list of what was subpoenaed from me:

CNN requested from every doctor, clinic, lab, or hospital I'd visited in the last decade any appointment record; record of complaints and symptoms; medical histories; consultation records; treatment records; medical records; medical charts; diagnostic tests; laboratory reports; MRIs; X rays; prescriptions; itemized statements of billings; charges and fees; payment records; insurance claims forms and reports; counseling notes; psychological evaluations, including notes and fees; neuropsychological reports and evaluations; psychiatric reports and evaluations; audio and/or video recordings of counseling and/or therapy sessions; all oral or written communication by the doctor to any other health care provider; and every other record prepared in the course of providing any form of care of attention, whether as an emergency room patient, inpatient, or outpatient, and also all other records constituting, referring to, or relating to any and all consultations, examinations, diagnoses, prognoses, opinions, recommendations, advice, counseling, testing, treatment, and/or therapy, provided by any health care provider.

If you claim that you are suffering from stress or other emotional damages as a result of your employer's discrimination (which is a standard claim in a discrimination lawsuit), your employer has a right to go through your entire mental and medical history.

Shortly after CNN fired me, I went to see a therapist for eight weekly visits. I'd wanted to run a reality check by her to see whether she thought I was strong enough to sue CNN. By our third meeting, I was assured that I was, and mentioned I had found a lawyer. "Tell your lawyer I don't keep notes," she said. "He'll be happy to hear that."

I didn't realize the full impact of what she'd said until months later, when CNN subpoenaed her "notes." She turned over one page, showing only the dates I'd seen her and the amount charged. She had known what was coming. I was lucky in that I had no history of therapy or treatment of any mental disorders. But what about the millions of people who do? At this stage, they are forced to choose between pursuing their lawsuit (and allowing the public to hear about their personal mental history) and dropping their case.

If you have a concern in this regard, bring it up to your attorney *before* you file the lawsuit. He or she will not only advise you what to expect but also may be able to assist you in protecting personal evidence from being made public. You walk a fine line here, because in order to help prove your case, you must document with medical professionals whatever stress or illness the ordeal has caused you. If, however, you are in *too much need* of therapy, the defense will attempt to paint you as a "nutcake."

The defense lawyers will attempt to show that other events in your life, and not the discrimination, are responsible for whatever stress you are under. If the discrimination did not cause the stress, then your employer will not have to pay for it.

In my case, CNN continually probed for reasons why I might be considered mentally unsound or unreasonably stressed out. For instance:

CNN: Can you tell me each action that CNN or any of its employees took that caused you emotional distress?

PANICCIA: This is—besides firing me? . . .

CNN: Have there been any other events in your life which have caused you emotional distress?

PANICCIA: Not of this nature. Not of this magnitude.

CNN: Of any magnitude?

PANICCIA: Well, every time I watch "An Affair to Remember," I cry. But I don't know what you mean by "any magnitude." A sad movie?

CNN: No, events in your life that have caused you emotional distress.

PANICCIA: What I mean is emotional distress meaning crying at a sad movie or—what degree of emotional distress?

CNN: I don't consider a sad movie an event in your life, Ms. Paniccia. I'm talking about things that happened to you in your personal life—school, work, things that you do in your life. Have there been any other events that have occurred that have caused you emotional distress to any degree?

PANICCIA: No. . . .

CNN: Did you feel any emotional distress in connection with any other prior employment that you have had?

PANICCIA: You know, sometimes when you go cover a plane crash . . . on the job, and you see a hundred dead bodies burned up and smelling the burning flesh, you lose a little sleep. And that's just part of the job. So you know, something like that would cause me emotional distress.

I remember I interviewed a guy with AIDS, and I was supposed to go back and call him a month later. And I took two months, and when I did, he had died. I was upset about that. That you could consider work related, but nothing that I think that you're inquiring about, which would mean job, personal life, or anything of that nature.

CNN: Did you ever consult any medical or health practitioners with respect to any emotional distress that you suffered?

PANICCIA: I think I have answered this question already. And what I said was there have been times when they will say do you have a stressful job, and I will say, yes, but I can usually handle it. And they may note, "She has a stressful job."

But no, I have never consulted them in terms of saying I have been fired or anything along those lines other than this particular time when I got fired by CNN.

You can expect to greet dusty skeletons as they're brought out of the closet and held up in full view for all to see.

Even when there are no skeletons, the defense will fish . . . and fish . . . and fish.

For example, CNN sent subpoenas to Pepperdine Law School. While a reporter, I had taught Communications/First Amendment Law at Pepperdine. After being fired from CNN, I'd instituted a Gender and Law class. CNN requested every record in the school's possession pertaining to employment, including files, papers, notes, memoranda, correspondence, and all documents stored on any form of computer or computer-readable storage media that in any way related to:

- Paniccia's job application, résumé, or other employment history
- references provided by or otherwise pertaining to Paniccia
- job interviews prior to the first day of work
- all representations by Paniccia regarding the reason for her termination from any employment
- any deliberation, thought, and/or consideration relating to the decision to employ Paniccia
- negotiations regarding any aspect of employment
- offers of employment
- terms, benefits, and conditions of employment
- employment contracts
- job title and status, application for changes in job titles
- job requirements
- job assignments and responsibilities
- requests for changes in job assignments or responsibilities
- promotions and transfers, requests for promotions and transfers, and responses to said requests
- evaluation, reviews, and communications of any kind, formal or informal, relating to job performance, conduct, or behavior by Paniccia
- formal and/or informal warnings to, reprimands of, and discipline regarding Paniccia

- investigations concerning the conduct, behavior, and job performance of Paniccia
- oral or written complaints, formal or informal, made by Paniccia
- responses of any kind to any and all oral and/or written complaints
- grievances, notes of grievance meetings or hearings, and results of grievance proceedings
- salary, wages, earnings, compensations, commission, bonuses, benefits of any kind, and any other form of income provided to Paniccia
- pension rights and benefits
- workers' compensation claims
- insurance-related documents
- termination, layoff, and separation from employment
- any lawsuits, complaints, charges, grievances, and other legal claims relating in any way to Paniccia's employment
- all other correspondence, notes, memoranda, and documents relating to any aspect of Paniccia's employment, regardless of whether they were authored by Pepperdine

Pepperdine dutifully circulated the subpoena to the payroll department, the provost's office, the dean's office, the associate dean's office, the assistant dean's office, the academic transcripts office, the employment/personnel records office, and any other department that might contain some records on me. In other words, practically the entire university was notified.

Fortunately, the deans and professors at Pepperdine were legally sophisticated enough not to be overly concerned upon receiving a subpoena. (And they had the courtesy to let me know that a subpoena had arrived. Not every employer will do so.)

But these subpoenas can be a menace to some women. Some employers, especially those unknowledgeable about the legal process, might become suspicious or upset over being handed a subpoena of this breadth. Or what if you've chosen not to discuss with your new employer the fact that you've charged your previous employer with discrimination? You can imagine what upset an unanticipated subpoena can cause.

If you are concerned about the effect a subpoena will have on any particular person, you might consider notifying them in advance, unless your lawyer advises you otherwise. Tell them something like, "I'm involved in a discrimination lawsuit, and it's my understanding that in this type of lawsuit, just about everyone I've ever known typically receives a subpoena. These people are fishing for whatever they can find on me. You might receive one, but please don't worry if you do. Just comply with it. I apologize if it causes you any great inconvenience."

VARIOUS MOTIONS

There are a number of motions that both the defense and your own lawyer may file before trial.

The defense may file a motion to strike in order to eliminate defendants or to limit your lawsuit in terms of the claims under which you are suing. For instance, you may sue for a violation of Title VII, a breach of contract, a violation of public policy, wrongful termination, and any of several other reasons. The defense will try hard to have most, if not all, of those causes of action eliminated from the lawsuit.

In my lawsuit, I counted more than one hundred pleadings, motions, responses to motions, notices of depositions, notices of related case, motions to request sanctions, motions to compel, oppositions to motions, and even an application by the defense submitted to the court requesting special permission to file a document longer than the usual fifteen-page maximum. All of these motions will be handled by your attorney.

SUMMARY JUDGMENT

The defense's motion for summary judgment may be the most pivotal point of your case. Summary judgment means that your case will be dismissed before trial because there are no issues of fact that can be decided by a jury. If the facts are not in dispute, then the defense asks the court to review those facts and determine that they simply do not constitute a violation of the law. Typically, this motion is filed after the evidence is produced and all the depositions have been taken.

Many employers are successful at this stage because of the preventative measures they've taken throughout your employment (making you an at-will employee, manipulating your performance reviews, anticipating lawsuits when documenting your in-house complaint, etc.).

They're also successful because defense lawyers typically focus their efforts from the very start on being able to succeed at this summary judgment stage. For instance, many of the questions they ask during deposition are specifically geared to elicit answers that fit neatly into their motion for summary judgment. They'll quote you (sometimes out of context) in the papers they file with the court asking for summary judgment.

Another reason employers prevail is a lack of knowledge and legal advice on the part of most employees during the early stages (especially when they file their EEOC complaints).

Defense lawyers contend they are successful because many of the cases they fight have no merit.

The results of summary judgment may be to dismiss the entire case or just some of the causes of action. Summary judgment is expensive for your employer; it can cost fifteen to twenty thousand dollars. It requires in-depth legal research and analysis of your entire case, including each piece of evidence and every line of the deposition transcripts.

SETTLEMENT

I once recited Robert Frost's "The Road Not Taken" to a friend who was a rock-and-roll disc jockey. I told her I was having to choose between two jobs, one in a big city and one in a lovely little town. I knew that the minute I made a choice it would irreversibly steer my life in a new direction, and there would be no going back. I recounted the poet's words in part, as he described his unhappy dilemma in having to choose only one of two diverging roads: "Yet knowing how way leads on to way, / I doubted if I should ever come back."

With all due respect to Robert Frost, she immediately quipped back with lines from "Stairway to Heaven," by Led Zeppelin:

> Yes, there are two paths you can go by
> But in the long run
> There's still time to change the road you're on.[17]

It's true. In a lawsuit it's called settlement.

Either side can propose settlement, and neither is bound to accept it.

If you are considering settlement, then first you must define what you want from your lawsuit. You must determine if what you want is what your employer is willing to give. It might be a certain amount of money, certain changes implemented in the workplace, reinstatement to your old job, or any other solution—as long as you both agree.

Your employer will determine whether to make you an offer of settlement, and if so, what kind and how much, based upon many different factors, including:

1. What are the merits of your case? What are the facts? How long have you worked there? Have there been any promises or policies violated? Does the employer have

any documentation that you did not properly perform your duties?

2. What kind of evidence do *you* have? Is there a smoking-gun memo, or other direct evidence? Is there evidence that a man or men were treated more favorably? Were there any inconsistent statements made by one of your managers or supervisors? Do you have statistics that reflect disparities in the way women are treated as compared to men?
3. What kind of a plaintiff are you? Are you credible? Are you likable? Is a jury likely to believe your story?
4. Does your employer have a legitimate, credible business reason for the adverse action taken against you?
5. Did you lodge a complaint within the company? If so, how did the company handle it? Have there been any prior complaints against the person or persons responsible for committing the discriminatory act against you? Does that person still work for the company? If not, he may be more likely to testify unfavorably toward the employer, and possibly reveal additional evidence of discrimination by higher-level managers.
6. What is the potential for damages? Remember, a Title VII claim is limited, but if the lawsuit is brought under your state discrimination law, your damages may be significantly more. Also, other claims, such as wrongful termination and violation of public policy, often call for significant punitive-damage awards.
7. Was there an EEOC investigation? If so, what was the outcome?
8. How will an ongoing lawsuit or a public trial affect others in the company? Will it lower or destroy morale if it's prolonged? Or if it settles too quickly, might managers feel as if the company does not back them up?

9. Will a trial bring adverse publicity that could hurt company profits? Or could it engender community resentment toward the company?
10. Is a jury likely to award a large sum of money, and thus encourage other employees to sue? If the company settles, will it get a reputation as being a pushover when it comes to charges of discrimination? Some companies have spent millions of dollars defending even the smallest of lawsuits, just to send the message to other employees that they are in for a fight. Big companies have resources to do this.
11. How much will it cost to defend the lawsuit?
12. Does the employer have insurance? In 1998, an estimated 50 percent of the Fortune 500 companies had Employee Practices Liability (EPL) coverage.[18] EPL policies cover legal fees and most damages awarded by a court or paid in settlement, *except for punitive damages!* An employer who suspects that a trial will bring a punitive-damage award may be motivated to settle and have it be covered by the policy, rather than be socked with punitive damages.

    Sometimes employers will continue to litigate until they reach policy limits, or make offers of settlement close to policy limits. Policy limits range anywhere from $10,000 to $50 million.

    Some states disallow EPL insurance for acts that are intentional on your employer's part. This is another risk an employer runs into by going to trial. If a jury finds *intentional* discrimination, the policy may not apply.

    Employers don't want employees learning what kind, if any, of EPL insurance they carry. Knowing this information can help you strategize your case.
13. In which court was the lawsuit filed—federal or state? Was it filed in a state that favors employers or a state that

favors workers? Is it a state that's known for large jury awards?

14. Who is the judge? Is he or she known for favoring either side?
15. Is your case going to be attractive to a plaintiffs' attorney, so that an attorney will work hard pursuing it?
16. Is your attorney known for being skilled at trial? Does the attorney usually take only credible cases? Or does he or she have a reputation for filing a lawsuit on frivolous grounds?

Settlement offers are not admissible during trial. This means that if your employer offers you an extremely large amount of money, you can't use that fact to imply to the jury that your employer has admitted wrongdoing. Nor can you use it to give the jury an idea of what your employer is willing to pay.

There's one more thing you should consider regarding settlement. If you are no longer employed there, but some of your witnesses are, then what will happen to them if you settle? Are they still experiencing the discrimination? Have they come forward to testify for you? Have they annoyed their boss(es) by doing so? If so, you definitely have a moral obligation to keep them in mind when settling your case.

Settlements can include all types of provisions, including a demand that those women still employed receive pay comparable to that of their male counterparts, are given the promotions they deserve, or are offered the opportunity to transfer out of a particular department where they've experienced harassment and discrimination. Settlements can also include getting discriminatory supervisors removed. I'm not telling you to be Joan of Arc, but it really would be a shame if, after all these women have done in coming forward to testify, they are left behind in the same (or worse) discriminatory work environment.

TRIAL

Trials vary so greatly that it would be impossible to give you a detailed description of what to expect in your own. And at this stage, you will have hired a lawyer whose job it is to take care of your legal needs. Let him or her do that.

When you are called on to testify, be open, honest, and to the point. Your lawyer will probably have rehearsed you somewhat so you feel comfortable answering questions in what might otherwise seem a stilted, or even scary, environment.

Trying to predict what the jury will decide is a bizarre experience. Some jury-selection experts make thousands of dollars per day doing so. Even so, one defense lawyer told me, "when all is said and done, the only thing predictable about jurors is that they're unpredictable."

Sometimes lawyers are dumbfounded when, after arguing what they believe is a legal "slam dunk" case, juries take it upon themselves to factor in humanity, social interaction, compassion, and a larger moral question of who was right and who was wrong.

APPEALS

If you win, your employer has the right to appeal the court's decision, in which case you will be paid nothing until the appeal is final.

Usually appeals are costly and lengthy. Whether your employer decides to appeal will most likely depend on the strength of your case, the size of your award, and how much money your employer is willing to spend.

Sometimes an employer will offer to pay you only a portion of the verdict in exchange for not filing an appeal. In that case, you and your lawyer should assess the likelihood that your employer will succeed on appeal.

In some courts, the judge has the ability to reduce the amount a jury awards you on the grounds that it's excessive.

If you lose the trial, you also have the option to appeal. Usually an appeal is not part of the original contingency agreement between you and your lawyer. You may or may not have to pay for the appeal, which can cost anywhere from $25,000 to $30,000 if you appeal to one higher court, and up to $50,000 if you appeal all the way to the Supreme Court. Supreme Court appeals are rare, and most levels of appellate courts refuse to hear the great majority of cases. On the other hand, should your case be heard on appeal and you win, your employer would probably be ordered to pay both trial and appellate costs.

Appeals can take anywhere from six months to five years, depending on how high up a case is taken.

The appeal court might reverse your verdict, or order that an entirely new trial be held, in which case both sides will be forced to spend more money.

AFTER TRIAL

One thing is certain: Your trial will be one of the most stressful times in your life, and it will forever change you. Former radio talk-show host Ginny Waters sued a San Francisco radio station after her show was canceled during her maternity leave. She endured a very public weeklong trial—one she says affected her life to an extent she never would have anticipated. Most trials do just that.

> It's all-consuming. You have to devote weeks to it, preparing and going through it, and I would come home and just burst out crying because I thought, "Here are these twelve strangers that I've never seen before, and my fate is in their hands." I went, "My God, these people are judging me in the truest sense of the word."
>
> But I learned so much from it. I learned that no matter what anybody says, you have to do what you have to do to protect yourself legally, and not be the nice guy. The radio station kept saying, "But Ginny's so nice. She's so nice." And they really thought they could get away with it because I am nice. But that shouldn't have to interfere with my rights. It's part of that women's syndrome that I want people to like me so I'm not going to make waves. Standing up for myself was

a really big deal. There are few places where you have to stand up more for yourself than when you're on trial.

I also learned that you have to be really accountable to anything you do or say because you never know when it can come back and slap you in the face. That's a scary thought, because I'm a very spontaneous person and I like to have a lot of fun. So to always be on your guard takes some of the fun out of work nowadays.

The most difficult thing was that I resented my close friends—not the ones who were involved in the case, but the ones outside of work. They weren't really there for me. They just couldn't have any way of knowing what I was going through, because they hadn't been through it themselves. That was really hard. People didn't understand the magnitude of what it was like to go through that emotionally, and you can't really expect them to.

Then there was this whole aftermath for the next couple of years where people were forming or re-forming their opinions of me because of how they got the information and how they heard the information.

This one woman who originally had told me what I was doing was right . . . I ran into her months later and she told me she didn't want to go to lunch with me. She said, "I saw what your trial put the general manager through, and it was awful." I thought, "My God. He didn't go through anything compared to what I did! He's the one who fired me!" But people will make their judgments.

The best part was after I won when the defense asked that the jury be polled. I only needed nine out of twelve. I found out that every single person on the jury had voted in my favor. I burst out into tears. I didn't know them and they didn't know who I was. But every single one of them voted in my favor.

In Closing

One must wait until the evening to see how splendid the day has been.

—Sophocles

Don't give up. If you are having a problem at work, don't give up. If you've read this book, then you know how many alternatives and choices are available to handle whatever problems you may be facing. You can decide for yourself the best route to take. But just don't give up.

I realize the advice I've given requires a lot of preparation on your part—constant homework to protect yourself and your rights. It may seem these tasks are cumbersome and time-consuming. But there's an old Chinese proverb: The more you sweat in peace, the less you bleed in war. This book, and all that it asks you to do for yourself, is about preparing for the worst, in anticipation of the best—in hopes that you can overcome any discrimination you encounter and correct the problem before it drastically and irreversibly affects your career.

An old cowboy once told me, "They'll never get rid of cowboys, because when we get to the end of the rope, we always tie a knot and hang on." Even if your problems seem insurmountable, tie your knot and stick around for a while. Women in the workplace are here to stay.

I wish you a long and successful career.

But most of all, I wish you peace.

Appendix

Although every effort has been made to ensure accuracy and completeness in these tables, the law in this area is constantly evolving. You should obtain legal assistance regarding your own state law.

TABLE I
State Discrimination Laws: Minimum Number of Employees Required

Most states stipulate a minimum number of employees for a private employer to be bound by the state's discrimination statute. Some states exclude household employees or family members when tallying the number of employees.

In most states, public employers (such as cities, counties, and other public entities) are bound by the statute regardless of the number of employees.

1. Alabama	No discrimination statute
2. Alaska	1

3. Arizona	15
4. Arkansas	9
5. California	5
6. Colorado	1
7. Connecticut	3
8. Delaware	4
9. District of Columbia	1
10. Florida	15
11. Georgia	No discrimination statute for private employees; only for state employees
12. Hawaii	1
13. Idaho	5
14. Illinois	15
15. Indiana	6
16. Iowa	4
17. Kansas	4
18. Kentucky	8
19. Louisiana	No discrimination statute
20. Maine	1
21. Maryland	15
22. Massachusetts	6
23. Michigan	1
24. Minnesota	1
25. Mississippi	No discrimination statute
26. Missouri	6
27. Montana	1
28. Nebraska	15
29. Nevada	15
30. New Hampshire	6
31. New Jersey	1
32. New Mexico	4
33. New York	4
34. North Carolina	15
35. North Dakota	1
36. Ohio	4

37. Oklahoma	15
38. Oregon	1
39. Pennsylvania	4
40. Rhode Island	4
41. South Carolina	15
42. South Dakota	1
43. Tennessee	8
44. Texas	15
45. Utah	15
46. Vermont	1
47. Virginia	More than 5 but fewer than 15; state employees must use EEOC
48. Washington	8
49. West Virginia	12
50. Wisconsin	1
51. Wyoming	2

TABLE II
State-by-State Employment-at-Will Exceptions

There are three major exceptions to the employment-at-will doctrine:

1. the existence of an implied contract—that is, a contract formed by oral statements or assurances, employee handbooks, or conduct of the parties.
2. wrongful discharge in violation of public policy, generally classified into one of the three categories:
   a. where employee is terminated for refusing to engage in an illegal activity
   b. where employee is terminated for reporting an illegal act such as discrimination
   c. where employee is terminated for exercising a legally protected right
3. breach of the implied covenant of good faith and fair dealing—that is, the duty upon each party to a contract to act in good faith and exercise fair dealing in fulfilling the obligations of the contract

Y—Courts in this state have recognized this at-will exception.

N—Courts in this state have not recognized this at-will exception.

L—Courts in this state have recognized limited application of this at-will exception, in which case the policy may vary from court to court.

State	Implied Contract	Public Policy	Good Faith
Alabama	Y	L	Y
Alaska	Y	Y	Y
Arizona	Y	Y	L
Arkansas	Y	Y	N
California	Y	Y	Y
Colorado	Y	Y	Y
Connecticut	Y	Y	L
Delaware	L	L	Y
District of Columbia	Y	L	N

State	Implied Contract	Public Policy	Good Faith
Florida	L	L	N
Georgia	Y	N	N
Hawaii	Y	Y	N
Idaho	Y	Y	Y
Illinois	Y	Y	N
Indiana	L	Y	N
Iowa	Y	Y	N
Kansas	Y	Y	N
Kentucky	Y	Y	N
Louisiana	N	N	N
Maine	Y	L	N
Maryland	Y	Y	N
Massachusetts	L	Y	Y
Michigan	Y	Y	N
Minnesota	Y	Y	N
Mississippi	L	L	N
Missouri	N	Y	N
Montana	Y	Y	Y
Nebraska	Y	L	N
Nevada	Y	Y	Y
New Hampshire	Y	L	L
New Jersey	Y	Y	N
New Mexico	Y	L	N
New York	Y	L	L
North Carolina	L	Y	N
North Dakota	L	L	N
Ohio	Y	Y	N
Oklahoma	Y	Y	N
Oregon	Y	Y	N
Pennsylvania	L	L	N
Rhode Island	N	N	N
South Carolina	Y	Y	N
South Dakota	Y	Y	N

State	Implied Contract	Public Policy	Good Faith
Tennessee	Y	Y	N
Texas	L	Y	N
Utah	Y	Y	L
Vermont	Y	Y	N
Virginia	N	L	N
Washington	Y	L	N
West Virginia	Y	Y	N
Wisconsin	Y	Y	N
Wyoming	Y	Y	L

TABLE III
State Human Rights Commissions

Some of the states listed below may also have Websites that provide information.

Alabama—none

Alaska
Alaska State Commission for Human Rights
800 "A" Street, Suite 204
Anchorage, AK 99501-3669
(907) 276-7474
(800) 478-4692

Arizona
Arizona Civil Rights Division
1275 West Washington Street
Phoenix, AZ 85007
(602) 542-5263

Arkansas
EEOC Little Rock Area Office
425 West Capitol Avenue, Suite 625
Little Rock, AR 72201
(501) 324-5060

California
California Department of Fair Employment and Housing
30 Van Ness Avenue, Suite 3000
San Francisco, CA 94102-6073
(415) 557-2006 (San Francisco)
(916) 445-5523 (Sacramento)
(800) 884-1684

Colorado
Colorado Civil Rights Commission
1560 Broadway, Suite 1050
Denver, CO 80202
(303) 894-2997

Connecticut
Connecticut Commission on Human Rights & Opportunities
1229 Albany Avenue
Hartford, CT 06112
(860) 566-7710

Delaware
Delaware Department of Labor, Anti-Discrimination Section
4425 North Market Street
Wilmington, DE 19802
(302) 761-8200

District of Columbia
D.C. Department of Human Rights and Business Development
441 Fourth Street, NW
Suite 970 North
Washington, DC 20001
(202) 724-1385

Florida
Florida Commission on Human Relations

325 John Knox Road
Building F, Suite 240
Tallahassee, FL 32303-4149
(904) 488-7082
(800) 342-8170

Georgia
Georgia Commission on Equal Opportunity
International Tower, Suite 710
229 Peachtree Street, NE
Atlanta, GA 30303
(404) 656-1736
—for state employees only

Hawaii
Hawaii Civil Rights Commission
Enforcement Division
888 Mililani Street, 2nd Floor
Honolulu, HI 96813
(808) 586-8640

Idaho
Idaho Commission on Human Rights
1109 Main Street
Owyhee Plaza, 4th Floor, Suite 400
P.O. Box 83720-0040
Boise, ID 83720-0040
(208) 334-2873

Illinois
Illinois Department of Human Rights
James R. Thompson Center
100 West Randolph Street, 10th Floor
Suite 100
Chicago, IL 60601
(312) 814-6245

Indiana
Indiana Civil Rights Commission
Indiana Government Center
100 North Center Avenue, Room N103
Indianapolis, IN 46204
(317) 232-2600
(800) 628-2909

Iowa
Iowa Civil Rights Commission
211 East Maple Street
Des Moines, IA 50309
(515) 281-4121

Kansas
Kansas Commission on Human Rights
Landon State Office Building
900 Southwest, 8th Floor, Suite 851-S
Topeka, KS 66612-1258
(913) 296-3206

Kentucky
Kentucky Commission on Human Rights
332 West Broadway, Suite 700
Louisville, KY 40202
(502) 595-4024
(800) 292-5566

Louisiana—none

Maine
Maine Human Rights Commission
51 State House Station
Augusta, ME 04333-0051
(207) 624-6050

Maryland
Maryland Commission on Human Relations
6 Saint Paul Street, 9th Floor, Suite 900
Baltimore, MD 21202
(410) 767-8600 (Baltimore)
(410) 313-6430 (Howard County)
(301) 883-6170 (Prince Georges County)
(800) 637-6247

Massachusetts
Massachusetts Commission Against Discrimination
McCormack State Office Building
1 Ashburton Place, Room 601
Boston, MA 02108
(617) 727-3990 (Boston)
(413) 739-2145 (Springfield)

Michigan
Michigan Department of Civil Rights
1200 Sixth Avenue, 6th Floor
Detroit, MI 48226
(313) 256-2663 (Detroit)
(517) 751-0325 (Lansing)

Minnesota
Minnesota Department of Human Rights
190 East Fifth Street
Army Corps of Engineers Center
St. Paul, MN 55101
(612) 296-5663
(800) 657-3704

Mississippi—none

Missouri
Missouri Commission on Human Rights
3315 West Truman Boulevard
P.O. Box 1129
Jefferson City, MO 65102
(573) 751-3325
(800) 877-6247

Montana
Montana Human Rights Commission
Department of Labor & Industry
616 Helena Avenue
P.O. Box 1728
Helena, MT 59624
(406) 444-2884
(800) 542-0807

Nebraska
Nebraska Equal Employment Opportunity Commission
State Office Building, 5th Floor
301 Centennial Mall South
P.O. Box 94934
Lincoln, NE 68509
(402) 471-2024

Nevada
Nevada Equal Rights Commission
1515 East Tropicana, Suite 590
Las Vegas, NV 89119
(702) 486-7161 (Las Vegas)
(702) 688-1288 (Reno)

New Hampshire
New Hampshire Commission for Human Rights
2 Chenell Drive
Concord, NH 03301
(603) 271-2767

New Jersey
New Jersey Division on Civil Rights
140 East Front Street, CN090
Trenton, NJ 08618
(609) 292-4605

New Mexico
New Mexico Human Rights Commission
1596 Pacheco Street
Santa Fe, NM 87505
(505) 827-6838

New York
New York State Division of Human Rights
Empire State Plaza Concourse
P.O. Box 2049
Albany, NY 12220
(518) 474-2705
(800) 427-2773

North Carolina
North Carolina Human Relations Commission
217 West Jones Street
Raleigh, NC 27603-1336
(919) 733-7996
—for private employees

North Carolina State Office of Administrative Hearings
424 North Blount Street
Raleigh, NC 27601
(919) 733-2691
—for public employees

North Dakota
North Dakota Department of Labor
State Capitol, 13th Floor
600 East Boulevard
Bismark, ND 58505
(701) 328-2660
(800) 582-8032

Ohio
Ohio Civil Rights Commission
Southeast Regional Office
1111 East Broad Street
Columbus, OH 43205-1379
(614) 466-5928

Oklahoma
Oklahoma Human Rights Commission
2101 North Lincoln Boulevard, Room 480
Oklahoma City, OK 73105
(405) 521-2360 (Oklahoma City)
(918) 581-2733 (Tulsa)

Oregon
Oregon Bureau of Labor and Industries Civil Rights Division
State Office Building
800 Northeast Oregon
Portland, OR 97201
(503) 731-4075 (Portland)
(503) 687-7460 (Eugene)

Pennsylvania
Pennsylvania Human Relations Commission
711 State Office Building
Broad and Spring Garden Street
Philadelphia, PA 19139
(215) 560-2596 (Philadelphia)
(717) 787-9784 (Harrisburg)

Rhode Island
Rhode Island Commission for Human Rights
10 Abbott Park Place
Providence, RI 02903
(401) 222-2661

South Carolina
South Carolina Human Affairs Commission
2611 Forest Drive
Columbia, SC 29204
(803) 737-7800
(800) 521-0725

South Dakota
South Dakota Division of Human Rights
118 West Capitol Avenue
Pierre, SD 57501
(605) 773-4493

Tennessee
Tennessee Human Rights Commission
530 Church Street, Suite 400
Nashville, TN 37243
(615) 741-5825

Texas
Texas Commission on Human Rights
8100 Cameron Road, Building B, Suite 525
P.O. Box 13493
Austin, TX 78753
(512) 837-8534

Utah
Utah Industrial Commission
Anti-Discrimination Division
160 East 300 South
Salt Lake City, UT 84110
(801) 530-6801

Vermont
Vermont Human Rights Commission
135 State Street, Drawer 33
Montpelier, VT 05633-6301
(802) 828-2480
—for state employees

Office of the Attorney General
Civil Rights Division
109 State Street
Montpelier, VT 05609-1001

(802) 828-3657
—for private employees

Virginia
Fairfax Human Rights Commission
12000 Government Center Parkway
Suite 318
Fairfax, VA 22035
(703) 324-2953 (Fairfax)
(703) 838-6390 (Alexandria City)
(703) 358-3929 (Arlington County)
(703) 792-4680 (Prince William County)
(703) 468-4265 (Montgomery County)
—for private employees

Virginia Equal Employment Opportunity Commission
1400 "L" Street Northwest, Suite 200
Washington, D.C. 20005
(202) 275-7377
—for state employees

Washington
Washington State Human Rights Commission
711 Capital Way, Suite 402
P.O. Box 42490
Olympia, WA 98504-2490
(360) 753-6770 (Olympia)
(206) 464-6500 (Seattle)
(509) 456-4473 (Spokane)
(800) 233-3247

West Virginia
West Virginia Human Rights Commission
1321 Plaza East, Room 106
Charleston, WV 25301
(304) 558-2616

Wisconsin
Wisconsin Department of Workforce Development, Equal Rights Division
201 East Washington Avenue, Room 407
Madison, WI 53702
(608) 266-6860
—for private employees

Wisconsin Personnel Commission
131 West Wilson Street, Room 1004
Madison, WI 53703
(608) 266-1995
—for state employees

Wyoming
Wyoming Department of Employment, Labor Standards Division
6101 Yellowstone, Room 259C
Cheyenne, WY 82002
(307) 777-7261

TABLE IV
Family and Medical Leave Act (in relevant part)

Section 2611. Definitions

(2) *Eligible employee*

(A) In general.

The term "eligible employee" means an employee who has been employed—

(i) for at least 12 months by the employer with respect to whom leave is requested; and

(ii) for at least 1,250 hours of service with such employer during the previous 12-month period.

(B) Exclusions.

The term "eligible employee" does not include—

(i) any Federal officer or employee; or

(ii) any employee of an employer who is employed at a worksite at which such employer employs less than 50 employees if the total number of employees employed by that employer within 75 miles of that worksite is less than 50.

(4) *Employer*

(A) In general. The term "employer"—

(i) means any person who employs 50 or more employees for each working day during each of 20 or more calendar workweeks in the current or preceding calendar year;

(ii) includes—

(I) any person who acts, directly or indirectly, in the interest of an employer to any of the employees of such employer; and

(II) any successor in interest of an employer;

(iii) includes any "public agency."

(5) *Employment benefits*

The term "employment benefits" means all benefits provided or made available to employees by an employer, including group life insurance, health insurance, disability insurance, sick leave, annual leave, educational benefits, and pensions, regardless of whether such benefits are provided by a practice or written policy of an employer or through an "employee benefit plan."

(6) *Health care provider*

The term "health care provider" means—

(A) a doctor of medicine or osteopathy who is authorized to practice medicine or surgery (as appropriate) by the State in which the doctor practices; or

(B) any other person determined by the Secretary to be capable of providing health care services.

(7) *Parent*

The term "parent" means the biological parent of an employee or an individual who stood in loco parentis to an employee when the employee was a son or daughter.

(9) *Reduced leave schedule*

The term "reduced leave schedule" means a leave schedule that reduces the usual number of hours per workweek, or hours per workday, of an employee.

(10) *Secretary*

The term "Secretary" means the Secretary of Labor.

(11) *Serious health condition*

The term "serious health condition" means an illness, injury, impairment, or physical or mental condition that involves—

(A) inpatient care in a hospital, hospice, or residential medical care facility; or

(B) continuing treatment by a health care provider.

(12) *Son or daughter*

The term "son or daughter" means a biological, adopted, or foster child, a stepchild, a legal ward, or a child of a person standing in loco parentis, who is—

(A) under 18 years of age; or

(B) 18 years of age or older and incapable of self-care because of a mental or physical disability.

(13) *Spouse*

The term "spouse" means a husband or wife, as the case may be.

Section 2612. Leave requirement

(a) In general

(1) *Entitlement to leave*

Subject to section 2613 of this title, an eligible employee shall be entitled to a total of 12 workweeks of leave during any 12-month period for one or more of the following:

(A) Because of the birth of a son or daughter of the employee and in order to care for such son or daughter.

(B) Because of the placement of a son or daughter with the employee for adoption or foster care.

(C) In order to care for the spouse, or a son, daughter, or parent, of the employee, if such spouse, son, daughter, or parent has a serious health condition.

(D) Because of a serious health condition that makes the employee unable to perform the functions of the position of such employee.

(2) *Expiration of entitlement*

The entitlement to leave under subparagraphs (A) and (B) of paragraph (1) for a birth or placement of a son or daughter shall expire at the end of the 12-month period beginning on the date of such birth or placement.

(b) Leave taken intermittently or on reduced leave schedule

(1) *In general*

Leave under subparagraph (A) or (B) of subsection (a)(1) of this section shall not be taken by an employee intermittently or on a reduced leave schedule unless the employee and the employer of the employee agree otherwise. Subject to paragraph (2), subsection (e)(2) of this section, and section 2613(b)(5) of this title, leave under subparagraph (C) or (D) of subsection (a)(1) of this section may be taken intermittently or on a reduced leave schedule when medically necessary. The taking of leave intermittently or on a reduced leave schedule pursuant to this paragraph shall not result in a reduction in the total amount of leave to which the employee is entitled under subsection (a) of this section beyond the amount of leave actually taken.

(2) Alternative position

If an employee requests intermittent leave, or leave on a reduced leave schedule, under subparagraph (C) or (D) of subsection (a)(1) of this section, that is foreseeable based on planned medical treatment, the employer may require such employee to transfer temporarily to an available alternative position offered by the employer for which the employee is qualified and that—

(A) has equivalent pay and benefits; and

(B) better accommodates recurring periods of leave than the regular employment position of the employee.

(C) Unpaid leave permitted

Except as provided in subsection (d) of this section, leave granted under subsection (a) of this section may consist of unpaid leave.

(d) Relationship to paid leave

(1) *Unpaid leave*

If an employer provides paid leave for fewer than 12 workweeks, the additional weeks of leave necessary to attain the 12 workweeks of leave required under this subchapter may be provided without compensation.

(2) *Substitution of paid leave*

(A) In general

An eligible employee may elect, or an employer may require the employee, to substitute any of the accrued paid vacation leave, personal leave, or family leave of the employee for leave provided under subparagraph (A), (B), or (C) of subsection (a)(1) of this section for any part of the 12-week period of such leave under such subsection.

(B) Serious health condition

An eligible employee may elect, or an employer may require the employee, to substitute any of the accrued paid vacation leave, personal leave, or medical or sick leave of the employee for leave provided under subparagraph (C) or (D) of subsection (a)(1) of this section for any part of the 12-week period of such leave under such subsection, except that nothing in this subchapter shall require an employer to provide paid sick leave or paid medical leave in any situation in which such employer would not normally provide any such paid leave.

(e) Foreseeable leave

(1) *Requirement of notice*

In any case in which the necessity for leave under subparagraph (A) or (B) of subsection (a)(1) of this section is foreseeable based on an expected birth or placement, the employee shall provide the employer with not less than 30 days' notice, before the date the leave is to begin, of the employee's intention to take leave under such subparagraph, except that if the date of the birth or placement requires leave to begin in less than 30 days, the employee shall provide such notice as is practicable.

(2) *Duties of employee*

In any case in which the necessity for leave under subparagraph (C) or (D) of subsection (a)(1) of this section is foreseeable based on planned medical treatment, the employee—

(A) shall make a reasonable effort to schedule the treatment so as not to disrupt unduly the operations of the employer, subject to the approval of the health care provider of the employee or the health care provider of the son, daughter, spouse, or parent of the employee, as appropriate; and

(B) shall provide the employer with not less than 30 days' notice, before the date the leave is to begin, of the employee's intention to take leave under such subparagraph, except that if the date of the treatment requires leave to begin in less than 30 days, the employee shall provide such notice as is practicable.

(f) Spouses employed by same employer

In any case in which a husband and wife entitled to leave under subsection (a) of this section are employed by the same employer, the aggregate number of workweeks of leave to which both may be entitled may be limited to 12 workweeks during any 12-month period, if such leave is taken—

(1) under subparagraph (A) or (B) of subsection (a)(1) of this section; or

(2) to care for a sick parent under subparagraph (C) of such subsection.

Section 2613. Certification

(a) In general

An employer may require that a request for leave under subparagraph (C) or (D) of section 2612(a)(1) of this title be supported by a certification issued by the health care provider of the eligible employee or of the son, daughter, spouse, or parent of the employee, as appropriate. The employee shall provide, in a timely manner, a copy of such certification to the employer.

(b) Sufficient certification

Certification provided under subsection (a) of this section shall be sufficient if it states—

(1) the date on which the serious health condition commenced;

(2) the probable duration of the condition;

(3) the appropriate medical facts within the knowledge of the health care provider regarding the condition;

(4)(A) for purposes of leave under section 2612(a)(1)(C) of this title, a statement that the eligible employee is needed to care for the son, daughter, spouse, or parent and an estimate of the amount of time that such employee is needed to are for the son, daughter, spouse, or parent; and

(B) for purposes of leave under section 2612(a)(1)(D) of this title, a statement that the employee is unable to perform the functions of the position of the employee;

(5) in the case of certification for intermittent leave, or leave on a reduced leave schedule, for planned medical treatment, the dates on which such treatment is expected to be given and the duration of such treatment;

(6) in the case of certification for intermittent leave, or leave on a reduced leave schedule, under section 2612(a)(1)(D) of this title, a statement of the medical necessity for the intermittent leave or leave on a reduced leave schedule, and the expected duration of the intermittent leave or reduced leave schedule; and

(7) in the case of certification for intermittent leave, or leave on a reduced leave schedule, under section 2612(a)(1)(C) of this title, a statement that the employee's intermittent leave or leave on a reduced leave schedule is necessary for the care of the son, daughter, parent, or spouse who has a serious health condition, or will assist in their recovery, and the expected duration and schedule of the intermittent leave or reduced leave schedule.

(c) Second opinion

(1) *In general*

In any case in which the employer has reason to doubt the validity of the certification provided under subsection (a) of this section for leave under subparagraph (C) or (D) of section 2612(a)(1) of this title, the employer may require, at the expense of the employer, that the eligible employee obtain the opinion of a second health care provider designated or approved by the employer concerning any information certified under subsection (b) of this section for such leave.

(2) *Limitation*

A health care provider designated or approved under paragraph (1) shall not be employed on a regular basis by the employer.

(d) Resolution of conflicting opinions

(1) *In general*

In any case in which the second opinion described in subsection (c) of this section differs from the opinion in the original certification provided under subsection (a) of this section, the employer may require, at the expense of the employer, that the employee obtain the opinion of a third health care provider designated or approved jointly by the employer and the employee concerning the information certified under subsection (b) of this section.

(2) *Finality*

The opinion of the third health care provider concerning the information certified under subsection (b) of this section shall be considered to be final and shall be binding on the employer and the employee.

(e) Subsequent recertification

The employer may require that the eligible employee obtain subsequent recertifications on a reasonable basis.

Section 2614. Employment and benefits protection

(a) Restoration to position

(1) *In general*

Except as provided in subsection (b) of this section, any eligible employee who takes leave under section 2612 of this title for the intended purpose of the leave shall be entitled, on return from such leave—

(A) to be restored by the employer to the position of employment held by the employee when the leave commenced; or

(B) to be restored to an equivalent position with equivalent employment benefits, pay, and other terms and conditions of employment.

(2) *Loss of benefits*

The taking of leave under section 2612 of this title shall not result in the loss of any employment benefit accrued prior to the date on which the leave commenced.

(3) *Limitations*

Nothing in this section shall be construed to entitle any restored employee to—

(A) the accrual of any seniority or employment benefits during any period of leave; or

(B) any right, benefit, or position of employment other than any right, benefit, or position to which the employee would have been entitled had the employee not taken the leave.

(4) *Certification*

As a condition of restoration under paragraph (1) for an employee who has taken leave under section 2612(a)(1)(D) of this title, the employer may have a uniformly applied practice or policy that requires each such employee to receive certification from the health care provider of the employee that the employee is able to resume work, except that nothing in this paragraph shall supersede a valid State or local law or a collective bargaining agreement that governs the return to work of such employees.

(5) *Construction*

Nothing in this subsection shall be construed to prohibit an employer from requiring an employee on leave under section 2612 of this title to report periodically to the employer on the status and intention of the employee to return to work.

(b) Exemption concerning certain highly compensated employees

(1) *Denial of restoration*

An employer may deny restoration under subsection (a) of this section to any eligible employee described in paragraph (2) if—

(A) such denial is necessary to prevent substantial and grievous economic injury to the operations of the employer;

(B) the employer notifies the employee of the intent of the employer to deny restoration on such basis at the time the employer determines that such injury would occur; and

(C) in any case in which the leave has commenced, the employee elects not to return to employment after receiving such notice.

(2) *Affected employees*

An eligible employee described in paragraph (1) is a salaried eligible employee who is among the highest paid 10 percent of the employees employed by the employer within 75 miles of the facility at which the employee is employed.

(c) Maintenance of health benefits

(1) *Coverage*

Except as provided in paragraph (2), during any period that an eligible employee takes leave under section 2612 of this title, the employer shall maintain coverage under any "group health plan" for the duration of such leave at the level and under the conditions coverage would have been provided if the employee had continued in employment continuously for the duration of such leave.

(2) *Failure to return from leave*

The employer may recover the premium that the employer paid for maintaining coverage for the employee under such group health plan during any period of unpaid leave under section 2612 of this title if—

(A) the employee fails to return from leave under section 2612 of this title after the period of leave to which the employee is entitled has expired; and

(B) the employee fails to return to work for a reason other than—

(i) the continuation, recurrence, or onset of a serious health condition that entitles the employee to leave under subparagraph (C) or (D) of section 2612(a)(1) of this title; or

(ii) other circumstances beyond the control of the employee.

(3) Certification

(A) *Issuance*

An employer may require that a claim that an employee is unable to return to work because of the continuation, recurrence, or onset of the serious health condition described in paragraph (2)(B)(i) be supported by—

(i) a certification issued by the health care provider of the son, daughter, spouse, or parent of the employee, as appropriate, in the case of an employee unable to return to work because of a condition specified in section 2612(a)(1)(C) of this title; or

(ii) a certification issued by the health care provider of the eligible employee, in the case of an employee unable to return to work because of a condition specified in section 2612(a)(1)(D) of this title.

(B) *Copy*

The employee shall provide, in a timely manner, a copy of such certification to the employer.

(C) *Sufficiency of certification*

(i) Leave due to serious health condition of employee

The certification described in subparagraph (A)(ii) shall be sufficient if the certification states that a serious health condition prevented the employee from being able to perform the functions of the position of the employee on the date that the leave of the employee expired.

(ii) Leave due to serious health condition of family member

The certification described in subparagraph (A)(i) shall be sufficient if the certification states that the employee is needed to care for the son, daughter, spouse, or parent who has a serious health condition on the date that the leave of the employee expired.

Section 2615. Prohibited acts

(a) Interference with rights

(1) *Exercise of rights*

It shall be unlawful for any employer to interfere with, restrain, or deny the exercise of or the attempt to exercise, any right provided under this subchapter.

(2) *Discrimination*

It shall be unlawful for any employer to discharge or in any other manner discriminate against any individual for opposing any practice made unlawful by this subchapter.

(b) Interference with proceedings or inquiries

It shall be unlawful for any person to discharge or in any other manner discriminate against any individual because such individual—

(1) has filed any charge, or has instituted or caused to be instituted any proceeding, under or related to this subchapter;

(2) has given, or is about to give, any information in connection with any inquiry or proceeding relating to any right provided under this subchapter; or

(3) has testified, or is about to testify, in any inquiry or proceeding relating to any right provided under this subchapter.

Section 2618. Special rules concerning employees of local educational agencies

(a) Application

(1) *In general*

Except as otherwise provided in this section, the rights (including the rights under section 2614 of this title, which shall extend throughout the period of leave of any employee under this section), remedies, and procedures under this subchapter shall apply to—

(A) any "local educational agency" (as defined in section 8801 of Title 20) and an eligible employee of the agency; and

(B) any private elementary or secondary school and an eligible employee of the school.

(2) *Definitions*

For purposes of the application described in paragraph (1):

(A) Eligible employee

The term "eligible employee" means an eligible employee of an agency or school described in paragraph (1).

(B) Employer

The term "employer" means an agency or school described in paragraph (1).

(c) Intermittent leave or leave on a reduced schedule for instructional employees

(1) *In general*

Subject to paragraph (2), in any case in which an eligible employee employed principally in an instructional capacity by any such educational agency or school requests leave under subparagraph (C) or (D) of section 2612(a)(1) of this title that is foreseeable based on planned medical treatment and the employee would be on leave for greater than 20 percent of the total number of working days in the period during which the leave would extend, the agency or school may require that such employee elect either—

(A) to take leave for periods of a particular duration, not to exceed the duration of the planned medical treatment; or

(B) to transfer temporarily to an available alternative position offered by the employer for which the employee is qualified, and that—

(i) has equivalent pay and benefits; and

(ii) better accommodates recurring periods of leave than the regular employment position of the employee.

(2) *Application*

The elections described in subparagraphs (A) and (B) of paragraph (1) shall apply only with respect to an eligible employee who complies with section 2612(e)(2) of this title.

(d) Rules applicable to periods near the conclusion of academic term

The following rules shall apply with respect to periods of leave near the conclusion of an academic term in the case of any eligible employee employed principally in an instructional capacity by any such educational agency or school:

(1) Leave more than 5 weeks prior to end of term

If the eligible employee begins leave under section 2612 of this title more than 5 weeks prior to the end of the academic term, the agency or school may require the employee to continue taking leave until the end of such term, if—

(A) the leave is of at least 3 weeks duration; and

(B) the return to employment would occur during the 3-week period before the end of such term.

(2) Leave less than 5 weeks prior to end of term

If the eligible employee begins leave under subparagraph (A), (B), or (C) of section 2612(a)(1) of this title during the period that commences

5 weeks prior to the end of the academic term, the agency or school may require the employee to continue taking leave until the end of such term, if—

(A) the leave is of greater than 2 weeks duration; and

(B) the return to employment would occur during the 2-week period before the end of such term.

(3) Leave less than 3 weeks prior to end of term

If the eligible employee begins leave under subparagraph (A), (B), or (C) of section 2612(a)(1) of this title during the period that commences 3 weeks prior to the end of the academic term and the duration of the leave is greater than 5 working days, the agency or school may require the employee to continue to take leave until the end of such term.

(e) Restoration to equivalent employment position

For purposes of determinations under section 2614(a)(1)(B) of this title (relating to the restoration of an eligible employee to an equivalent position), in the case of a local educational agency or a private elementary or secondary school, such determination shall be made on the basis of established school board policies and practices, private school policies and practices, and collective bargaining agreements.

TABLE V
State Age Discrimination Laws

The following states protect employees under age discrimination laws similar to the ADEA in the following age ranges:

18 and over: District of Columbia, Iowa, Kansas, Minnesota, New York, Oregon, and Vermont.

40 to 70: Arkansas (state employees only), Colorado, Delaware, Georgia, Indiana, Kentucky, Louisiana, Mississippi (state employees only), Missouri, Nebraska, North Carolina, Rhode Island, and Wyoming.

40 and over: Alabama, Alaska, Arizona, California, Connecticut, Florida, Hawaii, Idaho, Illinois, Maine, Maryland, Massachusetts, Michigan, Montana, Nevada, New Hampshire, New Jersey, New Mexico, North Dakota, Ohio, Oklahoma, Pennsylvania, South Carolina, South Dakota (state employees only), Tennessee, Texas, Utah, Virginia, Washington, West Virginia, and Wisconsin.

TABLE VI
Helpful Organizations, Websites, and Businesses

Following is a list of organizations, Websites, and businesses that offer assistance to women experiencing discrimination problems in the workplace. They provide counseling, legal assistance, literature, and/or hot lines. There may be local organizations in your area that provide assistance as well. You can usually find those by calling your local bar association, or a local law school. Some of the Websites listed below include lists of local organizations.

9to5, National Association of Working Women
231 W, Wisconsin Avenue Suite 700
Milwaukee, WI 53203-2308
(800) 522-0925—24-hour national hot line
E-mail: naww9to5@execpc.com
Website: www.feminist.com/9to5.htm

Provides assistance, counseling, and literature on sex discrimination and harassment in the workplace. Specializes in office workers.

American Association of University Women
Legal Advocacy Fund
1111 16th Street, NW
Washington, DC 20036-4873
(202) 785-7719
E-mail: laf@mail.aauw.org
Website: www.aauw.org

Funds sexual harassment cases brought by university women students, faculty, and staff against institutions of higher education. Also has a volunteer network of attorneys to assist university women.

Association for Union Democracy
Women's Project
500 State Street, 2nd Floor
Brooklyn, NY 11217
(718) 855-6650

E-mail to aud@igc.apc.org
Website: www.uniondemocracy.com

Provides support, attorney referrals, counseling, literature, classes, and legal advice to women, both union and nonunion.

Documented Reference Check (DRC)
1174 S. Diamond Bar Blvd.
Diamond Bar, CA 91765
(800) 742-3316
Website: www.badreferences.com

Documents and transcribes references from your current or past employers. Will also testify in court as to what was said about you. Works nationwide. Not a nonprofit organization. Charges a fee.

Equal Rights Advocates (ERA)
1663 Mission Street Suite 550
San Francisco, CA 94103
(415) 621-0672—Office
(800) 839-4372—Hot line for advice and counseling. Also offers Spanish-language services.
Website: www.equalrights.org

Offers assistance, information, and lawyer referrals on all discrimination issues and Family Medical Leave rights. In certain circumstances, will assist employees in drafting letters and filing internal grievances. In rare cases, may represent employees in lawsuits.

Feminist Majority Foundation
1600 Wilson Blvd., Suite 801
Arlington, VA 22209
(703) 522-2214—Office
(703) 522-2501—Hot line that provides advice on how to file a claim and deal with the EEOC.
Website: www.feminist.com

Provides information and referrals, and maintains a very thorough Website with many links to local women's help groups, including a sexual harassment resource list.

National Committee on Pay Equity
1126 16th Street NW, Suite 411
Washington, DC 20036
(202) 331-7343
E-mail: fairpay@aol.com
Website: www.feminist.com/fairpay.htm

Deals with wage discrimination. Offers literature, resources, and referrals to organizations in your area.

National Partnership for Women and Families (formerly Women's Legal Defense Fund)
1875 Connecticut Avenue NW, Suite 710
Washington, DC 20009
(202) 986-2600
Website: www.nationalpartnership.org

Answers questions and provides publications to assist women in meeting dual demands of work and family.

NOW Legal Defense and Education Fund (this is a separate organization from the local chapters of NOW, the National Organization for Women)
99 Hudson Street
New York, NY 10013
(212) 925-6635—Information and referral helpline
Website: www.afj.org/mem/now.html

Legal resource kit for sex discrimination and sexual harassment, and how to find a lawyer.

Women's Bureau, U.S. Department of Labor
200 Constitution Avenue, NW
Washington, DC 20210
(800) 827-5335—Work and family issues
(800) 347-3741—Fair pay issues
Website: www.dol.gov/dol/wb

Provides literature, referrals, publications, and other assistance on rights of working women.

Notes

CHAPTER 1

1. The law stated that a man could beat his wife as long as he did not use a switch thicker than his thumb—hence the term "rule of thumb." In 1868, however, at least one state decided that the Rule of Thumb was no longer applicable. The North Carolina Supreme Court determined that a man could beat his wife according to what class of woman she was. *See* State v. Rhodes, 61 N.C. 453 (1868). If she was from the "higher ranks . . . where education and culture have so refined nature, that a look cuts like a knife and a word strikes like a hammer," *id.* at 458, then a man must restrain his anger. If, however, she was from "the hovel, where neither delicacy of sentiment nor refinement of manners is appreciated or known," *id.* at 458–59, then a man could not "be responsible for rudeness or trifling violence." *Id.* The court further noted that a wife "should be able to purchase immunity from pain, by obedience to authority and faithfulness in duty." *Id.* at 459.
2. Women's Bureau, U.S. Dep't of Labor, *Women in Management, in* Facts on Working Women (Washington, D.C., Apr. 1997).
3. Id.
4. For a summary of studies that show working mothers assume primary responsibility for child rearing even in homes where both spouses work outside

the home in equally demanding careers, see ARLIE HOCHSCHILD AND ANNIE MACHUNG, THE SECOND SHIFT 277–79 (Avon Books 1990).

5. *See* K. A. Loughlin and W. A. Kayson, *Alcohol Consumption and Self-Reported Drinking-Related Problem Behaviors as Related to Sex, Work Environment, and Level of Education,* 67 PSYCHOL. REP. 1323–28 (1990); D. A. Parker and T. C. Harford, *The Epidemiology of Alcohol Consumption and Dependence Across Occupations in the United States,* 16 ALCOHOL HEALTH & RES. WORLD 97–105 (1992); *see also,* Mary E. McCaul and Janice Furst, *Alcoholism Treatment in the United States,* 18 ALCOHOL HEALTH & RES. WORLD 253–260 (1994) and Teresa McAleavy, *New Pieces of Alcoholism's Puzzle,* THE RECORD, All Editions, July 1, 1996 (quoting Dr. Paul Manowitz, associate professor of psychiatry and neurology at the University of Medicine and Dentistry of New Jersey (UMDNJ), Robert Wood Johnson Medical School, that alcoholism affects about one out of every ten men and one out of every twenty-five women).

6. "Men and women are neither similar—for many of these norms differ vitally across gender lines—nor similarly situated—for male control of the workplace has permitted male norms to prevail. These norms shape intangibles such as the 'appropriate' professional demeanor: the tone of voice, air of command, and the quickness to accommodate or anger that mark a 'successful' employee. They also dictate the acceptable forms of professional camaraderie, and prescribe the boundaries between the workplace and the rest of the world—boundaries that have defined the care of children as the province of those who are not workers." Kathryn Abrams, *Gender Discrimination and the Transformation of Workplace Norms,* 42 VAND. L. REV. 1183, 1189 (1989).

7. Judith Newmark, *What do sick kids crave? Survey: They want—and get—Mom,* CHI. SUN-TIMES, Dec. 1, 1996, at 48 (quoting consumer psychologist Selina Guber, president of Children's Market Research: "Nobody wants to be labeled as the mommy who stays out for every little thing. That's why many women lie. They say they are taking off for some other reason").

8. "Women have been expected to make their way by conforming to these norms. This expectation has emerged in part because demanding conformity to pre-existing norms is one way of protesting the access of women in the workplace. But it occurs mainly because the men who constitute the workplace, like most proponents of societal dominant standards, do not recognize the partiality of their norms. The preferences and perspectives of this group for so long have been considered 'the way things are done,' that most male workers have never considered the possibility that these choices could be

made differently. . . . The wisdom of conformity has been called into question." *See* Abrams, *supra* note 6, at 189–90.

9. *Industry Report,* 1998, TRAINING MAG., October 1998 at 43.
10. According to a report presented by the Federal Glass Ceiling Commission, issued by the U.S. Department of Labor in 1995 (hereinafter *Glass Ceiling Report*), 59 percent of the women surveyed said they had personally experienced discrimination on the job.

CHAPTER 2

1. Most newspapers no longer maintain separate "Help Wanted—Male" and "Help Wanted—Female" columns for fear of being held accountable under their state's or municipality's discrimination law. Whether or not a newspaper is held liable depends on the outcome of a somewhat complex legal analysis. Specifically, (1) do state and local discrimination laws, which prohibit employers from discriminating, apply to newspapers, which are technically not employers, and (2) even if the discrimination laws can be construed to apply to newspapers, aren't newspapers protected by the First Amendment so that the government is prohibited from interfering with what newspapers publish?

   Most courts have held that newspapers are, in fact, accountable under the discrimination laws because in publishing the ads, they "aid and abet" those who would commit discrimination.

   In addition, the U.S. Supreme Court, in *Pittsburgh Press Co. v. Pittsburgh Commission on Human Relations,* 413 U.S. 376 (1973), rejected an assertion by the *Pittsburgh Press* that it had a First Amendment right to publish help-wanted ads based on gender, even though the practice violated a local discrimination law. The court, in holding the *Pittsburgh Press* liable, ruled that the newspaper's advertising section was "commercial speech" and therefore entitled to a much lesser degree of First Amendment protection than the newspaper's editorial pages. The Court ruled that the government's interest in eliminating discrimination outweighed the newspaper's First Amendment right to engage in commercial speech, and ordered the publisher to discontinue its practice.
2. According to the 1997 *Liar's Index,* produced by Jude M. Werra & Associates, a Milwaukee-based consulting firm, the number of management- and executive-level candidates who misrepresent their academic credentials remains steady

at just under 15 percent. Other organizations estimate this number to be significantly higher.

3. *See* McKennon v. Nashville Banner, 513 U.S. 35 (1995).
4. *See* Tibbett L. Speer, *The Unseen Costs of Eldercare,* AM. DEMOGRAPHICS, June 1996, at 20. (Predicts that since women are much more likely to provide elder care, organizations with larger shares of women employees can expect higher elder care–related costs.)
5. These requirements are pursuant to an amendment to the Fair Credit Reporting Act, effective September 30, 1997, 15 U.S.C. § 1681 et. seq. (1997).
6. Dothard v. Rawlinson, 433 U.S. 321, 329 (1977) (citing Griggs v. Duke Power Co., 401 U.S. 424, 432 (1971)).
7. *Id.* at 329 (citing McDonnell Douglas Corp. v. Green, 411 U.S. 792, 801 (1973)).

CHAPTER 4

1. Elizabeth Faulkner Baker, *Protective Labor Legislation with Special Reference to Women in the State of New York,* 116 STUDIES IN HIST., ECON. AND PUB. LAW 58 (Faculty of Political Science, Columbia University eds., AMS Press, 1969).
2. The great irony about these "protective" laws is that they were aimed at protecting only white women. The slavery and poverty black women endured served only to disprove the invalid assumption that women were too weak and frail to perform manual labor, and thus in need of protective laws in the workplace. Moreover, even though our courts often spoke of the importance of protecting women since they were the bearers of our children, the court never once spoke about the importance of "preservation of the race" when it came to African-American women.

   Sojourner Truth, a former slave and abolitionist, gave a historic speech at the second annual convention of the women's rights movement in 1851 that was later recounted by various women's suffragettes. One rendition states that in response to a man who insisted women were too weak to do their share of manual labor, Sojourner Truth said:

   > *"Dat man ober dar say dat womin needs to be helped into carriages, and lifted ober ditches, and to hab de best place everywhar. Nobody eber helps me into carriages, or ober mud-puddles, or gibs me any best place!" And raising herself to her full height, and her voice to a pitch to like rolling thunder, she asked, "And a'n't I a woman? Look at me! Look at my arm!*

[And she bared her right arm to the shoulder, showing her tremendous muscular power.] I have ploughed, and planted, and gathered into barns, and no man could head me! And a'n't I a woman? I could work as much and eat as much as a man—when I could get it—and bear de lash as well! And a'n't I a woman? I have borned thirteen children, and seen 'em mos' all sold off to slavery, and when I cried out with my mother's grief, none but Jesus heard me! And a'n't I a woman?"

E. C. Stanton, S. B. Anthony, and Matilda Joslyn Gage, eds., *Sojourner Truth: Reminiscences by Francis D. Gage,* Akron Convention (May 28–29, 1851), *in* 1 History of Women's Suffrage, 1848–1861 (reprint ed. 1985).

3. The Equal Employment Opportunity Commission (EEOC) received 15,618 sexual harassment complaints in 1998—nearly triple the 6,883 complaints received in 1991.
4. Harris v. Forklift, 510 U.S. 17, 22 (1993).
5. *Id.*
6. Ellison v. Brady, 924 F.2d 872, 879 (9th Cir. 1991).
7. *See* Harris, 510 U.S. at 22.
8. Ellison, 924 F.2d at 879–81.
9. *See* Meritor Savings Bank v. Vinson, 477 U.S. 57, 69 (1986).
10. "[T]he fact that sex-related conduct was 'voluntary,' in the sense that the complainant was not forced to participate against her will, is not a defense to a sexual harassment suit. . . . The gravamen of any sexual harassment claim is that the alleged sexual advances were 'unwelcome.' . . . The correct inquiry is whether [a woman] by her conduct indicated that the alleged participation in sexual intercourse was voluntary." *Id.* at 68.
11. In Ball v. Postmaster General, EEOC Request No. 05930708 (May 12, 1994), the EEOC stated that "Title VII does not prohibit isolated instances of preferential treatment based upon consensual romantic relationships. An isolated instance of favoritism toward a 'paramour' may be unfair, but it does not discriminate against men or women in violation of Title VII, since both are disadvantaged for reasons other than their genders."
12. The U.S. Supreme Court ruled on this issue in March of 1998 in *Oncale v. Sundowner,* 118 S.Ct 998 (1998), where an oil rig worker complained that his fellow male workers were subjecting him to sexual insults and demeaning remarks, which constituted sexual harassment. In *Oncale,* Justice Scalia writes, "Courts and juries have found the inference of discrimination easy to draw in most male-female sexual harassment situations, because the challenged conduct typically involves explicit or implicit proposals of sexual activity; it is reasonable to assume those proposals would not have been made to someone

of the same sex. The same chain of inference would be available to a plaintiff alleging same sex harassment, if there were credible evidence that the harasser was homosexual. But harassing conduct need not be motivated by sexual desire to support an inference of discrimination on the basis of sex. A trier of fact might reasonably find such discrimination, for example, if a female victim is harassed in such sex-specific and derogatory terms by another woman as to make it clear that the harasser is motivated by general hostility to the presence of women in the workplace. . . . [S]he must always prove that the conduct at issue was not merely tinged with offensive sexual connotations, but actually constituted "discrimination . . . because of . . . sex." In addition, the behavior must be shown to have altered the conditions of the victim's employment: "Conduct that is not severe or pervasive enough to create an objectively hostile or abusive work environment—an environment that a reasonable person would find hostile or abusive—is beyond Title VII's purview." *Id.* at 1003.

CHAPTER 5

1. Women's Bureau, U.S. Dep't of Labor, *Twenty Facts on Women Workers, in* Facts on Working Women (Washington, D.C., Apr. 1999).
2. Testimony on Fair Pay Act July 21, 1994: Joint Hearing of Subcomms. of House Education and Labor and Post Office and Civil Service Comms., 103d Cong. 2d Sess. (1994), 1994 DLR 139d6 available in LEXIS, BNA Library, DLABRT File (statement of Judith L. Lichtman, President, Women's Legal Defense Fund) [hereinafter Hearing].
3. U.S. Dep't of Labor, Glass Ceiling Report (Washington, D.C., 1995).
4. A 1990 *Business Week* study of 3,664 business school graduates found that a woman with an MBA from one of the top twenty business schools earned an average of $54,749 in her first year after graduation, while a comparable man earned $61,400—12 percent more. Glass Ceiling Comm.,U.S. Dep't of Labor, *Executive Summary* (Washington, D.C., 1995).
5. *See* Price v. Lockheed Space Operations Co., 856 F.2d 1503 (11th Cir. 1988).
6. *See* 29 C.F.R. § 1620.26 (1994).
7. Hodgson v. Sears, Roebuck and Co., Fair Emp. Prac. Cas. (BNA) 749 (1972).
8. *See* Kouba v. Allstate Insurance Co., 691 F.2d 873 (9th Cir. 1982). The court in

Kouba went on to say, "In conclusion, the Equal Pay Act does not impose a strict prohibition against the use of salary." *Id.* at 878.

9. *See* Los Angeles Dept. of Water & Power v. Manhart, 435 U.S. 702 (1978).

CHAPTER 6

1. Justice Sandra Day O'Connor graduated third in her class from Stanford Law School and was rejected by all of the major law firms with which she had interviewed. Normally, candidates at the top of their class at Stanford would have their pick from among the best lawyer jobs in the country. O'Connor eventually found a lower-paying government position as a deputy county attorney in California.

   Chief Justice William Rehnquist attended Stanford Law School during the same years as O'Connor and graduated first in the class. Upon completing law school, Rehnquist accepted a prestigious one-year clerkship at the U.S. Supreme Court, a much sought after job that usually leads to immense career opportunities. In 1972, Rehnquist was appointed to the U.S. Supreme Court, where he now serves as Chief Justice. O'Connor was appointed to the Court nine years after Rehnquist, in 1981.

2. A 1993 follow-up study of the Stanford University Business School class of 1982 found that 16 percent of the men were CEOs, chairmen, or presidents of companies, compared to only 2 percent of the women. At the level below those posts, 23 percent of the men in the 1982 class were now vice presidents and 15 percent were directors, compared to 10 percent and 8 percent, respectively, of the women. GLASS CEILING COMM., U.S. DEP'T OF LABOR, (Washington, D.C., 1995).

3. One prominent headhunter told the commission, "Listen, I'm meeting my bottom line and I want to find the people that the client wants. My reputation is based on my track record of getting them candidates they are comfortable with. I can't bring in too many minorities and women." *Id.*

CHAPTER 7

1. Delta Airlines required its flight attendants to sign the following agreement upon being hired:

   > I hereby certify that I have never been married and that I shall terminate automatically and voluntarily my employment with Delta Airlines prior to the event of my entry into a contract of marriage any time during the Stewardess Training Course, after successfully completing the stewardess training class and prior to assignment of regular stewardess duties or after assignment to regular stewardess duties.

   A federal district court in Louisiana ruled that Delta was not violating the law by requiring its flight attendants to sign the agreement. Cooper v. Delta Airlines, Inc., 274 F. Supp. 781 (D. La. 1967).

   Four years later, when another flight attendant challenged a similar policy at United Airlines, a federal appeals court ruled that United could not fire a flight attendant who was married, but the airline could refuse to hire married women. *See* Sprogis v. United Airlines, 444 F.2d 1194 (7th Cir.), *cert. denied,* 404 U.S. 991 (1971). That rule has since changed.
2. The United State Supreme Court's protective concern for women was illustrated in *Muller v. Oregon*, 208 U.S. 412 (1908), in which the court upheld a law that forbade women from working more than ten hours a day because the "rigors of motherhood might be upon her." U.S. *Id.* at 421. As recently as 1984, in *Oil, Chemical and Atomic Workers International Union v. American Cyanamid Company,* 741 F.2d 444 (D.C. Cir. 1984), Judge Robert Bork allowed to stand a rule that required women to either get sterilized or quit their jobs at a factory that exposed them to potentially dangerous chemicals. Bork wrote that although women at the factory "were put to a most unhappy choice," the sterilization policy did not violate the law. *Id.* at 450. Some critics point out, however, that if this had really been a *true* concern for the race, then a similar rule should have been implemented for men as well, since working at the factory potentially jeopardized the health of their sperm. Bork was later nominated to the United States Supreme Court by President Bush, but his nomination was struck down by the U.S. Senate after several women legal scholars and others objected to his appointment.
3. International Union, UAW v. Johnson Controls, Inc., 499 U.S. 187, 195, 203 (1991) (citing Western Airlines v. Criswell, 472 U.S. 400, 412 (1985)).
4. According to a statement made by Alan R. Hinman, M.D., Director, National Center for Prevention Services, Centers for Disease Control and Prevention

on May 19, 1994, before the U.S. Senate House of Representatives Committee on Public Work and Transportation:

> [S]cientific literature suggests the possibility that female flight attendants may experience an increased risk of miscarriage, menstrual disorders, and other adverse reproductive experiences as a result of exposure to cosmic radiation. Computer modeling estimates from the Federal Aviation Administration (FAA) indicate that frequent air travel may expose pregnant flight attendants to ionizing radiation levels above those recommended as safe by the International Commission on Radiological Protection.

5. 42 U.S.C. §§ 12101–12213.
6. *Id.* at § 12102(2)(a) (1994).
7. "Reproduction falls well within the phrase 'major life activity.' Reproduction and the sexual dynamics surrounding it are central to the life process itself." Bragdon v. Abbot, 118 S. Ct. 2196, 2205 (1998).
8. Rena K. Uviller, *Fathers' Rights and Feminism: The Maternal Presumption Revisited,* 1 HARV. WOMEN'S L.J. 107, 109–11 (1978).
9. See, for example, *Phillips v. Martin Marietta Corp.*, 400 U.S. 542 (1971), where the U.S. Supreme Court found discriminatory a policy of refusing employment to female but not male parents of pre-school-aged children.
10. *United States Supreme Court Justice Ruth Bader Ginsburg Address: Remarks for California Women Lawyers, September 22, 1994, in* 22 PEPP. L. REV. 1, 3 (1994).
11. Kirsten A. Conover, *At Your Service,* THE CHRISTIAN SCIENCE MONITOR, Aug. 11, 1997, at 10.
12. According to the Glass Ceiling Commission Report, typical stereotypes about women include not wanting to work; not being as committed as men to their careers; not being tough enough; being unwilling or unable to work long or unusual hours; being unwilling or unable to relocate; being unwilling or unable to make decisions; being too emotional, not sufficiently aggressive, too aggressive, or too passive; and lacking quantitative skills.

    Fortune 1000 industrials and 500 service companies, however, refute these stereotypes, according to a Korn/Ferry survey. For instance, regarding the notion that women are not as committed to their careers as men, only a third of women have ever taken a leave of absence, and almost two-thirds of these leaves were for less than six months. Moreover, 82 percent of those leaves were for maternity or other family reasons. If maternity is controlled for, more *men* in the Korn/Ferry surveys took leaves of absence than did women.

Regarding the notion that women will not work long hours, executive women worked an average of fifty-six hours a week in a 1992 survey by Korn/Ferry. This was the same number of hours that their male counterparts reported working in a similar survey in 1989.

The stereotype that women cannot or will not relocate is also false. According to the 1992 Korn/Ferry study, only 14.1 percent of women refused to do so. Twenty-one percent of men, however, refused, according to the 1989 survey. Instead, it was discovered that women are not asked to relocate as frequently as men. The Glass Ceiling Commission concluded that the failure to provide this opportunity may prejudice their careers. U.S. DEP'T OF LABOR, GLASS CEILING REPORT (Washington, D.C., 1995).

13. California's law, commonly called the Family School Partnership Act, allows up to forty hours of unpaid leave per year for parents to attend school events. Minnesota has a similar law that allows sixteen hours a year to attend scholastic events that cannot be scheduled outside working hours. Most states, however, don't have laws of this type, although many are currently considering it. Congress has also made several failed attempts to pass a national law that would allow parents unpaid leave for school events. If passed, it would be an amendment to the Family and Medical Leave Act.
14. According to the organization 9 to 5 for Working Women, 95 percent of U.S. businesses are exempt from this law because they have fewer than fifty employees. As a result, only 43 percent of working women are covered under the act.

CHAPTER 8

1. In fact, many women are CEOs of the household! They are ultimately responsible for the smooth running of their "company." In addition, they often assume other executive-like positions, such as money manager, investor, transportation coordinator, bid taker, food resource manager, chef, purchasing agent, social director, therapist and counselor, travel agent, project coordinator, file clerk, interior designer, and time-management expert.
2. Ironically, as women mature, and presumably gain work experience, the wage gap between men and women grows larger. Young women between the ages of fifteen and twenty-four earn 93 percent of the wages earned by men of similar age, while women between the ages of fifty-five and fifty-nine earn only 62 percent of the wages earned by men their age. *See* Hearing, *supra* note 2, chap-

ter 45 (testimony of Michelle Leber, Treasurer, Nat'l Committee on Pay Equity). Older women also feel the effects of the wage gap when it comes to receiving pensions. According to the Older Women's League, the average annual private pension for retired women in 1998 was $4,679, whereas the average annual private pension for retired men was $6,442.

3. *Id.*
4. Loeb v. Textron, Inc., 600 F.2d 1003, 1013 (1st Cir. 1979).
5. *See* Carroll v. Talman Federal Savings & Loan Association, 604 F.2d 1028, 1031 (7th Cir. 1979).
6. Hopkins v. Price Waterhouse, 490 U.S. 228, 234 (1989).
7. *Id.* at 236.

CHAPTER 9

1. Roberts v. United States Jaycees, 468 U.S. 609, 619 (1984).
2. U.S. DEP'T OF LABOR, GLASS CEILING REPORT (Washington, D.C., 1995).

CHAPTER 10

1. Faragher v. City of Boca Raton, 118 S. Ct. 2275, 2293 (1998). *See also,* Burlington Industries, Inc. v. Allerth, 118 S. Ct. 2257 (1998).
2. *Id.*
3. Sparks v. Pilot Freight Carriers, 830 F.2d 1554 (11th Cir. 1987).
4. The American Management Association conducted a study for *The Washington Post* in 1996, finding that of 1,366 complaints, 49.7 percent involved the victims' peers or coworkers. Kristin Downey Grimsley, *Co-workers Cited in Most Sexual Harassment Cases,* WASH. POST, June 14, 1996, Financial Section.

CHAPTER 11

1. Electronic monitoring includes storage and review of e-mail; recording and review of telephone conversations; storage and review of voice mail messages;

storage and review of computer files; and video recording of employee job performance.

Only 74 percent of those companies that store voice mail messages tell their workers that they are doing so. Eighty-four percent of companies that monitor e-mail and 94 percent of those that record phone conversations inform their workers.

Electronic monitoring is most prevalent in the financial services sector, including the banking, brokerage, insurance, and real estate industries (68 percent of employers electronically monitor); followed by the business and professional service providers (51 percent); and wholesalers and retailers (47 percent).

The survey was conducted in January–March 1999. Human resources managers in 1,054 American Management Association companies participated, giving the survey a margin of error of +/–3.5 percent. The results mirror practices among the AMA's ten thousand corporate members, which together employ one quarter of the U.S. workforce.

2. Knox v. State of Indiana, 93 F.3d 1327, 1330 (7th Cir. 1996).
3. Dr. Anita Borg, founder of the Systers mailing list for female information professionals, conducted a survey in 1993 of 500 members. Twenty percent had experienced sexual harassment online. The women reported being badgered with sexual propositions and personal questions. Emma Mansell-Lewis, *Can Sisters Do It for Themselves?* COMPUTER WEEKLY, Oct. 19, 1995, at 56.
4. Title III of the Omnibus Crime Control and Safe Streets Act prohibits interception of wire and oral communications. 18 U.S.C. §§ 2510 et. seq (1998).
5. *See* Epps v. St. Mary's Hospital, 802 F.2d 412 (11th Cir. 1986).
6. Electronic Communications Privacy Act of 1986 (ECPA), 18 U.S.C. §§ 2510–2522, 2703–2711 (1998).
7. Fazo v. Nordstrom, No. 702450, Cal. App. Dep't Super. Ct. (Feb. 5, 1992) (cited in *California Jury Rules for Nordstrom on Employee's Invasion of Privacy Claim,* DAILY LAB. REP. (BNA) No. 25, at A-2 (Feb. 9, 1993)).
8. 29 U.S.C. §§ 2001–2009 (1998).

CHAPTER 13

1. This quote has often been attributed to Mark Twain. It is believed to have been said during a lecture tour during which he traveled around the United States

describing his adventures in the South Pacific. It does not, however, appear in any of his writings.

2. Faragher v. City of Boça Raton, 118 S. Ct. 2275, 2293 (1998). *See also,* Burlington Industries, Inc. v. Allerth, 118 S. Ct. 2257 (1998).
3. Ellen Warren and Nancy Millman, *Abuse on the Line: For Years, Women at Mitsubishi Say They've Endured the Degrading Deeds and Words of Coworkers. Now They're Doing the Talking,* CHI. TRIB., February 15, 1995, at 10.
4. *See* NLRB v. Weingarten, Inc., 420 U.S. 251 (1975). Under the National Labor Relations Act, a private-sector employer may not deny a bargaining unit employee's request for a union representative to be present at any meeting that might reasonably result in disciplinary action against the employee. 29 U.S.C. § 157 (1998). Similarly, public-sector union employees are protected by the Federal Service Labor-Management Relations Statute, 5 U.S.C. §§ 7101–7135 (1998).
5. Cotran v. Rollins Hudig Hall International, No. EC-014-711, Cal. Super. Ct. (1995) Jur. No. 161343, *available in* 1995 WL 691108 (awarding $1.7 million to alleged harasser for wrongful termination).
6. The Equal Employment Opportunity Commission reported in 1997 that retaliation claims are on the rise, having received 18,100 such charges in 1997, more than double the number from five years earlier. Press release: *EEOC Issues Guidance Clarifying Right to Protection Against Retaliation,* Washington, D.C., May 26, 1998.
7. Courts are split over which definition to use when deciding what constitutes an "adverse action" for the purposes of a retaliation claim. The particular definition listed is from the Equal Employment Opportunity Commission. *See* EQ. EMPL. OPP. COMM., *Retaliation* (No. 915.003 §§ 11 (D)(3)), *in* 2 EEOC COMPLIANCE MANUAL § 614 (May 20, 1998). Some courts, however, rule that an adverse employment action is any decision or action that is serious and tangible enough to alter the terms and conditions of employment. Other courts have ruled that it is any decision that results in an "ultimate employment action," such as hiring, firing, or promotion.

CHAPTER 14

1. McKennon v. Nashville Banner, 513 U.S. 352 (1995).
2. Three different definitions of "trade secrets" exist:

- The Restatement (First) of Torts, published in 1939, defines a trade secret as any formula, pattern, device or compilation of information, which is used in one's business, and which gives him an opportunity to obtain an advantage over competitors who do not know or use it. It may be a formula for a chemical compound, a process of manufacturing, treating or preserving materials, a pattern for a machine or other device, or a list of customers. RESTATEMENT (FIRST) OF TORTS, § 757 cmt. B (1939).
- The Uniform Trade Secrets Act (UTSA) defines a trade secret as information, including a formula, pattern, compilation, program, device, method, technique or process, that: (I) derives independent economic value, actual or potential, from not being generally known to, and not being readily ascertainable by proper means by, other persons who can obtain economic value from its disclosure or use, and (II) is the subject of efforts that are reasonable under the circumstances to maintain its secrecy. The UTSA has been adopted by forty-one states and the District of Columbia. Uniform Trade Secrets Act, 14 U.L.A. 437 (amended 1985) (1990).
- The Restatement (Third) of Unfair Competition (1995) defines trade secrets as "any information that can be used in the operation of a business or other enterprise and that is sufficiently valuable and secret to afford an actual or potential economic advantage over others." RESTATEMENT (THIRD) OF UNFAIR COMPETITION, § 39 (1995).

3. Due process rights arise from the Fifth and Fourteenth Amendments to the United States Constitution. These amendments prohibit state and federal governments from depriving any person of "life, liberty or property without due process of law." U.S. Const. amends V, XIV. The Fifth Amendment applies to actions by the federal government. *See* Mathews v. Eldridge, 424 U.S. 319, 332 (1976). The Fourteenth Amendment applies to actions by state and local governments. *See* Goldberg v. Kelly, 397 U.S. 254, 255–56 (1970). The Supreme Court has interpreted the guarantees of both amendments to provide equal safeguards and has used the term "due process" to include rights under either amendment. *See* Cleveland Board of Education v. Loudermill, 470 U.S. 532, 542–46 (1985) (discussing due process cases under both amendments without distinction); Arnett v. Kennedy, 416 U.S. 134, 164 (1974) (Powell, J., concurring) ("constitutional guarantee of procedural due process depends . . . on the presence of a legitimate 'property' or 'liberty' interest within the meaning of the Fifth or Fourteenth Amendment"). A property interest exists when the employee possesses a legitimate claim of entitlement to continued employ-

ment. *See* Board of Regents v. Roth, 408 U.S. 564, 577 (1972). In *Loudermill*, the Supreme Court held that a public employee who holds a constitutionally protected interest in his job must be granted a hearing before being terminated. Loudermill, 470 U.S. at 542, 545–46.

4. The liberty interest is implicated when discharge jeopardizes the employee's "good name, reputation, honor, or integrity." Roth, 408 U.S. at 573 (1972) (quoting Wisconsin v. Constantineau, 400 U.S. 433, 437 (1971)).
5. Federal Service Labor-Management Relations Statute, 5 U.S.C. § 7114 (1998).
6. Most employees are guaranteed this right under the Consolidated Omnibus Budget Reconciliation Act of 1986, 29 U.S.C. §§ 1161–69 (1998), most commonly known as COBRA. Similar provisions for public sector employees are found in the Public Health Service Act, 42 U.S.C. §§ 300-bb et seq. (1998). The only difference between the two laws is that private employees are allowed to sue for significant damages if an employer violates the COBRA requirements. Public-sector employees, however, are limited to only what money they may have lost as a result of the violation.
7. 29 U.S.C. §§ 621–634 (1998). The ADEA provides:

   It shall be unlawful for an employer—

   (1) to fail or refuse to hire or to discharge any individual or otherwise discriminate against any individual with respect to his compensation, terms, conditions, or privileges of employment, because of such individual's age;

   (2) to limit, segregate, or classify his employees in any way which would deprive or tend to deprive any individual of employment opportunities or otherwise adversely affect his status as an employee, because of such individual's age;

   (3) to reduce the wage rate of any employee in order to comply with this chapter.
8. The Older Workers Benefit Protection Act (OWBA) requires that any release signed to prevent claims under ADEA must have certain requirements. The OWBA provides that "an individual may not waive any right or claim [under ADEA] unless the waiver is knowing and voluntary." 29 U.S.C. § 626(f) (1998). The Act specifically requires employers to, at a minimum, draft the waiver in a manner calculated to be understood by an average individual, advise the individual to consult with an attorney, provide the individual at least twenty-one days to consider the agreement, and allow the individual to revoke the agreement within seven days.
9. Oubre v. Entergy Operations, 118 S. Ct. 838 (1998).

10. Lews v. Equitable Life Assurance Society, 389 N.W.2d 876 (Minn. 1986).
11. Miller v. Motorola, 202 Ill. App. 3d 976 (1998).
12. Cummings v. Walsh, 561 F. Supp. 872 (S.D. Ga. 1983).

CHAPTER 15

1. Even though his amendment to include women passed, Congressman Howard Smith (D-Va.) voted *against* the Civil Rights Act of 1964.
2. (42 U.S.C. §§ 200e-2(a)(1) (1988 & Supp. V 1993).
3. This was made clear in the Pregnancy Discrimination Act, passed by Congress in 1978. 42 U.S.C. § 200e(k) (1998).
4. Courts widely agree that discrimination based on sexual orientation is beyond the purview of Title VII. See, for example, *DeSantis v. Pacific Tel. & Tel. Co.*, 608 F.2d 327, 333 (9th Cir. 1979), where the court declared that "the courts have not designated homosexuals a 'suspect' or 'quasi-suspect' classification so as to require more exacting scrutiny."
5. Wilson v. Southwest Airlines Co., 517 F. Supp. 292, 304 (N.D. Tex. 1981).
6. *Id.* at 296.
7. The rationale for allowing the Playboy exception was noted in a concurring opinion in *Guardian Capital Corp. v. New York State Division of Human Rights,* 46 A.D.2d 832, 833 (1974) (citing Margarita St. Cross v. Playboy Club of New York, Appeal No. 773, Case No. CSF 22618-70).
8. The Equal Employment Opportunity Commission issued a response to the Hooters ad campaign, saying in part:

> Any legally sophisticated employer such as Hooters is well aware that the EEOC is prohibited by law from publicly discussing any pending litigation. As a result, we can neither confirm nor deny the existence of an ongoing investigation against Hooters or any other employer. EEOC, therefore, cannot respond to the public relations offensive recently initiated by Hooters.
>
> We feel it important to point out, however, that a private class action lawsuit—in which EEOC is not a party—was brought in December 1994 by individual men who believe that they were discriminated against by Hooters' hiring practices. The case is pending in federal court in the Northern District of Illinois (Chicago).
>
> Given the pendency of this private action, we fail to understand

what Hooters is seeking to accomplish through this expensive, well-orchestrated campaign other than to intimidate a federal law enforcement agency and, more important, individuals whose rights may have been illegally violated. Press release: *EEOC Comments on Hooter's Press Offensive*, Washington, D.C., November 21, 1995.

9. Wynn Oil Company v. Fernandez, 653 F.2d 1273 (9th Cir. 1981).
10. EEOC v. Sedita, 816 F. Supp. 1291 (N.D. Ill. 1993).
11. Courts have ruled that some height and weight restrictions are relevant in some cases, but that most of the requirements originally intact were "excessive" and needed to be toned down. For instance, many police departments used to have minimum-height requirements of 5'10". A less strict minimum-height requirement of perhaps 5'3" might serve to focus attention on a person's ability to do the job.
12. Both compensatory and punitive damages were made allowable by the Civil Rights Act of 1991.
13. BMW v. North America, Inc. v. Gore, 116 S. Ct. 1589 (1996).
14. Civil Rights Act of 1991.
15. EEOC v. Fremont Christian School, 609 F. Supp. 344 (N.D. Cal 1984), *aff'd*, 781 F.2d 1362, 39 FEP 1815 (9th Cir. 1986).
16. Congressional Accountability Act of 1995, 2 U.S.C. §§ 1301–1438 (1998).
17. Enacted as part of the Education Act Amendments of 1972 (20 U.S.C. §§ 1681–88, 1681(a) (1994)). Title IX was a response to Congress's growing concern about the problem of sex discrimination in educational programs. (*See* 118 Cong. Rec. 5804-15 (1972); H.R. Rep. No. 554, 92nd Cong., 1st Sess. 1–3 (1972).)
18. National Coalition for Women and Girls in Education, a coalition of more than fifty women's groups, including the American Association of University Women, issued June 23, 1997.

CHAPTER 16

1. 42 U.S.C. § 200e-5(e)(1) (1998).
2. *Id.* at 200e-5(f)(1) (1998).
3. *See* Delaware State College v. Ricks, 449 U.S. 250 (1980).
4. *Rapid Process Procedures Issue,* (No. 915.001, § 14.9(b), Fact Finding Conference) *in* 1 EEOC Compliance Manual § 14.

5. Ellen Warren and Nancy Millman, *Abuse on the Line: For Years, Women at Mitsubishi Say They've Endured the Degrading Deeds and Words of Coworkers—Now They're Doing the Talking,* Chi. Trib., Feb. 15, 1998, at 10.
6. *Id.*

CHAPTER 17

1. Ralph Nader and Wesley J. Smith, No Contest: Corporate Lawyers and the Perversion of Justice in America 231 (Random House 1996). The authors conducted several interviews with insurance company auditors who regularly monitor billing practices among law firms. According to Nader and Smith, "The auditors with whom we spoke all agreed that the following practices, if not routine, were not rare either, demonstrating that some lawyers believe that dishonesty is the best policy:
   - Lawyers billing unworked hours, sometimes more than there are in the day.
   - Senior partners billing their time for work actually performed by support personnel, work that therefore should have been billed at a substantially lower rate.
   - Firms charging for filling in the blanks in legal 'forms,' documents preprepared and used repeatedly as if the lawyer had created the documents from scratch.
   - Lawyers advising clients not to accept reasonable settlements so that the case, and the billing, can continue.
   - Lawyers taking unnecessary depositions.
   - Firms taking a markup for business expenses such as secretarial overtime, fax charges, long-distance phone calls, and the like. Expense markups can quickly add up to big profits for the firm. For example, real estate attorney Jay Dushoff tells the story of a large New York firm typesetting and printing fifty copies of a final loan document, without request or consent, and then charging the client $13,000. The client paid, because, as Dushoff put it, "We had no choice. We were in the economic position of being coerced." From the Pension Rights Center, Washington, D.C. Cutting Legal Costs for Business, 18 May 1981, cited in Nader and Smith, *No Contest.*
   - Lawyers living in luxury at the client's expense, such as using limousine services, staying in four-star hotels, and eating at expensive restaurants.

- Firms charging for using staff personnel to unnecessarily 'messenger' materials that could have been mailed or commercially messengered for a lowered price.
- Firms failing to provide detailed billing statements, making it impossible for clients to monitor the accuracy of the charges."

2. *Id.* Nader and Smith went on to say, "Perhaps for attorneys who spend their careers representing big corporations, lawsuits seem like no big deal. When an individual or small business sues or threatens to sue a large corporation, the impact is far less devastating than when the situation is reversed. . . ." *Id.* at 164.
3. Estimates vary roughly from 2 to 10 percent. Few legal publications have definitive data on this subject, because it is difficult to gather in any comprehensive manner. Many articles simply state that "a tiny percentage," "a small percentage," or "few cases" go to trial. The data may also vary depending on the area of the country in which you live.

CHAPTER 18

1. Between 1992 and 1996, employment cases involving civil rights filed in federal court doubled from 10,771 to 23,152. Amy Joyce, *Work and Careers: More Firms Are Buying Sexual Harassment Insurance Policies,* L.A. TIMES, March 26, 1998, Business Section at D3.
2. *EEOC Policy Statement on Mandatory Binding Arbitration of Employment Discrimination Disputes as a Condition of Employment,* §§ (7)(I), (7)(V)(B), released July 10, 1997, *reprinted in* DAILY LAB. REP. (BNA) No. 133 at E-4 (July 11, 1997) (setting forth position that agreements mandating binding arbitration of discrimination claims as condition of employment are contrary to the policy of the employment discrimination laws).
3. *Id.*, § (7) (V)(B).
4. *Id.*
5. *Id.*(citing Lisa Bingham, *Employment Arbitration: The Effect of Repeat-Player Status, Employee Category and Gender on Arbitration Outcome,* unpublished study on file with the author, an assistant professor at Ind. U. School of Pub. & Env. Affairs).
6. *EEOC Policy Statement on Mandatory Binding Arbitration of Employment Discrimination Disputes as a Condition of Employment,* § (7)(V)(B) (citing Reginald Alleyne, *Statutory Discrimination Claims: Rights 'Waived' and Lost in the Arbitration Forum,* 13 HOFSTRA LAB. L.J. 381, 428 (Spring 1996).

7. *Id.*
8. *Id.*
9. 28 U.S.C. § 1915 (1998).
10. The U.S. Supreme Court, in Wright v. Universal Maritime Service Corp., 119 S. Ct. 391 (1998), considered the issue of whether a worker was prohibited from filing a discrimination claim in federal court because his union contract stated that all disputes would be settled in arbitration. The Court held that the worker did *not* have to use the arbitration process. In upholding his right to sue in federal court, the court said, "[W]e find it unnecessary to resolve the question of the validity of a union-negotiated waiver, since it is apparent to us, on the acts and arguments presented here, that no such waiver occurred. . . . [W]e will not infer from a general contractual provision that the parties intended to waive a statutorily protected right unless the undertaking is 'explicitly stated.' More succinctly, the waiver must be 'clear and unmistakable' (quoting Metropolitan Edison Co. v. NLRB, 460 U.S. 693, 708). '[We] hold that the collective-bargaining agreement in this case does not contain a clear and unmistakable waiver of the covered employees' rights to a judicial forum for federal claims of employment discrimination." *Id.* at 395–397.

    The Court went on to hold, "We do not reach the question whether such a waiver would be enforceable." *Id.* at 397. The impact of this statement is that the law remains unclear as to whether even clear and unmistakable waivers of Title VII rights would be legal.
11. Some states are known for large and frequent punitive-damage awards. California leads the pack, according to a 1996 study by the Pacific Research Institute titled *Punitive Damages in California: A Review and Comparison of Evidence.* According to the U.S. Dept of Justice, the median nationwide of punitive damages is $50,000, whereas California's is $300,000.
12. Several studies were done on various federal circuits, funded by the federal courts themselves, some of which include *Second Circuit Task Force on Gender, Racial, and Ethnic Fairness in the Courts* (1997); *Eighth Circuit Gender Fairness Task Force Report* (1997); *The Gender, Race, and Ethnic Bias Task Force Project in the D.C. Circuit* (1995); *The Effects of Gender in the Federal Courts: The Final Report of the Ninth Circuit Gender Bias Task Force* (1993).
13. *Second Circuit Task Force on Gender, Racial, and Ethnic Fairness in the Courts* (1997). Twenty-nine percent of plaintiffs' attorneys and 11 percent of defendants' attorneys reported judges indicated that such cases are frivolous, unimportant, or undeserving of federal court time (sometimes/often/many times). When judges were asked whether they agreed that discrimination cases were undeserving of federal court time because "the issues are trivial," a majority

expressed disagreement or strong disagreement (53.4 percent). A substantial minority reported a neutral opinion on the issue (35.6 percent) and a small number (10.9 percent) suggested that they "agreed or strongly agreed."

14. *Second Circuit Task Force on Gender, Racial, and Ethnic Fairness in the Courts* (1997) determined that the issue raises "a concern; that, when an employment discrimination case is properly before a federal court, a judge's belief that the matter is too trivial for his or her attention may too easily translate into actual unfairness to a litigant as the case proceeds through the system in a form that disproportionately disadvantages women and members of minority groups. Whether this concern will prove to be well founded must await further study elsewhere."
15. According to the *Eighth Circuit Gender Fairness Task Force Report* (1997), "One-third of plaintiffs' attorneys and one-quarter of defendants' attorneys reported that discrimination cases had been pushed through the courts without adequate time (sometimes/often/many times)."
16. Fed. R. Civ. P. ro 23(a)(3) (1998).
17. "Stairway to Heaven," words and music by Jimmy Page and Robert Plant of Led Zeppelin, 1971.
18. Jolie Solomon, *An Insurance Policy with Sex Appeal*, NEWSWEEK, March 16, 1998 at 44.

Index

ABOUT THE AUTHOR

PATTI PANICCIA is a journalist and attorney who has personally lived through the experience of battling a multibillion-dollar Fortune 500 company after being discriminated against on the job. Her pregnancy discrimination case against CNN made national headlines and was settled in 1996 after two years of court hearings, appeals, and depositions. In 1997, she founded the Patti Paniccia Scholarship Fund, which financially assists law students responsible for parenting minor children.

She worked as a television news reporter for more than a decade, at CNN's Los Angeles bureau, KCOP-TV Los Angeles, and KEYT-ABC Santa Barbara. She is a member of both the California State Bar and the Hawai'i State Bar and is also an adjunct professor at Pepperdine Law School in Malibu, California, where she teaches a course on gender and the law.

Paniccia received an Emmy nomination from the Academy of Television Arts and Sciences in 1987 for an investigative series she did on the Los Angeles justice system's failure to adequately deal with infant abuse. In 1988, she was awarded the National Clarion Award from the Association for Women in Communications for outstanding reporting.

She received her Juris Doctor from Pepperdine School of Law and her B.A. in communications from the University of Hawai'i at Manoa. Prior to attending law school, she was ranked as one of the top women professional surfers in the world and spent four years competing on the women's international pro tour. She currently resides in southern California with her husband and two daughters.

You can visit Paniccia's Website at www.worksmarts.net.